At last, a complete and integrated approach to managing your stress

When asked why she wrote this book, Dr. Jackie Schwartz described the following experience:

"In my workshops and seminars, participants eagerly sought more information. "Where can I go," they'd ask, "to find out more of the practical kinds of things you teach?" I combed the bookstores and found a multitude of books on stress, but most of them had a single focus, emphasizing some proven way to decrease stress: diet is *the* answer, biofeedback is *the* answer, exercise is *the* answer.

"Nowhere did I find a book that presented the subject in a complex, interconnected way, affecting every aspect of life. Also, I knew from my experience that people wanted simple, effective measures to reduce stress. Plenty of books could provide the theory, but readers wanted to know how they could get through their next crisis without becoming ill, losing control, or seriously jeopardizing their jobs and intimate relationships.

"This book is my attempt to provide a solution to that need."

Letting Go of Stress

by Dr. Jackie Schwartz

PINNACLE BOOKS   NEW YORK

LETTING GO OF STRESS

Copyright © 1982 by Jackie Schwartz

An original Pinnacle Books edition, published for the first time anywhere.

First printing, April 1982

ISBN: 0-523-42028-5

Illustrations © 1982 by Diane Detrick Bavaro

Printed in the United States of America

PINNACLE BOOKS, INC.
1430 Broadway
New York, New York 10018

12   11   10   9   8   7   6   5   4   3

Life can only be understood backwards;
but it must be lived forwards.

—Soren Kierkegaard

To Norton
with whom I share my life.

In gratitude for introducing me to group dynamics,
baby-sitting our toddler and preschool girls when I went
away for my first residential group,
encouraging me to continue my education,
joining me in joining the gym when I felt "fat and forty"
and delighting me with surprise gourmet meals on
occasions when I felt like I didn't remember what the
inside of a kitchen looked like.

His support and encouragement made it all possible.

CONTENTS

Appendices

SELF-EVALUATION TESTS

ACKNOWLEDGMENTS

Some of the special people in my life who made it possible for me to write this book are:

My mother, Margaret Ruth Levy, whose indomitable spirit and courage provides inspiration throughout my life. Living her life free of sex-role stereotyping liberated me to know that I could savor whatever life had to offer instead of being limited to "woman's work."

My father, Ellie Alexander Levy, who first cherished me, appreciating me as a miracle, knowing that I would do wonderful things, even though he regretted that he wouldn't live to see me grow up.

My Uncle John Williams, who gave me the greatest gift any child could ever receive. He inspired me to believe that I could do whatever I wanted to do in this life. His gentle coaching and seemingly unlimited patience always made me feel very special.

My Aunt Lily Williams, who exemplified quiet dignity and propriety, unlimited generosity, all-accepting, uncomplaining, and invincible. She enabled me to appreciate the values of a simpler existence and Type B behavior long before I ever had words for it.

My daughters, Karen and Lisa, whose pride in their mom's efforts kept me going when I felt discouraged. I gratefully acknowledge their suggestions, incorporated in the book.

Getting into my chosen work, I have been blessed with the support and guidance of warm, genuine, caring, wise teachers who model congruent communication, respecting the rights of all individuals to be valued and listened to, introducing me to the omnipresent world of group process and expanding my creativity: Rosalind K. Loring, Joan K. Lasko, Paula Menkin, Eva Schindler-Rainman, Art Shedlin,

Robert Tannenbaum, and James F. T. Bugental. One of my most influential teachers, whose friendship and dependability I deeply cherish, is Richard P. Barthol.

Mentor and good friend Virginia Satir believed in me and encouraged me even during those times when I wondered what I was going to be when I grew up. The BP's, Family Camp families, and Avanta Network of colleagues trained by Virginia have enriched my spirit and broadened my life choices.

My clients and the participants in my workshops and seminars, who have shared so freely of their personal struggles and dreams, enabling me to know what truly matters in this life. As Consultant on Aging for the community-college system, I am especially grateful to my group of senior citizens, who shared with me their experiences in living a full, bountiful life, enjoying good health and peace of mind.

Friends John Thie and Roger Akers, who read and reread the segments on exercise, sharing their considerable knowledge. Betty Schwartz, Johanna Schwab, Gertrude Harrow, Jo Saltzer, Violette Jacobs, Donie Nelson, Violet Felix, Tom and Beverly Hanley, and Rory Roberts gave generously of their resources at times when I most needed them.

Colleagues who have shared generously with me their own discoveries for a more fulfilling life include:

Darri Heller, whose freedom of spirit elicits my joy in whimsy and inspires my sense of wonder and beauty in all living things.

Sam Farry, whose collaboration in early seminars refined my style of workshop presentation to a more sophisticated level.

Robert W. Hanna, who embodies self-caring coupled with compassion and giving of himself to others.

J. Stephen Colladay, exemplifying risk-taking and the quest for a more tension-free life, who shares his resources so freely.

My dear friend Janette Rainwater, who gave new meaning to the word "generosity" as she unstintingly supported, guided, facilitated, and fed me throughout the preparation of the manuscript. Her profound appreciation of my disciplined efforts inspired me with renewed dedication.

Freddy Northstar, who performed beyond anything humanly possible, turning out impeccable copy, showcasing my work.

My editor, Carole Garland, who consistently encouraged and inspired me, urging me to share of myself in presenting my teachings.

My partner, Reva Camiel, who insisted that I had a book to write, emphasized the importance of my applying my seat to the chair, and cheered me when I delivered the product. Her early critique of the manuscript provided essential redirection. Her creativity is inspiring.

FOREWORD

For the most part, *stress* is a word that signals danger to our physical and emotional health. It is often cited as a primary factor in many physical diseases and emotional difficulties. The usual advice is: "Avoid Stress." That's easy to say and to hear, but not that easy to accomplish, since it is seldom accompanied by instructions on how to do it. In fact, when people try hard to avoid stress, they usually create more stress which only worsens the situation.

This book offers useful answers. To start with, it clarifies the important fact that stress is energy. Stress is a natural consequence of interactions between individuals and their demands on, wishes for, and commitments to other human beings. Life carries many responsibilities and possibilities. We cannot cancel them. We need to learn how to live well with them.

Stress is normal. Like electricity, by itself it is neutral. It is the management and use of stress that determines constructive or destructive results.

Stress can become either a friend or an enemy, depending on the acknowledgment of its existence, the beliefs about its nature, and the conscious uses of its energy.

Jackie Schwartz, the author of *Letting Go of Stress*, has written comprehensively about this very complex subject. She has brought together the thinking and research of accepted theoreticians and practitioners relevant to the phenomenon of stress in a simple and effective way, and she links the findings of this research with practical experience. The results are sensible, easily applicable methods to help any person use the energy of stress constructively.

The book begins by identifying ways to recognize stress, followed by factual information that reduces fear through increased understanding. This opens the door for hope. Finally, there are clearly presented step-by-step exercises anyone can use to transform their reactions to stress. The result for everyone can be a life lived more fully rather than dying it day by day.

—Dr. Virginia M. Satir
Respected authority and pioneer
in the field of family therapy

PREFACE

He never grieved for his sister. He was the eldest of four children, only ten years old when his nine-year-old sister died after a brief illness. They had been inseparable. Their mother had dressed them in cute coordinated clothing, now captured in treasured, faded pictures. This unexpressed grief was the beginning of a lifetime of not expressing his feelings. Only a year later, he again knew loss.

His whole family was in a horrible automobile accident. The car turned over three times, killing one passenger immediately and seriously injuring all the others.

The boy's father, although apparently recovered, ultimately died as a result of his injuries. On his first day back at work, the father threw a blood clot. He encountered a difficult situation on that first day at work and, feeling that he was personally threatened, his body went into the "fight or flight" response; the increased blood pressure forced the blood clot to dislodge. He was dead at the age of fifty-nine, before he even reached the hospital. The doctors back then didn't know anything about the importance of thinning the blood, so the boy's father died of a stress response. His mother, who had suffered a broken neck and back injuries in the accident, attended her husband's funeral on a hospital gurney.

The little boy of eleven was told by well-meaning friends and family that he now had to be "the man of the family." His two remaining family members, his mother and two-year-old sister, were recovering from their own injuries. The loss, upheaval, and economic pressures caused by the father's dealth created a situation in which the family was fortunate to be able to survive as best they could in a country that was still in a deep economic depression.

Those strained times in that home did not allow the little

1

boy to express his own deep grief. "Being a man" meant he had to be strong, responsible, work hard, not complain or show weakness, never cry, take care of himself, and be considerate of others' needs.

He learned these lessons well. He could no longer be a carefree child playing with his favorite older cousin on the cousin's nearby farm. This had been a delight and constant adventure for him, so different from his city life. He got a job as a box boy at a local market, working after school and on weekends. He was very sociable, and he appreciated the satisfaction of being able to work in a place where repeat customers befriended him. He liked to joke with them and "kid around."

In high school he played a clarinet in the band. He never went out for any sports, and didn't consider himself especially athletic. His favorite subject was wood shop, in which he excelled, although he considered it too low status to make it his life work. Even though he was self-conscious about his adolescent acne, he was very popular with the girls. The attractive little boy had grown into a tall, slim, well-built, handsome young man.

Whenever he had a fight with a girlfriend, he became irritable, tense, and angry at the world. He developed the habit of rhythmically clenching his teeth, and his cheek would pulsate to reveal his anger and tension. He seemed incapable of knowing how to talk about his feelings.

His mother wanted him to go to college, but he wasn't much of a student. He was seventeen when World War II broke out, and it gave him a good excuse to duck out of the college he'd been attending for a few months. He enlisted in the Navy for his four years, serving in the Philippines. Here again, it was important to be strong and tough. He took up smoking, a habit he retained throughout his lifetime. Except for the malaria that would continue to plague him after the war, he was discharged physically unscathed in 1945.

Even though college would have been economically attractive on the G.I. Bill, he still didn't want to go to school. He truly didn't know what he wanted to do with his life, and he floated from one job to another. Capitalizing on his good looks and his social ease, he became a salesman. He got his first decent job through a charitable uncle but stayed in that job for less than a year.

At twenty-two he married the first woman who ex-

2

pressed an interest in him. She was only nineteen. When the marriage ended after less than two years, he felt a sense of failure. He didn't have a good job or a college education, and now his marriage was over.

Three years later he married a former model who was several years older than he, attracted to her because of her good looks and tasteful style of dress. Everyone commented on what a good-looking couple they were, but good looks were not enough to ease the interpersonal strains that soon erupted in their relationship. She liked to spend money, and he always felt that he didn't earn enough as a salesman. He feigned wealth and status by leasing cars and hosting expense-account dinners, but underneath it all he felt like he just wasn't good enough.

He gained a lot of weight, smoked two packs of cigarettes a day, drank a great deal of coffee, and was very impatient, impulsive, and unsure of himself. His work as a salesman was very stressful and his income was unpredictable, based as it was on commissions. Although he was a skilled craftsman who enjoyed woodworking and heavy construction, he didn't do any vigorous physical exercise on a regular basis. He was a perfectionist about everything he did, always demanding the very best performance from himself.

A very generous and likable man, he would do anything for a friend or a neighbor. He had a hard time saying "no," and frequently he found himself loaded down with demands from others. He would escape by going fishing, a boyhood pleasure he cherished throughout his lifetime, but these escapes weren't enough.

His cheeks still pulsated when he ground his teeth. His brow had become furrowed with deep lines, reflecting both his anxiety and his eagerness to please. He was continually between forty and sixty pounds above his desired weight.

His mother died of a massive heart attack when he was forty, and he felt like he had lost his best friend. Although his wife didn't know it, his mother had always bailed him out financially, lending him a twenty-dollar bill here and there to tide him over. It helped him save face with his wife, for whom he never seemed to have enough money.

He wasn't interested in learning about or doing anything to reduce his stress. Predictably, he had a heart attack at forty-six. He got to the hospital in time and survived, which spurred him to re-evaluate his life.

3

His marriage had been unbearable for a long time, and now, with his new desire to live, he divorced his wife of twenty-five years. He had met a woman twenty years younger than he who brought him the greatest happiness he had ever known. She was a financially and socially independent professional woman, very bright, open to new experiences, secure in her career, upwardly mobile. She was easygoing, nondemanding, generous, loving, and accepting—very different from his former wife. He took to her as a dry sponge takes to water.

His new wife, too, was fat, but they made no visible effort to restrict their diet. He continued to smoke and drink coffee, and kept his high-stress job. Other than remarrying, he made no significant attempt to improve his lifestyle. He never lived to see his sons grow up. He died at fifty-two of a massive heart attack.

This death of a salesman is a true story. I am his "baby" sister, the lone survivor of that family.

Our legacy of two parents' deaths from heart disease did not serve as adequate warning to my brother. He lived his life as if he were invulnerable to stress. It is a tragedy that my brother didn't know how to reduce his stress in ways that he could incorporate into his daily life. Another tragedy is that he didn't really understand how important it is to do just that.

This book could have saved his life.

I have written this book to help people learn how to develop a lifestyle of wellness. It provides practical information and an action program with specific steps to improve your life.

I have seen how well my clients and the people in my seminars respond to these practical suggestions. Clearly, it is time to get something into print to reach the people whom I might never meet.

When I first became interested in knowing more about coping with stress, I felt it was a natural marriage of my two different areas of expertise: consulting with organizations and seeing clients as a psychotherapist.

When people weren't happy in their jobs and the organizational system bred chaos and discontent, the whole system suffered in every way. The unhappiness and dis/ease of employees affected their home lives. Those who were experiencing trouble in their marriages or were preoccu-

4

pied with other personal problems became less capable workers.

Further, I wanted to know more so that I could personally benefit. Too well I knew this truth: *life is what happens to you while you are busy making plans.*

I know what it is like to be incapacitated and endure pain caused by physical injury. I know what it is like to live with physical limitations. I know what it is like to feel rejected by a loved one. I know what it is like to feel driven and desperate because of the uncertainty of income. I know what it is like to feel weak in character and disappointed in myself when I succumb to self-destructive practices. I know what it is like to feel despair and hopelessness about a loved one. I know what it is like to feel trapped in a job I don't like. I know what it is like to terminate a long-term relationship that is no longer nourishing. I know what it is like to fail. I know what it is like to grieve the deaths of close friends and loved ones. I know what it is like to not be able to relax properly when I fall into old, dysfunctional coping patterns.

On the bright side, I know, too, how healing the warmth and support of good friends and loved ones can be. I know what it is like to feel grateful that I can be physically fit and enjoy my body. I know what it is like to be able to ask for help. I know what it is like to love myself. I know what it is like to fully own my power. I know what it is like to be patient and allow things to unfold. I know what it is like to feel loved and cherished. I know what it is like to set goals and discipline myself to achieve them. I know what it is like to experience divine bliss in contact with nature. I know what it is like to feel the deep satisfaction that comes from using all my resources fully, taking pride in my work. I know what it is like to feel personally and professionally respected and sought after.

I share these aspects of myself with you, dear reader, to underscore a lesson that was, for me, many years in coming: *no one has everything.* I grew up believing the "Santa Claus theory," so ably expressed by Dr. Virginia Satir— that if I worked hard enough, was good, clean, earnest, good looking, smart, kind and polite enough, I would be rewarded with the best of everything. My life would be perfect, free of pain, full of joy. This isn't the way it works. Both the theory and Santa Claus are myths. The illusion of

5

perfection we sometimes envy in our heroes and heroines is just that: an illusion. Repeatedly I find that I have only to scratch the surface to uncover the humanness of any idol. That humanness is a basis for connecting and identifying with that person, as I have had similar feelings.

With this backlog of personal history and my earnest desire to live a long, healthy life, I set out to learn as much as I could about stress. Working with colleagues at first, I helped present workshops, emphasizing the costs of interpersonal stress from my own perspective as a psychotherapist and human-relations consultant. My years as an administrator of a public-service agency grounded me in the day-to-day demands of a large system. I felt privileged that my clients and co-workers so openly shared their concerns with me. From this, I was able to develop some understanding of how much stress is self-induced, how people sometimes limit themselves unnecessarily, and what changes were possible.

My first publication, in 1978, was *The Relaxation Log*, a self-help tool to enable people to cope with stress. When I spoke at conventions or universities, people in the audience would express a desire to go home and tell their spouses what they had learned, so I developed two audio cassette tapes. The first contains a half-hour lecture explaining just what stress is, why it is such a problem today, and what can be done about it. The second side contains a progressive relaxation. People liked this tape, but some complained that they didn't always have a half-hour in which to practice relaxation techniques. As a result, I developed the second tape, "Brief Relaxation Techniques for People Who Never Have Time to Relax." On the reverse side is a fifteen-minute progressive relaxation. I put these two tapes together in one package, called *Relaxation—Relief from Tension.*

In my workshops and seminars, participants eagerly sought more information. "Where can I go," they'd ask, "to find out more of the practical kinds of things you teach?" I combed the bookstores and found a multitude of books on stress, but most of them had a single focus, emphasizing some proven way to decrease stress: diet is *the* answer, biofeedback is *the* answer, exercise is *the* answer.

Nowhere did I find a book that presented the subject in a complex, interconnected way, affecting every aspect of life. Also, I knew from my experience that people wanted simple, effective measures to reduce stress. Plenty of books could provide the theory, but readers wanted to know how they could get through their next crisis without becoming ill, losing control, or seriously jeopardizing their jobs and intimate relationships.

This book is my attempt to provide a solution to that need. When I get stuck in an old, negative way of coping, I recall one of these techniques to enable me to feel better, and then I can restore my energies and address the problem. I hope this book will serve you well in your journey toward a more rewarding life.

Jackie Schwartz
October 1981
West Los Angeles, California

INTRODUCTION

Congratulations! By reading this book, you're taking a positive step toward alleviating the excessive tension and anxiety engendered by the "stress epidemic" that is plaguing us. If you're one of the many people who are experiencing an overload of stress—which might be showing up in high blood pressure, tension headaches, insomnia, intestinal disturbances, or increased susceptibility to colds and flu—then clearly you're looking for an alternative. That's certainly no way to live, even if you've got plenty of company. Just because it's usual doesn't mean it's normal.

How did all this come about? Karl Albrecht notes in *Stress and the Manager* that American life as we know it has undergone significant changes in this century:

1. From rural to urban living.
2. From stationary to mobile.
3. From self-sufficient to consuming.
4. From isolated to interconnected.
5. From physically active to sedentary.

Then and Now

In the eighteenth and nineteenth centuries, life was much simpler. Think about this picture. People slept beneath homemade quilts, awakening naturally at the first sounds of morning, rising with the dawn. They dressed simply in preparation for their day's work in clothes made of natural fibers, perhaps homespun.

They had definite jobs to do, maybe the same work their parents had done before them. They grew up watching and learning, knowing well what kind of work their parents did, knowing that some day they might be doing that same

8

job. They knew all the people in their community and saw them whenever there was a special occasion for a social gathering, which wasn't very often.

Their food was homegrown, and if they didn't grow all their food themselves, they bartered with a neighbor, perhaps swapping eggs for corn. Older and younger family members lived together, and children had a feeling of security and identity. There was a lot of caring expressed between the generations. There weren't any telephones or automobiles, and timepieces were scarce. And, of course, there was no income tax. There weren't many interruptions in their lives; their days were relatively predictable.

Everyone worked hard because heavy physical labor was often a necessary part of their work. A lot of physical exercise, like chopping wood and beating rugs, was a regular part of their lives. At the end of the day, their work was done. Because fuel was regarded as a precious commodity, they went to bed not long after sunset. They slept soundly, naturally, restoring their bodies. Others didn't expect any more of them.

Certainly, life was far from perfect then. But there were fewer sources of stress, and people were better equipped to handle the stress that is a part of every person's life.

Contrast this scene with life today. Now most people are packed into densely populated areas, living and sleeping scant yards from others with whom they have no significant relationship or whom they don't even know. They are awakened by a mechanical alarm, the first of many mechanical devices that influence or even govern their daily lives. They dress in clothes that are usually made of synthetic materials. Breakfast is often something out of a package, washed down with instant coffee and imitation orange juice.

Then they either hop into a metal and glass "isolation tank" or cram into a subway, bus, or commuter train to be transported to work, which is often located far from where they live. This daily ritual stirs their competitive and survival senses as they struggle through heavy traffic or contend with crowds of others heading for work. By this time they're fighting the clock, fighting for their own safety zone, alert to dangers that may slow them down or impinge on their space.

Once at work they may be locked into a very specialized job, perhaps interdependent with others for a total product,

9

probably part of a large project. They may never even see the completed product, and their contribution may be swallowed up in the process. The workplace itself may be fraught with sources of stress that they either don't notice or meekly accept.

A coffee break is hardly a time for restoring energy. That's when most people have a cup of coffee, perhaps with a doughnut and a cigarette, in another crowded place where peace and quiet are unknown. Conversation probably centers on the work situation, and the "break" is in name only.

Lunch may consist of a "blue-plate special" put together for the convenience of the restaurant and exemplifying the typical American diet with its emphasis on high fat, high salt, high sugar, white flour, and food additives. If they don't have time to get out of the office for lunch, they may order something to be sent in so that they can work while they eat, gulping down French fries and a soft drink while they remain absorbed in their work, unaware of the stress reaction created by eating poor foods. If they're already feeling overstressed, their lunch break only adds to it.

Back at work, the pressures build as conflicting demands are made upon their time and interruptions increase, giving them the feeling that they'll never get everything done. Characteristically, the signs of stress surface, and in order to continue working, they may mask the pain by popping some pills. Fatigued at the end of the work day, they head for home, again battling traffic or the crowds on mass transit, wrung out by the day. They may stop on the way home for a drink or two to unwind.

The person who spends his day at home is subject to a different kind of stress. He may go through an entire day without seeing anyone with whom he can share concerns and problem-solve, experiencing strong feelings of isolation and alienation. Too much ambiguity rather than too much structure may be the cause of his stress.

To those who work, home presents a new set of demands for time, expertise, and interpersonal needs, and is no longer a retreat from the pressures of the day. Instead, their day is capped off with three or four hours of television. Mindless situation comedies or "adventure" shows full of crime and violence fill their time, followed by the generally distressing news program in which they learn of worldwide social and political uncertainties and turmoil they can do nothing about, reinforcing their feelings of powerlessness and hopelessness.

Does all this sound familiar? It's estimated that we are subjected to a hundred times more stress than our grandparents and great-grandparents. People then paid attention to their responses to stress, which were the result of specific identifiable, separate events. In contrast, much of our stress results from ambiguous ongoing situations over which we have no control, creating generalized anxiety and subsequent self-induced stress as we ponder "What if. . . ?" We are responding to stress so much of the time that we hardly notice we're functioning in an almost constant state of stress overload. Many people rarely relax fully, so they are unaware of their tension and are always in an agitated state. To find out how you respond, you may wish to complete "What Are Your Stress Symptoms?" in Appendix A.

The Anatomy of Stress

What, then, exactly is stress? According to Hans Selye, whose lifelong work has been in this area, stress is the nonspecific psychological and physiological response of the body to any new demand made upon it. Anything—pleasant or unpleasant—that interferes with the body's equilibrium is a *stressor*, or source of stress. Whether you're fired or promoted, hit with a brick or caressed by a lover, you experience stress. Your body has the same reaction every time. Any change, positive or negative, evokes stress. Selye calls positive stress *eustress* and negative stress—which most of us think of when we think of stress—*distress*.

In *Stress Without Distress,* Selye defined this stress syndrome as the General Adaptation Syndrome (GAS). First your body goes into the "alarm reaction" to fight the demand—the well-known "fight or flight" response. Next there is the "resistance stage," in which the body adapts to the demand. The stress response raises the level of resistance to the stressor that provoked it and to other stressors like it, and resistance to other types of stressors tends to decline. For a while, you feel more capable, resistant, and energized. Finally, the "exhaustion stage" sets in, when overadaptation to continued stress may cause the body to fall prey to stress-linked illnesses.

Some people so enjoy the "high" they get from being in

11

the resistance stage of the GAS that they perpetuate it by engaging in one activity after another that is stress-producing for them. These "stress seekers" choose highly exciting, competitive activities as their way of relaxing, such as the thrill of a hockey match, gambling, going to a nightclub, or engaging in a competitive sport or, for that matter, in any activity and making it competitive. Typically, stress seekers simply don't know how to relax and may in fact fear the "letting go" that accompanies deep relaxation. Their strong need to be in control dominates their actions. Sadly, they are often unaware of the cumulative effect of constantly subjecting themselves to new stressors. When they get their standard cold in January, they believe it's because it's the "cold season," overlooking the preceding weeks of frenzied, highly stressed activities.

Another way of thinking about all this is to look at Jeff Bisch's cartoon.

At the top of the Stressmobile is (1) the input valve for all of life's stressors—job, family, customers, inflation, the environment, etc. How you respond to these stressors depends on (2) your "awareness and choice value." You'll notice that the cutaway view of the interior of the Stressmobile reveals that you need a certain amount of stress to help you reach your goal. When that level is exceeded, however, you need to obtain some (3) stress relief by taking a vacation, relaxing, following proper guidelines for exercise and nutrition, and having varied interests. If you don't get any relief from excessive stress, you'll reach (4) the overflow level, which will affect whatever is your weakest point. This tension and anxiety may show up as a headache, ulcer, or coronary, which you may try to avoid or ignore with drugs or alcohol.

Now let's look at what actually happens when your body experiences the "fight or flight" response. It releases a quick spurt of adrenalin, and your adrenal glands become enlarged and discolored. The lymphatic gland, crucial to the immune system, shrinks intensely. Numerous blood-covered stomach ulcers appear. Your cardiovascular system speeds up, your breathing rate and heart rate increase 25%, your blood pressure rises, and more cholesterol is released into your bloodstream. Chemicals that cause the blood to coagulate are released into your bloodstream to help your body form scabs more easily in case of an ensuing injury. Your heart beats more forcefully, perhaps even

12

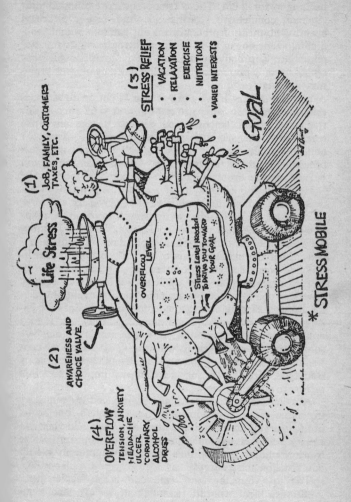

(1) **Life Stress**
JOB, FAMILY, CUSTOMERS TAXES, ETC.

(2) AWARENESS AND CHOICE VALVE

(3) **STRESS RELIEF**
- VACATION
- RELAXATION
- EXERCISE
- NUTRITION
- VARIED INTERESTS

(4) **OVERFLOW**
TENSION, ANXIETY HEADACHE
ULCER,
CORONARY
ALCOHOL
DRUGS

OVERFLOW LEVEL

Stress Level needed to Drive you TOWARD Your Goal

GOAL

* STRESS MOBILE

13

irregularly. Adrenalin dilates the bronchi to allow a maximum intake of oxygen, as your need for oxygen is momentarily increased. Blood goes from your extremities to your vital organs, leaving your hands and feet cooler and lowering your skin temperature. Your gastrointestinal functioning slows down, your sweating increases, and your pupils dilate to provide a maximal field of vision. All your senses become more acute. Even the patterns of your brainwaves change.

Now your body is fully in gear for "fight or flight," that critical alarm response to stress, but you can't stay in this stage very long. Generally you advance to the resistance level, when the symptoms of "fight or flight" disappear and your body seems to adapt so well that you may feel like you're functioning normally. Often, mistakenly, you believe that the problem has been overcome.

How well you are able to advance to the resistance level depends upon how much adaptive energy you have. Everyone is born with a genetically determined amount of adaptive energy. Theoretically, we could be expected to live to a hundred, but few of us do. Selye speculates that this is because our adaptive energy is continually being drained in order to combat stress. Too often, we use adaptive energy to combat stressors that we don't even think about, such as excessive noise, overcrowding, pollution, interruptions, distractions, high mobility with its consequent loss of a stable supportive community, commuting in heavy traffic, increased social and community demands, threats to our personal safety, general fear of nuclear destruction and economic collapse, and, of course, the self-inflicted stressors of smoking, alcohol and substance abuse, improper eating, and inadequate exercise.

Another kind of stressor is that which comes from having either too little or too much stress in one's life. *To be productive and energized, the amount of stress in your life should be in an acceptable range,* so that you are neither overloaded nor understimulated. This diagram may help you visualize this concept.

Too little stress, or *stress underload*, is the "cabin fever" syndrome. With too little stimulation, variety, and challenge in your day, you may begin to question your value. This could apply to the worker on an assembly line who repeats the same monotonous task with little social interaction, and it is a serious concern of the recently retired. In

14

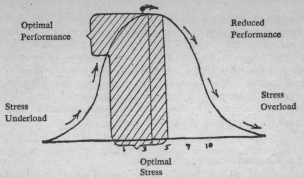

Optimal
Performance

Reduced
Performance

Stress
Underload

Stress
Overload

1 3 5 7 10

Optimal
Stress

contrast, with too much stress, or *stress overload*, you may feel oppressed because of too many demands, too much to do in too little time. Your best may not be enough, and this may trigger feelings of inadequacy. In order to achieve *optimal performance*, you need to function in a band of optimal stress, not too little and not too much. Wise managers create this kind of working environment.

Whether we are subject to too much or too little stress, stress that is environmental or self-induced, or stress arising from the overwhelming unprecedented social changes, it is *all* loaded onto the major life changes that always take a heavy toll!

Marriage, physical injury, leaving home for the first time, the birth of even a much-wanted child, divorce, moving to a better neighborhood, the loss of a loved one through death or breaking off a relationship are all sources of stress. Selye defines aging as the sum total of scars upon the body. True physiological aging isn't determined by how long we live but by how much of that given supply of life energy is drained by the demands of stress.

How each person responds to stress depends upon many variables: heredity, personality, diet, personal habits, pressures from job or personal life, physical condition, and so forth. Our current state of mind, how we anticipate the stressful event, our familiarity with the event, and our success in using stress-reduction techniques all influence our response.

With so many variables, it's difficult to predict how much stress is required at any given time to produce fatigue or collapse in any one individual. Our capacity to respond well to extraordinary stressors is tremendous and

15

amazing. What constitutes a stressful event for one person—making a speech or going on a business trip, for instance—may not be at all stressful for another. Selye emphasizes that it's not so much what happens to us but, rather, how we respond to it. That's our "awareness and choice valve." It's our ability to cope with the demands upon our lives, not the quality or intensity of those demands that counts. The stressor itself is less important than our ability and preparedness to meet it.

The Consequences of Stress

Over half of all illness can be traced to stress. Heart disease, high blood pressure, colitis, asthma, sleep disorders, kidney disease, peptic ulcers, rheumatoid arthritis, obesity, anxiety, depression—even cancer—are some of the more common stress-linked illnesses. The evidence is startling.

We've known for quite a while that the medical profile of a person likely to have a heart attack is an older, physically inactive male with high blood pressure and high serum cholesterol. He smokes, he's overweight, he has diabetes, and he has a family history of heart disease. In their research on Type A behavior, Meyer Friedman and Ray Rosenman have demonstrated that stress is an equally important cause of heart attacks.

At the Cancer Counseling and Research Center in Fort Worth, Texas, Carl and Stefanie Simonton have found a high correlation between cancer and the loss of a love object six to eighteen months prior to the onset of cancer symptoms. Those people who respond to such a loss with feelings of helplessness and despair are prime candidates for cancer. The Simontons identify the "cancer personality" as one characterized by (1) poor self-image, or lack of self-esteem; (2) self-pity, or feeling sorry for oneself; and (3) resentment, or the inability to forgive and forget.

Clearly, different people respond differently to stress. Each person has his own vulnerable spot. Past trauma, either psychological or physical, and heredity lay the groundwork for future weak spots. You probably already know your own ways of responding to stress, and you probably know, too, what your body is most vulnerable to. Besides your own personal characteristics and background, how much stress you can handle varies from time to time, re-

16

flecting both the situational factors and the amount of support you feel you have at the time.

Stress cannot be avoided; it is an integral part of everyone's life. You'd be like a limp noodle if you were free of stress! Used positively, stress can be an ally, enabling you to perform at your peak when you need to. A crucial deadline, an artistic performance, hostessing a party, and an athletic competition are examples of those times when you must do your best.

The problem, then, is how to increase your adaptive energy so that you can better respond to stress. Selye refers to two types of adaptive energy: deep adaptive energy and superficial adaptive energy. *Deep adaptive energy* is like stocks and bonds, the equity in your home—what you can count on as assets but is not readily available. *Superficial adaptive energy*, on the other hand, is quite accessible, like the money in your pocket or checkbook, immediately available to "pay" for your response to stress.

Deep adaptive energy is limited to what we're born with, and superficial energy normally drains off deep adaptive energy. You can, however, increase your superficial energy by utilizing proven techniques and acquiring beneficial behavior that will decrease *your* tension and add to your energy.

Dealing with Stress

That's what this book is all about: how to increase your ability to respond to stress through an examination of the crucial areas in understanding and managing stress. Stress knows no boundaries. What happens at home affects you at work, and what happens at work affects you at home. This book will give you the vital information and practical suggestions necessary to enable you to live a more stress-free life, both at home and at work.

Basically you have three choices in dealing with stress:

1. You can remove the stressor from your environment.
2. You can get out of the stressful environment.
3. You can learn to use relaxation techniques to directly counter the toxic effects of a stressful environment.

17

All three options will be dealt with here. I would like to be able to tell you I have a magic wand that can take away all your excessive stress, but, alas, that's not the case. Some of you are unable to escape from extraordinary sources of stress, such as living with a handicapped child, caring for an aged relative, trying to scrape by on too little income in inflationary times, or living in a home that's too crowded for your growing family. However, *you can change your response to these stressors*, which will have a beneficial effect and perhaps enable you to become aware of new options.

Just reading this book will not in itself make it happen for you. I invite you to discard honored restrictions about book care. This is a book designed for you to write in, making it your own personal copy. The final chapter asks you to violate another sacred rule by clipping out the pages. Giving yourself permission to do so can be very freeing.

In some ways this is like a cookbook. What's on the printed page has no value unless you take the necessary steps to make the procedures real for you: reviewing the material and deciding what's best for you, making your plan of action, and going wherever you need to go or doing whatever you need to do to carry out your plan. In order to get tangible results from *Letting Go of Stress*, you must make the commitment to do what is necessary to create a lifestyle of wellness.

Doctors generally define "health" as the absence of disease. By that definition, many of us may be healthy, but what we're striving for is a positive, preventive approach, which is what wellness is all about. Ironically, although the health of the American populace has increased during the twentieth century as a result of more effective immunizations and control of childhood diseases, wellness has decreased as a result of the changes in the American lifestyle.

Sometimes people need to do something dramatically different to reach a point at which they are willing to examine the personal cost of stress in their lives.

When I work with top executives, I find it most helpful to schedule a residential weekend during which we focus on understanding the nature of stress and learning the skills of deep relaxation and self-management. Away from our typical "life in the fast lane," we begin with a nondemanding Friday-evening session.

Many of these executives find that, for the first time,

they can relax without alcohol. In small groups of twelve to fifteen people, an atmosphere of trust prevails, giving each person opportunity to discusss his own concerns, organizational as well as personal.

The weekend is a time to unwind, to alternate the stimulation of being in an experiential-group situation with quiet time to go for a walk in the countryside or enjoy some recreational reading—all very different from a usual frenetic weekend at home. Here the executives learn about wellness and enhancing interpersonal skills. Many of the techniques covered in this book are presented, providing practical measures for effective stress reduction. They come to understand their own self-induced stress. By the end of the retreat, after having re-examined their life goals and present health practices, they create their own action plans. Generally, I meet with them again in a follow-up session a month later. From each other, they receive support for their efforts in creating more rewarding lives.

Getting away for a weekend to participate with others in learning how to live a more stress-free life is ideal, but for most people it is impractical. However, you can make the same kind of dedication in small amounts of time on a regular basis to achieve similar results. You *can* make it happen for you.

From my experiences in counseling clients and planning programs to enable people to live fuller, more satisfying and joyful lives, I have identified six major areas as crucial to understanding and managing stress:

> Awareness
> Nutrition
> Exercise
> Communication
> Relaxation
> Lifestyle Management

Recognizing the lack of an all-purpose personal pronoun befitting both sexes, I shall at times refer to "him" or "he" and at other times to "her" or "she" in an attempt to speak to all readers.

HOW TO USE THIS BOOK

This book contains two major divisions: the first half provides background and supporting information about each of the six subjects critical to *Letting Go of Stress*: Awareness, Nutrition, Exercise, Communication, Relaxation, and Lifestyle Management.

The overview of each area includes a self-evaluative test to enable you to determine which of these areas is most relevant to your concerns. Before you read the entire book, I suggest you complete the self-evaluative tests. How you do on the tests will enable you to discover the sections of the book to which you need to pay special attention.

The remainder of the book consists of the daily program. Each day for fifteen days you are given information and a practical "how-to" procedure in each of the six areas. If, when you take the self-evaluative tests, you find you need to focus your action plan on one particular segment, such as "awareness," you can then go through each of the fifteen days doing the exercises in awareness. If so, you may need to spend only fifteen minutes a day to reduce your tension.

Following the daily segments is a chapter entitled "Developing Your Personal Action Plan." The final chapter is called "Feedback," and is my opportunity to learn from you what you have found to be most helpful.

AWARENESS/OVERVIEW

What color are your mother's eyes?

What phase is the moon in tonight?

How high in the sky was the sun this morning when you first left your house?

Right at this moment, what parts of your body are making contact with the floor and the chair?

Right now, what noises do you hear as you read these words?

All these questions have to do with awareness. Sharpening your awareness means increasing your consciousness of what is going on within you and around you. The strong odors of a printing shop or a dry cleaners, the harsh noise of heavy construction equipment, the drone of a tractor, the blare of a loudspeaker, the whine of traffic, the roar of a diesel truck—all are part of our contemporary lives.

When I ask people what it's like to work in places where they are constantly subjected to such stressors as noises and fumes all day, their usual response is, "Oh, I don't even notice it any more." We also become accustomed to and ignore other kinds of stressors—such as an unsatisfying personal relationship, a disappointing job, or continual physical pain.

"Two magic questions" posed by Janette Rainwater in *You're in Charge: A Guide to Becoming Your Own Therapist* will enable you to become more self-observant.

1. *What is happening right now*? What am I thinking? What am I doing? What am I feeling? How am I breathing?

I suggest you answer these questions as if you were objectively observing another person and were able to perceive everything going on both inside and outside that per-

22

son. Avoid making any judgments and don't be emotional. Notice especially how you are breathing.

2. *What do I want for myself right now?*

Here you need to examine the benefit you receive from casting yourself in a certain role. For instance, if you see yourself as the helpless victim at the hands of willful wrongdoers, you need to discover how that role flatters you. Do you enjoy being center-stage in a melodrama?

These two magic questions will enable you to know yourself better, which is the key to all awareness. Most of the time, we pay attention to the things our minds are involved with, ignoring what our senses can tell us. The first step in reducing stress is to become aware of our sources of stress.

The Relaxation Log

A pocket-size aid to enable you to become more aware of what's happening in your life is *The Relaxation Log*, which was published in 1978.* It is a daily checklist that enables you to become aware of:

- your sources of stress
- how you experience that stress in your body
- what you are doing to alleviate it
- what behavioral changes you need to make to experience less stress.

The Relaxation Log is completely reproduced in Days 2, 4, and 5 of "Awareness."

Awareness of Sources of Stress and Physiological Indicators of Stress

1. Without referring to the Log, write down what you consider to be your sources of stress.
2. Write down, too, how you experience stress in your body—what physiological changes you're aware of when you feel overloaded.
3. Now refer to Day 2 of "Awareness" in the daily program, which gives that portion of the Log. How

---

* Jackie Schwartz, *The Relaxation Log*, Kasriel Productions (1908 Benecia Avenue, Los Angeles, CA 90025), 1978.

many new items did you add to your list after you saw the Log? (As tempting as it may be to turn immediately to that segment, I suggest that you complete this self-evaluation before doing so, as a way of finding out just how aware you are.)

To Score:

0 to 4 additional items = High degree of awareness
5 to 8 additional items = Moderate degree of awareness
9 + additional items = Low degree of awareness

The Relaxation Log has been designed so that you can keep track of these items for a two-week period in order to discover your particular patterns and, from them, to learn which areas need more attention. After the initial two weeks, you may wish to put the Log away for two months and then, again, use it as a daily checklist for another two weeks.

Using the Log this way will enable you to see what changes you may or may not be making to reduce your tension and increase your energy. If you're undergoing an especially stressful period, you may wish to keep it on an ongoing basis as a helpful guide to what's happening internally and behaviorally in your life.

Using the Relaxation Log is one way to learn how your sources of stress are interrelated, how your body responds, and what you may or may not be doing about it. For instance, if you suffer from muscular tension and notice that you tighten up as you become more aware of your sources of stress, you may find that this discomfort makes you more anxious and tense, which in turn causes your muscles to tighten up even more. Then you experience even more pain, which causes more tension, forming a very destructive cycle. *All muscular tension is self-produced.* Do you find that you're becoming more tense as you contemplate these interrelationships? Where in your body do you feel that tension right now? Is that a familiar feeling? If so, you may wish to refer to the "Relaxation" sections of the daily program to obtain some relief.

The Interrelatedness of Stress

How your body's reaction to stress is tied in with your sources of stress is an example of how you function as a system. A "system" can be defined as an interrelated group of people or things that, together, make up a whole. Every system is (1) made up of component parts that are (2) linked together in a particular way in order to (3) accomplish a common purpose. If anything goes wrong in any part of the system, the whole system is affected. Further, each system is usually made up of several subsystems, and the same principle applies: if anything goes wrong in any part of the subsystem, then the whole subsystem, and ultimately the whole system, is affected.

For instance, the chair on which you are sitting is a system comprised of four legs, a seat, a back, and perhaps armrests. If one of the legs is broken, then the whole system is impaired.

An individual person is also a system. If you have a blister on your thumb, you're painfully aware of how much it affects almost everything you do. If you have a cold, your respiratory and lymphatic subsystems place greater demands upon your body, and your whole system is affected.

Your total system is comprised of your mind, your spirit, and your body. *How you think affects how you feel.* Think about this for a moment. I have a big juicy lemon I've just picked from my garden. Now I'm cutting it in half, and the juice oozes over the cutting board. I take the lemon and press my tongue against it, sucking the sour juice. Okay, what did your mouth do while you read this? Chances are that you salivated just as if you were the one tasting the sour lemon juice. Your body was reacting because of your mind. That's the same kind of link that's demonstrated in biofeedback.

In the daily program you'll explore your family and your workplace as systems. These interrelationships are diagrammed below. The whole picture represents your life system. A change in any of the subsystems affects the system as a whole: *if any part of the system or subsystem is experiencing stress, that stress will affect the entire system.*

In the sections on "Awareness" that are part of the daily program, some new ideas may be presented along with some opportunities for you to expand your awareness. As

25

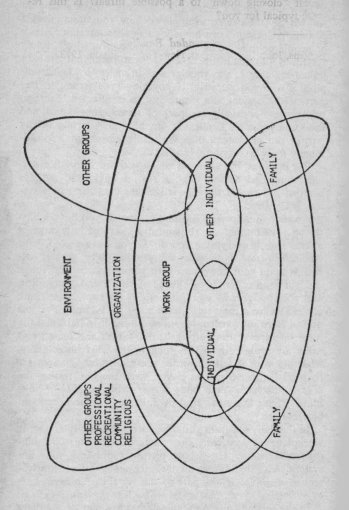

**THE SYSTEM'S NATURE OF
STRESS INFLUENCES**

26

you anticipate those experiences, do you find yourself responding with excitement and eagerness or do you feel yourself "closing down" to a possible threat? Is this response typical for you?

Recommended Reading
Stevens, John O. *Awareness*. New York: Bantam, 1973.

NUTRITION/OVERVIEW

We can't get away from it. It seems that in almost everything we read, we learn of some new approach to diet and nutrition. For most people, "diet" is synonymous with a method of weight reduction, and if being overweight is not their problem they may not pay much attention to what they put into their mouths.

Here I'm concerned with the bigger picture—everything we introduce into our bodies, including food, drugs, alcohol, and smoking. The bald truth is that each of us is responsible for what we choose to put into our bodies. Availability, tradition, and peer pressure form an unholy triad of enemies that interferes with selecting and enjoying only those foods and substances we know are good for us. Even though there is disagreement on some issues, such as the importance of cholesterol, eggs, coffee, and vitamin supplements, it's important to raise both these issues and others on which there is consensus.

To get an indication of your wellness in this area of your life, I suggest you complete the following self-evaluation, which I developed, along with some segments from Tom Isgar's self-test on nutrition.

WHAT DO *YOU* INGEST?

Respond to the following statements by placing a number on the line preceding each one. Select the number that best describes your behavior.

6=Always
5=Frequently
4=Often
3=Occasionally

29

2=Seldom
1=Never

—— 1. I read the list of ingredients on the foods I buy.

—— 2. I educate myself about good nutrition.

—— 3. I eat at least one uncooked fruit or vegetable each day.

—— 4. I eat red meat fewer than four times each week.

—— 5. I include fiber (roughage) in my diet each day.

—— 6. I drink fewer than five soft drinks each week.

—— 7. I drink fewer than three cups of coffee or tea (with the exception of herbal teas) each day.

—— 8. I avoid eating refined foods.

—— 9. I avoid salt.

——10. I avoid foods cooked in saturated fats.

——11. I avoid sugar.

——12. I avoid refined flour.

——13. I avoid MSG and other additives.

——14. I avoid bacon, ham, sausage, luncheon meats, frankfurters, and most regular cheeses.

——15. I avoid saccharin.

——16. I avoid avocados, nuts, olives and peanut butter.

——17. I occasionally fast.

——18. I take vitamin and mineral supplements in moderation each day.

——19. I drink eight glasses or more of water each day.

——20. I chew my food thoroughly.

——21. I am able to avoid foods I know I should limit or avoid entirely.

——22. I refrain from alternately binging and dieting.

——23. I eat food publicly (without secrecy).

——24. I avoid "eating on the run."

——25. I refrain from cleaning my plate.

——26. I avoid eating when I'm feeling tense, bored, or anxious.

——27. I avoid skipping meals.

——28. I eat when I am hungry, rather than when the clock tells me.

——29. I avoid using artificial aids, such as pills or shots, to control my appetite.

——30. I avoid eating when I am angry, depressed, or frustrated.

——31. I am aware of the side effects of drugs I take,

such as birth control pills or medication for high blood pressure.
——32. I take aspirin or other pain medications.
——33. I take other patent medicines, such as antacids, cold remedies or laxatives.
——34. I take tranquilizers.
——35. I take sleeping pills.
——36. I have a few (alcoholic) drinks before or during my meals.

Total your point score and enter here:——————

(Statements 1 through 19 concern *positive food intake;* statements 20 through 30 concern *positive eating behaviors;* statement 31 concerns a *positive health practice;* statements 32 through 36 concern *negative health practices.* All the subjects mentioned in these statements are discussed in this overview.)

If your total score is less than 143, I suggest you examine these health practices more closely.

Any answers of 1 or 2 on statements 1 through 31 indicate that you could improve these health practices.

Any answers of 5 or 6 on statements 32 through 36 indicate that you could improve these health practices.

The Perils of Alcohol and Cigarettes

Most of this overview is concerned with the food and drugs we use. However, since alcohol and cigarettes are problems for such a large percentage of the population and since both of these substances heap more stress upon the body, I'd like to address them first.

Alcohol is one of the oldest, most common tension relievers knows. "Having a drink to relax" is such a widespread practice that many people don't know how to relax without a drink. Unfortunately, having a drink doesn't take away the source of stress. In fact, it only creates more of a stress reaction, weakening the body and making the person even more vulnerable to stress. As one Alcoholics Anonymous spokesman put it, "If you drink because you have a problem, you have two problems—your original problem and alcohol."

Cutting down on or eliminating hard liquor is advocated

31

by many, but—on the positive side—drinking a glass of white wine with dinner can actually lower blood cholesterol, and the caloric value will not interfere with a desire for more nutritious foods. Unfortunately, a great number of people are unable to limit themselves to a single glass of white wine.

Alcoholism has been called industry's $40 billion hangover, including in that figure the cost to business and industry of alcohol-related problems. The problem drinker misses an average of twenty-two work days a year. His chance of having an accident is two to four times greater than that of the nondrinker, and three times as many medical benefits are paid to alcoholics. Philip Goldberg in his 1978 book *Executive Health*, estimated the average loss to a company to be one-fourth the drinker's annual salary.

Even if they aren't alcoholics, people who drink excessively subject themselves to high health risks. Because of their decreased mental alertness, coordination, and judgment, drinkers are implicated in nearly half of this country's 80,000 annual traffic fatalities. Further, alcohol lowers the body's resistance to infectious diseases.

Figures on the costs—emotional, physical, and financial—of being an alcoholic are readily available. What's often overlooked, though, is the cost to the alcoholic's family.

Some of these costs are enumerated by my colleague Sharon Wegscheider, in *Another Chance: Hope and Health for the Alcoholic Family:*

Stress wreaks much of the same havoc with the Enabler's (spouse's) health that alcohol does with the Dependent's (alcoholic's). Only the symptoms differ. She experiences one or several of the familiar stress-related conditions—digestive problems, ulcers, colitis; headaches and backache; high blood pressure and possible heart episodes; nervousness, irritability, depression. If her symptoms are mild, her doctor may write them off as neurotic or menopausal. But for the alert practitioner, the Enabler's physical complaints can offer the first crack in the family's wall of silence, the first opportunity for a professional to intervene.

We are fortunate to be living in a time when effective treatment programs for alcoholics and their families are available. Intervention programs that require residential treatment for the alcoholic and emphasize family participation have achieved dramatic positive results.

Now that you've been reminded of the perils of drinking, it's time to look at smoking. The shocking fact is that *cigarettes are the number-one cause of cancer in the United States*. So much has been said about the evils of smoking that you may think you've heard it all, but here is information that may be new to you.

Although most people are aware of the association of smoking with lung cancer and chronic lung diseases such as emphysema, less than half the population realizes that *smoking is one of the four major risk factors for heart attacks and strokes*. (The other three are higher blood pressure, higher serum cholesterol, and Type A behavior.)

Each of these major risk factors increases the chance of having a heart attack three times. Thus if you smoke and have high blood pressure, your chances of having a heart attack are increased six times. If you have a high serum cholesterol level, too, then you've increased your chances nine times!

One reason that smoking is a major factor in heart disease is that it contributes to the buildup of fatty arterial deposits of atherosclerosis. That means that there's less room for your blood to flow and a higher likelihood that a clot could cut off the blood flow altgether. A one-pack-a-day smoker has a 20 percent greater incidence of stroke.

Another reason is that *there is less oxygen available* when you are "under stress" and need it. For a one-pack-a-day smoker, the reduction of oxygen supplied to the heart and brain may be as much as 15 percent. It takes four to six hours to expel the carbon monoxide from the body, or overnight for heavy smokers.

Smoking as long as six hours before flying can seriously impair a pilot's eyesight, manual dexterity, reflexes, and ability to estimate time intervals. Decreased oxygen *increases the demand upon the heart, lungs, and blood vessels*—exactly the opposite of aerobics.

The risk of smoking means, in general, a *70 percent increase in the probability of dying at any age*—100 percent for a two-pack-a-day smoker. As a rule of thumb, each cigarette knocks about five minutes off the smoker's life. For someone with an average habit, that adds up to six or seven years. Meanwhile, smokers lose more work days because of

33

illness than nonsmokers and spend more time in the hospital.

In contrast, it's encouraging to know that, after a relatively short time people who *do* quit smoking are no more susceptible to heart disease than nonsmokers.

Maybe you already knew these things and have tried to quit. Giving up smoking has to be one of the hardest things for anybody to accomplish, harder than giving up alcohol or heroin. Nine out of ten smokers say they'd like to quit, and six out of ten say that they have tried but haven't succeeded. In spite of these odds, approximately 15 million people in the United States have quit smoking in the past fifteen years; 2 million quit in 1980 alone.

If you'd like to quit, you may wish to look into the programs offered by your local YMCA or the American Cancer Society. SmokEnders is a commercial venture that claims that only six out of a hundred participants ever smoke again. An approach that combines behavioral changes and group support seems to work best.

Alcohol and cigarettes are the two most obvious self-inflicted enemies of good health. Now let's turn our attention to less visible enemies: the food and substances that make up most of our daily diets.

How to Improve Nutrition: The McGovern Report

With the move away from staples and toward synthetic and highly processed foods since World War II, the food habits of Americans have changed dramatically. A blizzard of styrofoam packaging, disposable bottles, crinkly paper bags, aluminum containers, plastic pouches, and tin cans is testimony to our overabundant use of fast foods, convenience foods, and junk foods. We have become a nation that eats on the run, tending to neglect such former bases of security and predictability as a good breakfast and a family dinner. The shift away from a hearty breakfast to a heavy evening meal, however, is considered detrimental to our well-being.

Another change is the increasing number of meals eaten in restaurants, which further reduces our awareness of how food is prepared and where it comes from. With 51 percent of American women now in the work force, more emphasis is placed on speed and convenience at the expense of wholesome, nutritious meals and eating habits.

34

There is a great deal of controversy about what constitutes a "good diet." Unfortunately, many physicians are ill qualified to be informative, because nutrition is not a required subject in most medical schools. One attempt to provide an accepted guideline is the report of the Senate Committee on Nutrition and Human Needs, chaired by Senator George McGovern, popularly called the McGovern Report. In order to formulate a national nutrition policy, this committee recommended that the department of Health, Education, and Welfare spend a "specific amount" annually on introducing clinical nutrition training into the curriculum of every medical school by 1980. The committee also recommended that we:

- reduce fat and cholesterol consumption (including both animal and vegetable fats)
- reduce sugar consumption
- reduce salt consumption
- increase consumption of fruits, vegetables, and whole grains
- decrease consumption of meat, substituting poultry and fish

The stated purpose of these changes is to reduce the risk of heart disease, hypertension (high blood pressure), gall bladder disease, liver disease, and cancers of the breast and colon. The report advises that our eating habits "may be as profoundly damaging to the nation's health as the widespread contagious diseases of the early part of the century." Let's look at just how these dietary changes can increase our well-being.

Reduce Fat and Cholesterol Consumption

The McGovern Report's recommendations to reduce fat and cholesterol consumption are consistent with those advocated by Nathan Pritikin et al. in *Live Longer Now: The First One Hundred Years of Your Life*, writing of their experiences at the Longevity Center in Santa Monica, California. Many of us grew up in homes where our parents wanted to give us plenty of protein and calcium by having us eat eggs, cheese, whole milk, butter, meat, and ice cream. Such a diet is also high in cholesterol and saturated fats, which tend to increase deposits of fat (serum cholesterol) in the arteries. High-fat diets have also been linked to breast cancer.

The average American diet consists of 42 percent fat, which the McGovern Report suggests should be reduced to 30 percent. Pritikin goes even further, believing that it should be reduced to 5 to 10 percent, citing the correlation between high cholesterol in the foods we eat and high serum cholesterol.

According to a 1958 article in the AMA *Journal,* one of the first links between diet and serum cholesterol was established during the Korean War, when autopsies revealed that men as young as eighteen to twenty years of age showed clear signs of the buildup of fatty deposits in their arteries. Autopsies of 300 American soldiers revealed that 77.3 percent already showed evidence of heart disease. Their average age was twenty-two.

Until then, it was thought that heart attacks affected only older people, mainly men, and didn't "happen" until they reached their late forties or so. Finding out that diet and serum cholesterol could be related caused doctors to suspect that arterial buildup is a lifelong process that is affected by early-childhood eating patterns.

Pritikin believes the lower the fat, the lower the amount of cholesterol in our bodies. The average American consumes 600 to 750 milligrams of cholesterol per day. Pritikin's diet allows only five milligrams, and his "maintenance diet" only 100 milligrams, per day. Pritikin believes that 90 percent of heart disease can be prevented by changing to his low-fat/low-cholesterol diet, and claims that patients on his diet-and-exercise program have actually reversed atherosclerosis (narrowing of the arteries). Many medical doctors have supported his claims. Previously such a reversal was considered impossible.

These foods are high in cholesterol:

egg yolks	red meat
whole milk	ice cream, ice milk
butter	luncheon meats
most regular cheeses	sausage
ham	bacon
frankfurters	palm oil
commercial baked goods	organ meats—liver, kidney,

coconut oil   heart, brains, sweetbreads
shellfish

The McGovern Report took a big step when it recommended that we should reduce unsaturated as well as saturated fats in our diets. Despite the commercials, margarine is not necessarily better for you than butter. In fact, unsaturated fats (present in margarine, avocados, peanut butter, seeds, and nuts) increase another type of fat in the blood, triglycerides, and the arteries become filled with sludge. All fats that are liquid at room temperature, such as salad oil, are unsaturated fats and should be avoided.

Reduce Sugar Consumption

Sugar, sugar, everywhere sugar. Without diligently monitoring your food, you will find it almost impossible to get through a day without sugar. It's in:

catsup	jello
soft drinks	most breads
cocktails	processed foods—soups,
crackers	fruit, vegetables
some mustards	most breakfast cereals

You have to be a true detective to find a breakfast cereal without sugar, including those labeled "natural." Whether it's called sugar, turbinado, brown sugar, raw sugar, molasses, fructose, sucrose, syrup, dextrose or even honey—it's all still sugar and all processed in a similar way in your body.

The same is true of refined starches, such as white bread, spaghetti and other pasta made from white flour, pastry, rice, and noodles. Your body converts all of these foods to sugar once they're digested. It's no wonder that *the average American consumes over 100 pounds of sugar a year—about two pounds a week*. That makes it the third major ingredient consumed in the American diet, right after milk and meat. Three-quarters of the sugar consumed is in the form of processed foods.

The McGovern Report recommends reducing sugar intake by 40 percent, and Pritikin advises eliminating it altogether.

Besides the calories, what's so bad about too much sugar? If tooth decay and blood sugar's link with the life-changing diseases of diabetes and hypoglycemia aren't frightening enough, consider that sugar has been linked to heart disease. It apparently raises the level of fat in the blood, increasing the amount of low-density lipoproteins, which carry and deposit cholesterol in the blood vessels. In his book *Sweet and Dangerous*, John Yudkin, professor of biochemistry at the University of London, noted that patients with coronary artery disease and with peripheral vascular disease had a substantially higher sugar intake than the control group. In *Type A Behavior and Your Heart,* Meyer Friedman and Ray Rosenman advise anyone with tendencies toward Type A behavior or coronary artery disease avoid all but small quantities of sugar and other simple carbohydrates.

But what about all those candy commercials advocating sugar for quick energy? Yes, your body *does* need sugar, which is turned into glucose to fuel your brain. It does *not* however, need refined sugars, which play havoc with your pancreas' output of insulin and your blood-sugar level, creating wide fluctuations in your energy level. Your body can best use the natural sugars from complex carbohydrates, which release a slow, steady stream of glucose at a rate your body can optimally handle, normalizing your energy level.

Reduce Salt Consumption

Right up there with sugar is the prevalence of salt in food. Only recently has salt been removed from baby foods, to which it had been added years ago to keep mothers from complaining that the food lacked taste. But who knows, they may be adding salt from their saltshakers to "make the food taste right" for their babies. We're so accustomed to eating food with salt that when we eat something without salt it tastes dull, if it hasn't been tastefully seasoned with herbs and spices. Those who are put on salt-restricted diets complain at first, but readily adjust to the natural flavors of food. These foods are high in salt:

most regular cheeses	sauerkraut
frankfurters	salted popcorn

38

luncheon meats	biscuits, muffins
turkey franks	dehydrated potatoes
potato chips	peanut butter
buttermilk	frozen peas
frozen fish	cornflakes
commercial baked goods	bouillon
cakes made from mixes	canned vegetable juice
sausage, ham, bacon	melba toast
crackers	pickles
salted nuts	pancakes, waffles
canned soups	canned corn, beans, peas,
canned tuna	and most other canned
instant cereals	and frozen garden
bran flakes, All-Bran	vegetables
consomme	

Salt, the cheapest and most available seasoning, is used in almost everything we eat. Almost all snack foods, such as crackers, pretzels, chips, and cheese, are high in salt. Dehydrated foods (such as beef jerky), and smoked and processed meats are high in salt. Foods containing baking soda also contain salt. Even antacids and soda water contain salt. These vegetables have a naturally high salt content: celery, beets, dandelions, kale, mustard greens, and spinach.

Salt is directly linked with hypertension (high blood pressure), one of those big-four risk factors for heart disease. Most Americans take in six to eighteen grams of salt per day; some authorities estimate that the average is 14.5 grams per day. The McGovern Report suggests that salt intake be reduced by 50 to 85 percent, to about three grams a day. Pritikin agrees, recommending no more than two or four grams a day.

Our desire for salt is a learned, not a natural, taste. Once you become accustomed to a natural diet in which you use very little salt, your taste buds will be most sensitive to how much salt there is in almost every kind of food. Your body does need salt, but that need can be met by eating natural foods, almost all of which contain some salt.

Increase Consumption of Fruits, Vegetables, and Whole Grains

Foods rich in complex carbohydrates—whole grains, coarse raw vegetables, and fresh fruits—are generally lacking in diets that emphasize convenience. Grains and vegetables require time to prepare, and fresh vegetables and fruits must be eaten within a limited time period. This is in sharp contrast to "instant" packaged foods and the virtually unlimited shelf life of most prepared foods, which last indefinitely because of the additives and preservatives they contain. The advantages of complex carbohydrates, however, are many.

They take longer to digest, which results in the release of glucose, which can best be utilized by the brain. Unlike fat or protein, only carbohydrates are completely utilized, converting into energy carbon dioxide (which is expelled by breathing) and water (which is excreted in urine, feces, and sweat). Complex carbohydrates are most valuable when they have undergone minimal processing and refinement. *They supply us with necessary vitamins, minerals, dietary fiber, and energy, and are much better sources of protein than meat, fish, eggs, and milk.*

Fiber (roughage) is needed to facilitate the movement of food through the alimentary canal at a faster speed. People whose diet is rich in complex carbohydrates rarely complain of constipation. This faster "transit time" is linked to prevention of colon and rectal cancers, diverticulosis, hemorrhoids, appendicitis, and hiatus hernia. In *Nutrition and Physical Degeneration*, Weston Price says that the closer our diet is to that of primitive man, the healthier we will be. Another advantage is that a diet rich in complex carbohydrates tends to make you feel full and gives you a great deal of quantity for few calories. It's for this reason that fresh fruits and vegetables are preferable to fruit or vegetable juices.

Between 40 and 45 percent of the calories in the average American diet come from carbohydrates, but most of them are refined sweets and sugars (simple carbohydrates). Pritikin believes that carbohydrates are the best things you can eat—the *complex* carbohydrates, that is, found in whole grains, vegetables, and fruits—and advocates a diet consisting of 80 percent entirely complex carbohydrates. Contrary to what most people might expect, you will lose weight on such a diet.

Decrease Consumption of Meat, Substituting Poultry and Fish

Many people regard a thick, juicy steak as the height of luxury and self-indulgence, an indication that they can afford the best and are being good to themselves. Nothing could be further from the truth. That steak, loaded with saturated fats and cholesterol, isn't such a good source of protein after all. As much as 70 percent of the calories in a "choice" grade of cooked, untrimmed steak is fat, which is reduced only to 45 percent even after the steak is trimmed.

Further, the cattle-raising industry uses a great many hormones in order to get its product to market more rapidly, and you eat those hormones right along with the meat. Organ meats (liver, brains, kidneys, heart, and sweet-breads) are also loaded with saturated fat and cholesterol. The impurities collected by an animal's liver remain there even after it's cooked, making it a particularly poor choice.

Fish and the white meat of chicken and turkey, prepared without skin and with all visible fat removed, provide more protein than beef, and with fewer calories and less fat. Regrettably, even poultry and fish are not free of hormones and toxins.

Dealing with Overweight

Let us now direct our attention to one of the most important food-related problems: overweight.

We Americans are the most overweight people in the world. Conservatively, 80 to 90 percent of the U.S. population is more than 5 percent overweight. Stress and excess weight form a vicious cycle. When people are tense, bored, and anxious, they tend to eat too much. Stress contributes to poor digestion, which, in turn, creates even more stress for the body.

Further, susceptibility to stress-linked illnesses increases with excess poundage. If you're 25 percent overweight, your chances of having a heart attack are about two and a half times greater than that of someone whose weight is

41

normal. An obese person's heart must pump nourishment to a large quantity of tissue, putting an extra demand upon the heart and blood vessels. This is turn raises the risk of stroke, diabetes, hypertension, and heart disease. Here are some suggestions to help you become more aware of your eating habits and shed some excess pounds in a sensible fashion.

Keeping a Food Awareness Log, described in Day 1 of "Nutrition" in the daily program, will enable you to discover many things about your food patterns. First of all, you can find out *how you feel at the time you are eating.*

Many people seek food for comfort when they're going through some kind of emotional upset. If someone said something to upset them, if they feel anxious about having to make a decision, if they've just experienced a disappointment, if they regret something they either did or didn't do, if they feel lonely and unloved—these are just some of the reasons behind compulsive eating.

As children, most of us learned to associate food with pleasure. "Come on, I'll buy you an ice cream cone," were comforting words to a child who had skinned his knee. "If you don't behave yourself, you won't get any dessert," threatened the scolding parent.

We learned that if we were good we'd be rewarded with food, and that if we didn't feel well food would make us feel all right again. It's no wonder, then, that many of us turn to food when we're feeling unhappy, anxious, or tense. If things are really bad, you may be like the "hollow-leg" adolescent boy: you eat only one meal—all day long. During the "fight or flight" response, gastrointestinal functioning slows down; despite this, man is the only animal to eat when "under stress."

Second, your Food Awareness Log can also serve as a starting point to keep track of *how many calories you consume.*

The dictionary defines a calorie as "a unit of energy." That doesn't sound momentous enough to cause droves of people to center their lives around calories, but indeed they do. Unfortunately, even more people don't pay enough attention to the caloric content of their food.

When you consume more calories than you expend through your day's activities, you gain weight. It takes a lot of exercise to burn up calories. Eventually, exercise contributes to your desire for and maintenance of a slimmer body, but losing weight primarily through exercise is an awesome task. To give you an idea, you'd have to run four miles in thirty-two minutes to burn 450 to 500 calories. You can take in that many calories in a few minutes—one piece of pecan pie has 430 calories, and a chocolate milkshake has 500.

Fad diets and crash programs will not lead to long-term weight control. Worse, some of them may be harmful to your health—mental and physical. The most recent outstanding example was the very popular liquid protein diet, which upset the body's balance to such a degree that it sometimes caused an irregular heartbeat, and was occasionally fatal.

In any one year, 40 million Americans are dieting. Many engage in the "rhythm method of girth control"—alternately virtually starving themselves and, soon disenchanted, going on a binge. When you find yourself saying that you'll soon "go on a diet," those very words imply that at another point you'll "go off your diet." Instead, you should realize that you need to adopt healthier patterns of eating to live a more stress-free life.

Rather than saying "I'm going on a diet," say "I'm going to adopt eating habits that contribute to my wellness lifestyle." To achieve permanent weight loss, the changes you make in your eating habits should be pleasurable, diversified, and sociable. You need to devise a program you can *live* with.

Finally, your Food Awareness Log will enable you to discover *which situations encourage you to eat*.

Picture this scene. You stop by Sandy's house to wait for Marion to join you for the movies. Sandy puts out a bowl of potato chips. You settle down on the couch for some good talk, and before you know it, the bowl is empty. The two of you have finished that big bowl, hardly aware of it.

You were responding to *environmental cues*. The food was there, an accepted part of "making you feel at home," and without thinking about it, you simply ate and ate. An environmental cue is when you are in a specific situation or place and are "conditioned" to eat because that's what you usually do in those circumstances. This kind of unconscious eating has little to do with physiological hunger; rather, it's habitual response to a particular situation.

Popcorn at the movies, a cup of coffee while you read the paper, Crackerjacks at the circus, a doughnut during the Friday staff meeting, cotton candy at the county fair, a pastry when you pass the bakery, a hot dog and beer at the ballgame, an ice cream cone on a hot day—these are all learned responses to particular situations.

Debunking Some Myths

Your Food Awareness Log can be a big asset in learning about why, what, how, and when you eat. The next three daily segments concern some popularly held myths about food: your body needs as much protein as it can get, "milk is good for every body," having a cup of coffee will help you relax, and the Food and Drug Administration (FDA) protects you.

How Much Protein Do You Need?

Most Americans think of a reducing diet as high in protein and low in starch or carbohydrates. You've already seen how beneficial complex carbohydrates can be, in spite of all you've been told about avoiding starches. Because of the emphasis on high-protein diets, we tend to believe that protein is a very good thing—the more the better. Not so.

No more than 8 to 10 percent of our caloric intake needs to be in protein. Most Americans consume up to twice that amount. When more than 16 percent of your calories are in protein, out of an average daily intake of 2,300 calories, you go into negative mineral balance, which means your body actually loses important minerals, such as calcium, iron, zinc, phosphorus, and magnesium. Most Americans are in a negative-mineral-balance state.

A primarily vegetarian diet can supply more than enough high-quality protein if complementary vegetables are mixed. Frances Moore Lappe's *Diet for a Small Planet* is an excellent place to learn more about this.

Milk Is *Not* Good for Every Body

We have recently become aware that the generally accepted amount of calcium we need is too high. There is *no* correlation between calcium intake and bone thickness, even though bone thickness (and bone calcium) vary with age, according to Stanley Garn, an anthropologist at the University of Michigan, in his book, *The Earlier Gain and Later Loss of Cortical Bone in Nutritional Perspective*.

In a 1981 article in the *Los Angeles Times*, Robert Marcus, assistant professor of medicine in Gerontology and Endocrinology at Stanford University, was quoted as saying that "walking and running and that type of activity are the best things we can do with respect to providing a physical stimulus to keep bone mass at a high level." So if you're concerned about the dangers of osteoporosis (reduction in bone mass), get some physical exercise.

Another reason to drink less milk after the age of five is that most people lose the enzyme required for the proper breakdown and absorption of lactose, which can cause bloating, stomach cramps, and/or diarrhea. Nobody benefits from the high fat content of whole-milk dairy products, and people would be wise to limit their consumption of dairy products to nonfat milk, low-fat cottage cheese, and yogurt. One cup of nonfat milk provides 296 mg. of calcium; one cup of low-fat cottage cheese provides 180 mg. of calcium. One cup of yogurt made from partially skimmed milk contains 272 mg. of calcium; one cup of yogurt made from whole milk contains 251 mg. of calcium.

You can get some of the calcium your body needs from whole-grain cereals and certain vegetables, such as greens, artichokes, broccoli, and chard. One cup cooked collard greens provides 289 mg. of calcium. One cup cooked spinach provides 212 mg. of calcium. One cup of cooked rhubarb provides 212 mg. of calcium. One cup cooked dandelion greens provides 252 mg. of calcium. Marcus recommends one gram of calcium per day for women before menopause and one and a half grams after menopause, as menopause increases the need for calcium.

Coffee Will *Not* Help You Relax

Coffee causes the body to react in the "fight or flight" stress-alarm response. The villain here is caffeine, which is found in many sources other than coffee. Your metabolism speeds up as adrenalin increases. That's what you experience as the "pick-up" when you have a cup of coffee.

The other harmful effects of coffee are less well known. It has been linked directly to heart disease by increasing the free fatty acids in the blood, which can contribute to atherosclerosis and other degenerative diseases. It can also lead to conditions that increase the possibility of a fibrillation type of heart attack. Caffeine raises blood pressure.

Better known is the link of caffeine to birth defects. This last threat to health has provoked controversy regarding the Food and Drug Administration's identifying coffee as "dangerous to your health." Most recently, coffee in particular, not caffeine itself, has been linked to cancer of the pancreas.

Another important aspect of coffee is that it *increases* the need for Vitamin B_1, thiamin. Thiamin, called the "tranquility vitamin," is essential to good mental health. Caffeine also weakens the lower back. If you already have lower-back problems, you'll only increase their severity by drinking coffee. Even so-called decaffeinated coffee contains enough caffeine to negatively affect the lower back. Caffeine increases the amount and concentration of stomach acid, which contributes to ulcers.

If you're in the habit of drinking one or two cups of coffee first thing in the morning, you may discover that you get a headache if you can't have your coffee. Perhaps you've heard people say, "I must have my coffee first thing!" In a way, they're right. Going without coffee can cause withdrawal symptoms, as your body can become addicted to the caffeine in coffee or tea. Caffeine causes the blood vessels to constrict, and when you don't get your caffeine "fix" your blood vessels may dilate, causing a headache.

Although you wouldn't think of giving coffee to a young child, you might freely give a cola drink, cocoa, or a chocolate bar, all of which contain caffeine. Caffeine is also used in a variety of headache, cold, and pep pills. Anacin, for instance, consists of a combination of approximately six and two-thirds grains of aspirin and one-third grain of caffeine per tablet. It is advertised to be vastly superior to five-grain aspirin tablets, but the value of caffeine in controlling headache pain is reportedly without significant support. Read the labels to find out just what it is that makes you "feel better."

Too much caffeine can cause nervousness, irritability, agitation, headache, rapid breathing, twitching, insomnia, ringing in the ears, and flashes of light. Perhaps you know this syndrome as "coffee nerves."

The FDA Will *Not* Always Protect You

Now that Americans consume more processed foods than fresh foods, they may be unwittingly contributing to destructive internal pollution. If we could only see the additives the same way we can smell noxious fumes, we'd be more alert to their danger and more careful about putting them into our bodies. Some additives are flavor enhancers, preservatives and antioxidants, color additives, and emulsifiers, stabilizers, and surfactants.

Food processors use these additives to make their products more cosmetically attractive, enhance shelf life, retard spoilage, provide consistency of texture, and improve flavor. All of this greatly benefits the food processors, making their product salable over a longer period of time, but they would be hard-pressed to demonstrate that additives benefit the consumer.

Preparing foods from fresh vegetables and fruits is more of a bother than using canned, packaged, or frozen products, but the extra time and effort could make a big difference in how you feel. In their own way, food additives affect the body much as medications.

But perhaps you believe you don't have to worry about the safety and purity of the foods you eat because Uncle Sam's Food and Drug Administration (FDA) oversees food processors to insure that all foods are fine for us to eat. Right? *Wrong!*

In 1958 the FDA established the Generally Recognized as Safe (GRAS) list, consisting of hundreds of additives that had been in use long enough to be considered harmless even though they had never been tested. These substances were free of any restrictions that apply to other food additives and were made totally available for use in foods for which they had been approved. Many more substances have been added to the GRAS list over the years, often as a result of a decision by the manufacturers themselves— not the FDA—that a particular food additive is safe.

This means that there are some additives in our foods that have never been subjected to independent scientific investigation to determine their safety for human consumption. Two of the most well-known additives formerly on the GRAS list are cyclamate and saccharin. In the late 1960s

47

when studies linked cyclamates with bladder cancer in rats, almost three out of four families in the United States were consuming it in such products as Metrecal, ice cream, Diet Pepsi, jams, Kool-Aid, and even vitamin pills for children.

Most people, however, didn't know they were consuming it because the FDA had decided that additives on the GRAS list need not be listed on the label of the product! This means that, unknowing, you're probably eating and drinking an alarming number of additives. Food processors may choose to list as few additives as they wish from the GRAS list, perhaps in a misleading ploy to make the consumer believe he fully knows what he's getting.

One of the most pervasive of all food additives is the flavoring agent monosodium glutamate, commonly known as MSG. To find a prepared or processed food without MSG is quite a challenge, as it's in almost all sauces, seasoning salts, frozen and canned foods, crackers, soups, and mayonnaise, and is used liberally in Chinese cooking. This additive, secure on the GRAS list, was dangerous enough to be banned from all baby foods. It's been linked to arthritis, water retention, and headaches in human beings and to irreversible brain damage in infant laboratory animals. Despite these findings, it's still on the GRAS list, and processors are under no obligation to list it on their labels.

The Indispensability of Water

From the self-evaluation test at the beginning of this overview you should have gleaned these important bits of information: your body needs a lot of water, and it's wise to give your gastrointestinal system a rest occasionally with a fast of diluted fruit and vegetable juices.

Apart from the oxygent in the air we breathe, water is the most important thing human beings must have. Water constitutes between one-half and three-quarters of an adult's body weight; the percentage is even higher in babies and young children, and in lean rather than obese persons. The water that fills individual cells (intercellular fluid) constitutes three-quarters of the total body water.

Although water is generally not thought of as a nutrient, it is absolutely essential to every bodily function. Every chemical change in the body takes place in the presence of water. In addition, water is the basis of every body fluid—blood, lymph, digestive juices, sexual emissions, perspira-

48

tion, urine, and feces. It acts like an oil in an engine, lubricating and preventing friction between moving parts. It regulates the body temperature through evaporation from the lungs and as a result of perspiration.

The primary user of water in the body is the kidneys, since it is the kidneys through which waste products are excreted. Once this task is completed, water is made available within the body for other purposes. Water also plays a crucial role in enabling your body to effectively balance the demands made upon it by excessive stress. Whether you have sprained an ankle, feel like you're catching a cold, have had to work into the wee small hours on a project, or have had a fight with your lover, your body needs water. It helps your body's lymphatic system to cleanse out the impurities and overload caused by the additional stress.

Here's a formula to determine how much water you need. If you're healthy, your body needs a third of an ounce of water for every pound of body weight. If you're experiencing any kind of stress, you need twice that amount. Effectively, that means that if yours is a typical urban high-stress life, you need two-thirds of an ounce of water for every pound of body weight every day. That adds up to a great deal of water. And that water should be just that, the purer the better—not just any liquid. It's best to drink water between meals, to avoid diluting the digestive enzymes necessary for processing your food.

Unfortunately, the only people who follow such advice are usually those who have already experienced some kidney problems. If there were wider awareness of the benefits of high water intake in preventing skin from drying and aging, I believe more people would be drinking more water.

I had recently been the victim of a rear-end collision when I first found out about my body's need for water. At about the same time I learned that my prized special blend decaffeinated coffee weakened my lower back muscles. I knew it was mandatory to change these habits, and yet I didn't want to feel deprived, so I compromised with myself.

I truly loved the flavor of coffee, and the thought of giving it up altogether was too much. I bargained that I could have coffee only when I could have espresso, which automatically ruled out most coffee in offices, at coffee breaks, from vending machines, in people's homes, and in most restaurants. This meant that I had my espresso about once every six or eight weeks on my regular business trips to San Francisco. That was two years ago. Now I rarely even have espresso when it is available, as I'm so aware of the negative effects of coffee. I'd rather have a strong back and a strong heart.

The thought of drinking all that water didn't appeal to me either, but I found that if I heated the water and drank it from my oversize coffee mug, I was still going through the satisfying motions of sitting down "to relax" with a cup of coffee. Knowing the power of autosuggestion, I told myself I was having something good for me—nourishing, satisfying, and healing. I began to look forward to my cup of hot water after dinner and in the morning. Actually, it's three cups of hot water in the morning. It takes a lot of planning to work in a large quantity of water during a day.

I advise my clients to keep a carafe of water on their desks so that they can fill their coffee cups with something that's good for them. If they prefer to have it cold, fine, although, room-temperature water is easier on the body (ice puts a strain on the pancreas). One of my clients has on her desk a goblet and a crystal decanter, which she refills throughout the day. Subject to bladder infections, she has learned the importance of water the hard way.

The Benefits of Fasting

To most people fasting is the same as starving. In truth, your body has a great reserve of food, enough to keep you going for three or four weeks. Some authorities recommend fasting as a way of taking the strain off the digestive system. For example, *Physical Culture* magazine states that "fasting is an excellent agent for purifying the blood, and the majority of people who fast usually experience an increase in their ability to think more clearly." Because digesting food requires a lot of energy, when your body is relieved of the chore of digestion, you naturally feel lighter and more vibrant. Your body doesn't have to contend with the fluctuations in blood-sugar level caused by food intake, and it stabilizes at a higher level of functioning, causing you to feel energized.

One of my clients, a former dancer, fasts every Monday on fruit juices diluted half and half with water. She feels she's giving her body a day of rest after a weekend of heavier-than-usual eating and drinking. She's also careful to drink a minimum of two quarts of water, which supplies her with minerals, prevents dehydration, and stifles any feelings of hunger. She puts in a regular workday and feels no ill effects from abstaining from solid food for the day. In fact, she welcomes it.

You may wish to investigate further the benefits of fasting, and familiarize yourself with the different kinds of fasts available. Homeopaths recommend using an intestinal cleanser, available from health food stores, during fasting.

The Danger of Drugs

Now it's time to explore that other all-too-typical staple of American life: drugs, common legal drugs.

When you go to the doctor because you're not feeling well, an accepted, perhaps required, part of the ritual of healing is that he prescribe something for you. If he doesn't give you a prescription, you might think he's not taking your problem seriously. Most of us have grown up with the expectation that if we get sick, the doctor will "fix it," and part of how he fixes it usually involves prescribing some kind of medication. Few people know that 80 percent of the problems seen by a doctor are self-limiting: even if you didn't see a doctor you'd get better.

As a people, Americans want instant results. We look to drugs as a way of obtaining fast relief from any pain. In 1977, 37 million pounds of aspirin were sold, and tension headaches were the most frequently reported complaint. The number of sleeping pills consumed by Americans is staggering—27 million prescriptions in 1976, about a billion doses.

Aspirin is the most commonly used pain reliever. It lessens inflammation, reduces fever, relieves pain, is relatively nonaddictive, and its side effects are minimal if it's used according to directions. On the other hand, aspirin can produce stomach bleeding and abnormalities in liver and kidney functioning. It also interferes with the clotting function of platelets, the substance in blood that helps to form clots and stop bleeding. If you have ulcers or iron-deficiency anemia or are taking blood-thinning medication for diabetes or gout, you probably shouldn't take aspirin unless your doctor specifically instructs you to.

Barbiturates, the most commonly prescribed sleeping pills, quickly lose their effectiveness as tolerance develops.

One study revealed that Seconal starts to lose its effectiveness after just four nights of use. Clearly, sleeping pills are not the solution for sleep disorders. Further, sleeping pills suppress Rapid Eye Movement (REM) sleep, those critical active periods when most dreaming occurs, recurring at ninety-minute intervals. Dreaming is essential so that the unconscious mind can resolve the activities of your day. Ironically, when sleeping-pill users stop using these drugs, the body makes up for the REM sleep it has lost by an avalanche of vivid dreaming. This "REM rebound," which typically lasts for a week or two, causes a barrage of nightmares that are so frightening most people find them intolerable, often causing them to resume taking sleeping pills in order to sleep. In effect, they have become addicted, and many authorities consider dependence on sleeping pills to be more serious than heroin use.

Valium is one of the most widely prescribed drugs in the world. Twenty-five million people in the United States regularly take Valium—that's about one in nine. Librium and Valium have made their producer, Hoffman-La Roche, the world's largest drug manufacturer, comparable in size to General Motors. Unfortunately, Valium is also the most commonly misused drug, and it is responsible for more drug-related illnesses and deaths each year than any other drug—even alcohol. When taken in large doses over a long period of time, it can also produce or significantly increase depression. When properly used, these tranquilizers may be helpful in treating the kind of pain in which anxiety, agitation, and muscle spasm are prominent. Unfortunately, when used over an extended period of time, they can also produce such side effects as jaundice, blurred vision, nausea, changes in blood clotting, constipation, and hallucinations. Addiction can be a major problem.

There is no drug available that is completely free of side effects, and yet these potential dangers are rarely explained to patients. A drug-free lifestyle can be achieved through proper nutrition, a regular exercise program, relaxation techniques, finishing any "unfinished business" you have with others by appropriately expressing your anger or resentment, and effectively goal-setting.

In *Ninety Days to Self-Health*, C. Norman Shealy, an internationally respected neurosurgeon, suggests that you obtain answers to these questions when your doctor prescribes a drug:

1. What are the risks? (Get percentages.)
2. What are the risks if I don't take this drug?
3. Is there any alternative?
4. Are there any interrelations with other drugs I'm taking? (A pharmacist may be in the best position to answer this last question.)

Recommended Reading and Listening

Airola, Paavo. *How to Get Well*. Phoenix: Health Plus, 1974.
————. *How to Keep Slim, Healthy, and Young with Juice Fasting*. Phoenix: Health Plus, 1971.
Beiler, Henry G. *Food Is Your Best Medicine*. New York: Random House, 1965.
Brown, W. J.; Liebowitz, David; and Olness, Marlene. *Cook to Your Heart's Content: On a Low-Fat, Low-Salt Diet*. New York: Van Nostrand Reinhold, 1976.
Cheraskin, E.; Ringsdorf, W. M. Jr.; and Brecher, Arline. *Psychodietetics*. New York: Bantam, 1976.
Geisinger, M. *Kicking It: How to Stop Smoking Permanently*. New York: Grove Press, 1978.
Graedon, Joe. *The People's Pharmacy: A Guide to Prescription Drugs, Home Remedies, and Over-the-Counter Medications*. New York: St. Martin's Press, 1976.
Keller, Jeanne. *Healing with Water*. West Nyack, N.Y.: Parker, 1968.
Kraus, Barbara. *The Dictionary of Sodium, Fats, and Cholesterol*. New York: Grosset and Dunlap, 1974.
Lappe, Frances. *Diet for a Small Planet*. New York: Ballantine, 1971.
Miller, Emmett E. "Smoke No More" audio cassette tapes. Available from Emmett E. Miller, 945 Evelyn Street, Menlo Park, Calif. 94025
Price, Weston A. *Nutrition and Physical Degeneration: A Comparison of Primitive and Modern Diets and Their Effects*. Santa Monica, Calif.: Price-Pottenger Foundation, 1945.
Pritikin, Nathan, and McGrady, Patrick M. Jr. *The Pritikin Program for Diet and Exercise*. New York: Bantam, 1980.
Rodale, J. I., and staff. *The Complete Book of Minerals for Health*. Emmaus, Pa.: Rodale Press, 1977.
Staff of *Prevention* magazine. *The Complete Book of Vitamins*. Emmaus, Pa.: Rodale Press, 1977.

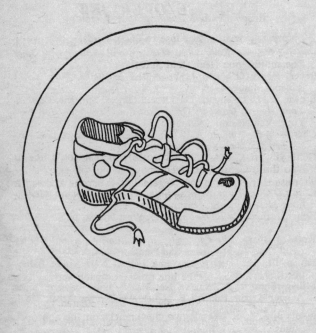

EXERCISE/OVERVIEW

Before I start, I have to lose twelve pounds.
My work schedule is too erratic to fit it in.
The mornings are too cold and dark.
I'm afraid I'll activate that old injury.
I'm too tired when I come home at night.
I don't have anyone to accompany me.
There's no point in starting until my work load eases up a bit.

Do you have a favorite excuse or two that you'd like to add to those commonly given above to put off exercising? Exercise is like eating your vegetables: everyone knows it's good for you, but sometimes it's so hard to do. See how you rate on the following self-test.*

PHYSICAL EXERCISE EVALUATION

Put a checkmark on the line preceding each activity you *presently practice.*

If you presently practice the activity indicated in statements 3, 5, 8, or 10, put *two* checkmarks on the appropriate lines.

Then total your checkmark responses and write this number on the line provided for "Total number of activities presently practiced."

---

* Adapted from *The Wellness Workbook,* by John W. Travis and Regina Sara Ryan, pp. 34–35. © copyright 1981. Used with permission. (Available at $9.95 paper from Ten Speed Press, Box 7123, Berkeley, CA 94707.) Scoring devised by Jackie Schwartz.

—— 1. I climb stairs rather than ride elevators.

—— 2. I include moderate physical effort (gardening, child care, standing all day) in my daily activities.

—— 3. I include strenuous physical effort (construction work, farming, hauling) in my daily activities.

—— 4. I jog at least one mile twice a week (or equivalent).

—— 5. I jog at least one mile four times a week (or equivalent).

—— 6. I regularly walk or ride a bicycle for exercise.

—— 7. I participate in a strenuous sport once a week.

—— 8. I participate in a strenuous sport more than once a week.

—— 9. I do yoga or some form of stretching and limbering exercise for fifteen to twenty minutes at least twice a week.

——10. I do yoga or some form of stretching and limbering exercise for fifteen to twenty minutes at least four times a week.

——Total number of activities presently practiced.

A score of 6 or more indicates that you are protecting your health.

A score of less than 6 indicates that you should seriously explore ways to make vigorous exercise a more regular part of your life.

It's a vicious cycle. If you don't exercise regularly, you get out of shape, you gain weight, you feel lethargic, and your body can't handle the demands of vigorous exercise—and yet that's when you need it most. It's most important, therefore, to *begin an exercise program after first consulting with your doctor about what limitations you should set for yourself.* Forget that you used to be able to run a mile in high school. That was then, and now, thirty years later, your arteries and waistline have no memory of your former athletic achievements.

Over the course of history, the physiology of human beings has changed little. However, the Industrial Revolution and, more recently, ever-increasing automation have eliminated the need for the physical activity that was formerly accepted as part of life. Now our lives are basically sedentary; we tend to work at desks or on assembly lines in the business world and use automated "labor-saving" appliances in the home. Back when people had to do hard physical work all day, it made sense that their leisure time should emphasize rest and quiet relaxation. Our leisure time is still primarily comprised of rest and inactivity, and that's in addition to our sedentary work, which typically demands very little from us physically.

Planning for Exercise

Introducing exercise into our sedentary lives needs to be a methodically planned activity. It's simply not likely that, in the course of a regular day, it will just happen that we get enough exercise.

Almost any kind of exercise is better than none. I say "almost" because you should be cautious about going out to play a strenuous game of tennis on Sunday morning every couple of weeks if that's the only exercise you ever get. That sudden burst of adrenalin could be too much for your normally sedentary body.

You can't afford to begin an exercise program until you first determine what shape you're in. It's quite possible that you've been sedentary for so long or that your arteries have become so narrow that launching an exercise program could be too much of a shock to your system. This is especially true if you're past forty years of age and you (1) ever experience chest pains upon exertion; (2) have ever had high blood pressure; (3) haven't had a physical examination from a doctor in the past three years; or (4) currently walk less than two and a half miles per day.

Your doctor should be aware of the first three items on that list. The last is one that might be news to you. If you're extremely sedentary, you may actually walk that little in a day, which puts you in the highest-risk category for heart attack and stroke in terms of physical activity.*

Your body needs different kinds of exercise.

- You can do some simple *stretching exercises or calisthenics* to keep your body limber.
- You can do *exercises to relieve muscular tension,* often caused by maintaining a certain posture or po-

---

* This is the "inactivity" that qualifies as a Minor Risk Factor in heart disease, referred to later in this overview.

sition for extended periods of time while working at a desk, standing at a counter, or slouching in a chair watching TV.

- You can do *cross crawls or walk* to stimulate both hemispheres of your brain simultaneously. "Cross crawls" are exercises that use opposite sides of the body at the same time—for example, your left leg moves at the same time as your right arm, which is the same combination of movements as in walking. These exercises enable the linear, logical, arithmetic, and speech functions of your brain's left hemisphere to merge with the pictorial, intuitive, artistic, and tactile functions of your brain's right hemisphere. When you're suffering stress overload, your thinking becomes more narrow in focus. Doing cross crawls for two or three minutes, as described in detail in Days 14 and 15 of "Exercise," enables you to use all your brain while you alternately stimulate and relax your muscles. If you're angry or have an important decision to make, doing cross crawls or taking a walk without having anything in your hands (a purse, notebook, or even a piece of paper) will clear your mind. Some experts recommend that all important decisions be made only after a period of using both the upper and lower extremities in an opposite, cross-crawling pattern.
- You can do *anaerobic exercise* if you want to develop the ability to perform at a high level of energy output for very short periods of time. This is fine if you want to be a sprinter, but useless for cardiovascular fitness.
- You can do *weight-lifting (resistive isotonic) exercises or pushups* if you want to build up your muscles. These may make you stronger and more attractive, but they can dangerously increase your blood pressure.
- You can do *isotonics*, where one muscle is pushed against another, if you want to build up your muscle tone. These cause less increase in blood pressure but are just as valueless as resistive isotonic exercises for cardiovascular conditioning.
- You can do *aerobic exercises* for cardiovascular fitness. Your body needs this kind of exercise.
- You can do *Hatha Yoga* for general toning and

conditioning of all systems in your body, including cardiovascular. Yoga emphasizes stretching and breathing exercises.

Exercises to Avoid

Everyone should be cautious about and probably avoid doing the following three exercises from Hatha Yoga, all of which irritate or make vulnerable the cervical vertebrae, the little bones in your neck that help support your head. The first is the popular *head roll*, in which you relax your neck muscles and allow your head to rotate all the way around in a slow motion. Although this might feel good at the moment, the vertebrae close down the intervertebral foramina (the openings for the nerves in the spine), thereby putting pressure on the nerves.

The second exercise to avoid is the *plough position* used in yoga, where you lie on your back, holding your knees close to your chest, and rock back and forth, eventually stretching your extended legs over your head. Here the majority of the body's weight rests on the delicate cervical vertebrae.

The third exercise to avoid is the *yoga headstand*. Here, too, the body's weight is pressing on the cervical vertebrae. If you choose to do a headstand using one of the specially designed supports that distribute your weight onto your shoulders, fine. Otherwise, no. If you've ever had a whiplash or other back injury, you know the importance of protecting these delicate vertebrae and your nerves.

The Benefits of Aerobics

Now back to what's good for you. Aerobics refers to rhythmical exercise of the large muscles, performed in a regular, sustained, and vigorous manner. "Regular" means that it has to be at least three times a week. "Sustained" means that it has to be a minimum of twenty minutes and preferably forty-five minutes. A quick spurt of activity, as in basketball or tennis, cannot produce this "training effect." "Vigorous" means that your heart functions between 70 to 85 percent of its maximum heart rate. Your maximum heart rate is obtained through a standard formula, described in Day 6, which takes into account your age and resting heart rate.

The three most common forms of aerobic exercise are jogging, lap swimming, and riding a stationary bicycle. If you can find a place to ride a bike where you don't have to stop for traffic lights, pedestrians or traffic, then that's fine, too. Walking briskly at a pace of thirteen to fifteen minutes per mile and running are also aerobic exercises. Cross-country (Nordic) skiing is excellent. Kenneth Cooper found that the Norwegian cross-country skiers had the best cardiovascular fitness of any group he tested, due to their ability to ski cross-country, often with packs on their backs, for hours at a time. Even jumping rope, using a trampoline and vigorous dancing, such as folk dancing or "jazzercise," can be aerobic exercises if they are done vigorously enough.

Let's look at the risk factors of heart disease.

Major Risk Factors	Minor Risk Factors
Higher cholesterol	Obesity
Higher blood pressure	Inactivity
Smoking	Gout
Type A behavior	Diabetes Mellitus

And *heredity* underlies everything else.

As mentioned in the overview of "Nutrition," the major risk factors increase your likelihood of having a heart attack threefold. As detailed below, aerobic exercise tends to neutralize these risk factors, and diet can control gout and diabetes.

Aerobic exercise is essential to attaining a high level of wellness.

- It's required to maintain peak cardiovascular and pulmonary conditioning.
- It's a natural antistress experience and can result in an improved psychological outlook as well as obvious physiological improvements. Fifteen minutes of brisk walking produces more relaxation at the muscular level than a tranquilizer.
- It increases the amount of oxygen in the blood, thereby reducing the number of heartbeats required to nourish your body. (Your body uses more oxygen when it's in the "fight or flight" state.)
- It increases your lung capacity. You'll breathe more

easily because the muscles in your chest wall will be stronger.

- It decreases your blood pressure and lowers your heart rate, allowing your heart to beat more strongly and pump more blood per stroke. A lower heart rate is comparable to a more efficient pump or lower rpm's in an engine. It can do the same job by working less hard, and should therefore last longer.
- It increases circulation by increasing the size of the blood vessels and building a network of auxiliary capillaries. Blood flow to the heart and the brain is increased, improving mental functioning.
- It lowers serum cholesterol. It increases your high-density lipoproteins, an "anti-risk" factor associated with lower incidence of cardiovascular deaths.
- It is recommended for building stronger bones, better posture, and better skin. Walking and running provide the stimulus to keep the bone mass at a high level, minimizing the likelihood of osteoporosis in the aged.
- It causes a redistribution of body weight. Your weight on the scales may not change very much as your fat turns to muscle, but you'll be able to wear smaller clothing sizes.
- It's ideal for the Type A personality, as it's a natural outlet for tension, anxiety, and pent-up feelings of aggression.
- It causes the brain to release endorphins, a chemical which acts as a natural tranquilizer and pain-killer.
- It contributes to better sleep.
- It contributes to a better sex life.
- It has a calming effect upon the mind, as no mental activity is required to sustain the rhythmic pattern.
- It increases stimulation in the right hemisphere of the brain, allowing for greater creativity.
- It decreases appetite immediately afterward.
- It contributes to the adoption of positive lifestyle choices, such as improved diet and giving up smoking.

This overwhelming list of benefits may be enough to get you out of bed to exercise instead of turning off the alarm for an extra forty winks. As is true of all the other aspects.

of this book, before beginning to exercise you should first identify the problem, selecting what best fits you, make a commitment to carry through, overcome your inertia to just get started, monitor your progress, and maintain a regular program. Besides feeling better, a powerful side benefit of exercise is that you'll feel so virtuous! I also recommend that you read about the benefits of aerobics in any of the excellent books available.

Avoiding Injury

What's that? You're aware that you have some fears about beginning a program of brisk walking or jogging? Are you reluctant to begin for fear of injury? Unfortunately, many people are injured due to exercise that is entered into carelessly, excessively, or without proper guidance. The biggest worry, of course, is that you'll have a heart attack. You can allay this fear by having a physical exam before you start. A stress-electrocardiogram as part of your physical will tell you (and the doctor) the condition of your arteries and blood supply. A regular resting electrocardiogram (EKG), unfortunately, detects single-vessel coronary disease only about 15 percent of the time. The Masters two-step test, in which you are monitored while taking a step up and a step back, will pick up single-vessel coronary disease only about 35 percent of the time. The stress-EKG, however, will detect single-vessel problems as much as 93 percent of the time. The stress-EKG is conducted on a treadmill or a stationary bicycle.

One of the most common causes of self-inflicted injuries is setting expectations for yourself that are too high, in terms of either time or distance, which can result in fatigue or actual muscular injury. One way to find out if your jogging pace places too great a strain on your heart is to take the "talk test." You should be able to carry on a conversation while you're jogging; if it requires too much effort to do so, you're overextending yourself.

Your goal, remember, is to get your pulse rate up to 75 percent of your maximum heart rate (that's your *ideal* "working heart rate"), and you might be able to accomplish this by walking. Once you've gotten your pulse to a working heart rate, you can increase either your speed or your distance—but don't overdo it. Never increase your mileage by more than 25 percent a week. If you go four miles one week, you should go no more than five the next.

Injuries to the feet and ankles are common for joggers who don't take preliminary precautions. With every step you take as you run, you put a pressure equal to approximately three times the amount of your weight on your feet. Thus if you weigh 150 pounds, you're putting 450 pounds of pressure on your feet. This is one reason you should get slim and stay slim. Runner Jim Fixx, author of *The Complete Book of Running*, gives this formula as a general rule: the ideal weight for a runner in good condition is two pounds per inch, which is lean to the point of gauntness if you're very tall. When my husband was training for his first marathon and had attained his ideal running weight, friends and family—especially family—would ask with concern how long had he been ill! We associate good health and well-being with a body that's well filled out, and we still like our babies plump.

The body isn't meant to run on hard surfaces, like city streets. Instead, it's best to run on cushioned surfaces, such as grass or a high school or college track. Running on hard packed sand is another option. However, beware of running at the water's edge, as the shore slants and running on an uneven surface can also cause injury. Some jogging programs are conducted through fitness centers that are equipped with carpeted, banked tracks. All-purpose gyms may conduct their jogging programs on a hardwood floor, which provides some resiliency. If bad weather keeps you from going outside, you can jog in place on a carpeted surface.

Well-designed jogging shoes are available at sporting-goods stores and specialty shops that cater to runners. If you're interested in walking, jogging, or running, invest in a good pair of running shoes. They may be expensive, but they're your most important investment. Besides, spending a lot for a pair of well-designed shoes may help you realize that your body is worth taking care of, and once you've got the shoes you can begin in earnest. Regardless of where you run—inside on carpeting or outside on grass, a track, or packed sand—*always wear your running shoes*. They're designed to support your feet and minimize injury.

To decrease the possibility of injuring your legs, it's wise to learn how to set down your feet properly. Heel first or

63

flat-footed are recommended positions, and you should not land on your toes. It may look most graceful, but it doesn't allow the calf muscles to stretch out.

Proper warm-up and cooling-down exercises are exceedingly important in reducing injuries and increasing joint mobility, making your body more flexible. A supervised exercise program or one of the excellent books on running will detail which exercises are essential to stretching your muscles before and after a run in order to minimize injury.

A sharp pain at the front of your waist, on either side, is commonly called a "side stitch" but is actually a spasm of the diaphragm. (The diaphragm is a muscle like a piece of elastic sheeting that stretches across the chest, separating the chest cavity from the abdomen.) The stitch occurs when you are breathing shallowly and can be eliminated by learning how to breathe properly. You need to find your own natural rhythm for breathing and forcefully expelling the air every fourth, sixth, eighth, or tenth step. You don't have to worry about the process of breathing in—that will take care of itself. Simply remember to exhale forcefully in a regularly repeated pattern and proper breathing will become automatic for you.

In *The Sportsmedicine Book,* Gabe Mirkin gives two simple rules to avoid injury: (1) stop running when you feel pain that gets worse, and (2) follow an easy-hard, easy-hard training schedule, where you run hard only every other day. The body needs forty-eight hours to recover.

What to Wear

Special clothing, which may or may not be necessary, is available for joggers. Women should wear brassieres especially designed for active sports to avoid skin irritation and injury to delicate tissue during a long run. Those designed without a fastener, the kind that slip on over the feet, are preferable. Using Vaseline on toes, feet, and any other areas that might become chafed (such as under a brassiere) will minimize irritation.

To avoid becoming overheated during jogging, wear clothing that is well ventilated, comfortable, loose-fitting, and nonbinding. Avoid wearing plastic cover-ups or heavy warm-up suits, which reduce or eliminate ventilation and increase perspiration. Some people wear these as a way to attain a temporary water loss, which shows up momentarily on the scale as a weight loss. Drinking water will immediately put the weight back on, however. Since your body temperature will rise during vigorous activity, it's best that perspiration act as the natural cooling agent it is intended to be by evaporating on the skin and thus lowering your temperature.

Okay, now you know how good aerobic exercise is for you, what precautions you should take, what to avoid, and what to wear. The daily programs include many different kinds of exercises to increase your wellness, but because of its supreme importance to your total wellness, the emphasis is on aerobic exercises. The areas of the body most vulnerable to muscular tension—neck, shoulder, and lower back— also receive special emphasis, and simple exercises to stretch away tension are included. Some cross-crawl exercises are given to stimulate both halves of your brain, which is essential when you're feeling overstressed and unable to think clearly. They're great, too, to keep you limber.

Enjoy your reading and your exercising!

Recommended Reading

Cooper, Kenneth. *The New Aerobics.* New York: Bantam, 1970.

Farquhar, John. *The American Way of Life Need Not Be Hazardous to Your Health.* New York: Norton, 1978.

Fixx, James. *The Complete Book of Running.* New York: Random House, 1977.

Hittleman, Richard. *Introduction to Yoga.* New York: Bantam, 1969.

Lance, Kathryn. *Running for Health and Beauty: A Complete Guide for Women.* New York: Bobbs-Merrill, 1977.

Mirkin, Gabe. *The Sportsmedicine Book.* New York: Little, Brown: 1978.

Mitchell, Curtis. *The Perfect Exercise.* New York: Simon and Schuster, 1976.

Royal Canadian Air Force Exercise Plans for Physical Fitness. New York: Pocket Books, 1972.

Spackman, Robert R. *Exercise in the Office.* Carbondale, Ill.: Southern Illinois University Press, 1968.

Spino, Michael. *Beyond Jogging: The Innerspaces of Running.* Millbrae, Calif.: Celestial Arts, 1976.

Thie, John F., Marks, Mary. *Touch for Health.* Los Angeles: DeVorss, 1980.

COMMUNICATION/OVERVIEW

When is the last time you felt that you were truly understood—when you talked with someone who genuinely seemed to understand what you were feeling? Most of us can remember such an occasion because "connecting" with another person is somewhat of a rarity. Without it, though, we tend to feel quite separate, which leads to feelings of being misunderstood and sometimes to an aching loneliness. Just knowing that another person understands what it's like to be in such a predicament or to feel a certain way reduces our feelings of isolation.

To find out how well you communicate, I suggest you complete the following self-evaluation.* Some of these statements have explanatory notes. If the statement does have a note, please refer to it before responding. Some of the statements are really two in one. This was done to show an important relationship. If only one of them is true for you, give yourself two points.

WELLNESS AND COMMUNICATING

Respond to the following statements by placing a number on the line preceding each one. Select the number that best describes your behavior.

4 = Very, always, or usually
3 = Often

---

* Adapted from *The Wellness Workbook* by John W. Travis and Regina Sara Ryan, pp. 39–40, © copyright 1981. Used with permission. (Available at $9.95 paper, from Ten Speed Press, Box 7123, Berkeley, CA 94707.) Scoring devised by Jackie Schwartz.

2 = Sometimes, maybe
1 = Occasionally, rarely
0 = No, never, or hardly ever

—— 1. I am able to initiate a conversation on my own.
—— 2. I am able to communicate with strangers.
—— 3. I can introduce a difficult topic and stay with it until I've received a satisfactory response from the other person.
—— 4. I enjoy communicating and am interested in what others have to say.
—— 5. I enjoy silence.
—— 6. I have at least three friends with whom I can communicate intimately.
—— 7. I can communicate my weaknesses to others when appropriate.*
—— 8. I am aware of how other people are likely to react when I initiate a communication.*
—— 9. I consider my thoughts and feelings with care before responding to others.
——10. I am aware of how I communicate with others nonverbally.*
——11. I am aware when I'm responding to my internal "tapes" rather than thinking independently.*
——12. I communicate clearly with friends and family.
——13. I am not asked to repeat myself or speak more loudly.
——14. Instructions I give to others are carried out properly.*
——15. I assert myself to get what I need rather than feel resentment toward others for taking advantage of me.
——16. I am aware of situations when I want to blame others rather than accept that I may be wrong.*
——17. I admit my mistakes when I am aware of them.*
——18. I can let go of my negative judgments of others, and I can accept that they only are doing what they think is best.*
——19. I am aware of my defense mechanisms.*
——20. I am able to listen to and objectively consider opposing viewpoints.*
——21. I am a good listener.*
——22. I don't try to change the subject during a conversation in order to win.*

68

———23. I am aware of my tone of voice, facial expression, and body language when communicating with others.*

———24. I like myself and can accept my "failings" rather than "beat up" on myself because I think I'm unworthy.

———25. I don't interrupt or finish others' sentences for them.

———26. I am not responsible for keeping (making) other people happy.*

———27. I take charge and control a situation when it is appropriate.*

———28. I let others take charge and control a situation when it is appropriate.*

———29. I cooperate with others when it is necessary for several of us to take charge of a situation.*

———30. I am able to let go of control and allow a situation to work itself out through means I don't fully understand.*

———31. I let go of mental labels and judgments I attach to persons and things in my environment, and instead see them for what they are.

———32. I am aware of the psychological games people play.*

———33. I am aware of the psychological games I play with others.

———34. I can stop playing a psychological game and instead communicate directly.*

Total your point score and enter here:———

If your total score is less than 85, you may wish to improve your communication practices.

Notes to the Evaluation

7. Trust is more readily established when we are open about our limitations.

8. This doesn't mean you let other people control your behavior, but that you initiate communication in a way that is likely to accomplish its purpose.

10. When highly verbal people expand their range of communication modes, it enables them to meet situations more satisfactorily.

11. Our supply of self-chosen "tapes" (i.e., internal messages such as "You shouldn't be acting so silly") is hard to turn off, but being aware of when they are operating can give us more control in a situation.

14. If many different people frequently don't, consider the fact that you may not be giving instructions clearly.

16, 17, 18. "Right-wrong games" can impede communication as well as thinking.

19, 20, 21, 22. Defense mechanisms (phobias, overreacting, not listening, changing the subject, etc.) allow us to keep our world view intact. Letting go of them can be painful, but is rewarding in the growth it produces.

23. Most communication occurs via the nonverbal modes, and being aware of this can speed the process of communication. Trying to take responsibility for another person usually doesn't serve either person in the long run.

26. Each of us, regardless of how inadequate we may make ourselves seem, is ultimately responsible for our own happiness.

27, 28, 29, 30. Control is an important form of communication. Being able to deal with it in a balanced way provides us with more options.

32, 33, 34. Psychological games, as defined by Eric Berne in *Games People Play*, are complex unconscious manipulations that result in the players attracting negative attention and feeling bad.

* * *

One of the first steps to improving communication is to become more aware of what is true for you, what is happening for you. Many fail to recognize that there are two parts of reality to everything we experience:

1. What we are thinking or doing and how we may be reacting to something.

70

2. How we feel about it.
If we were to draw this, it could look like this.

Thoughts, Actions

Feelings

Sometimes the feelings stay beneath the surface and only the words predominate. At other times our feelings are so strong that they overshadow any words.

Learning to Express Ourselves: Keeping a Journal

Perhaps you've had the experience of seeing someone who has just suffered a minor injury, like burning her hand on a hot plate or dropping something heavy on her foot. When you ask her how she is, she replies, "I'm just fine!" Her words don't match the red color and tense muscles of her face as she strains valiantly not to reveal her true feelings. This is called a "double-level message." As the observer, you are confused as to which message to respond to: her words or her obviously pained feelings. If her reply were something like, "Oooh! I hurt myself, and I feel so clumsy," then she would be sending a straight, or "congruent," message.

Feelings accompany everything we do. When the feelings are much stronger than whatever it is that we're doing, we may find it more useful to talk about our feelings than about *what* we're doing. If we refrain from talking about our feelings when they're strong it means we're putting a great deal of energy into "keeping the lid on" in the belief the others won't or shouldn't know how we feel. (Appendix E reveals how common this characteristic is.) For many, talking about or being in touch with feelings is not considered appropriate, and, indeed, our society places little value on how we feel. Mainly we are encouraged for what we produce, not how we feel about it.

Keeping a journal is one way to improve your ability to be in touch with and express your feelings. A journal can be your own special place for recording your thoughts and feelings, serving as a marker in time for what is going on in your life at any given time.

71

That brings me to a very important point. Your journal should be for your eyes only. Once you regard it as something that someone else might read, you will automatically censor your thoughts and feelings. If you fear intruding eyes, be resourceful in finding a suitable place to keep it.

Anything that has strong feeling content can be a source of learning for you and is therefore ripe for inclusion in your journal. Some people use it only when they feel confused and need to "talk over a problem with a friend"; the journal serves that role nicely. In fact, your journal is your true friend, to whom you can tell anything that's important to you.

However, it's also valuable to take the time to write in your journal when things are going very well, so that you don't record only the trying times of your life. When you're in a situation where you're meeting new people or seeing sights for the first time, the journal gives you an opportunity to record those first impressions. After you're more familiar with them, your impressions will probably change, and it might be helpful if you note what initially attracted or repelled you.

I've found that if I'm having trouble figuring out a problem or clarifying my feelings about a situation, writing in my journal enables me to present (through pictures or words) what's important to me. I can look back at it much later—even years later—and, because I took the time to record exactly how I was feeling at the moment, where I was, and what time of day it was, the whole experience is as fresh as yesterday. A real benefit, too, is seeing how much I've changed or stayed the same since the original entry.

Day 1 of "Communication" in the daily program deals with starting your journal.

An alternative to writing in a journal is to record your thoughts and feelings by using a tape recorder. A very dear friend of mine commuted an hour each way on the freeway to her job in a prison. Her work was very draining, as she had to be exceedingly alert and in control at all times, and she was constantly vulnerable to the threat of personal injury. She used her commuting time to record her thoughts and feelings on a daily basis. She obtained a clip-on microphone that attached to her clothing, and plugged her tape recorder into the cigarette lighter receptacle. *She made several important discoveries.*

She found that she could not lie to herself. She couldn't say, for example, that "today wasn't such a bad day," because her stomach would knot up as she said it. She became sensitive to her bodily reactions as she verbalized her thoughts, which enabled her to better express her feelings.

She also discovered that it didn't matter if she thought that she had nothing important to say. Once she began her stream-of-consciousness monologue, the strong underlying feelings would surface—feelings that, at most other times, she found difficult to express.

It also didn't matter if she didn't talk about things in the order of importance that she had planned. If she interrupted herself with "Oh, the traffic is backing up now," she might start again in an entirely different place. That was okay, because the truly important messages were delivered. She found that there was no "wrong" way to reveal herself.

The very act of this daily ritual provided an essential safety valve for this woman in her high-stress job. Through this process, she became aware of the heavy toll the job was taking on her well-being. After several months, she left the job.

Getting in Touch with Your Beliefs

In addition to becoming more in touch with your feelings by means of a journal or tape recorder, another important ingredient in effective communication is to *understand your belief systems*. The messages you send yourself are most powerful in determining how you feel about yourself, how much stress you experience, and how well you communicate with others. If you anticipate that bad things will happen to you, it's likely that they will, and that will in turn color whatever messages you send yourself about what you perceive. For instance, if you see a stranger in a car parked outside your home, you may assume the worst and think that he's there to inflict some harm. Accordingly, you would approach him with suspicion and some degree of hostility. On the other hand, if you experience the world as a friendly place and expect the best from people, you wouldn't be surprised if he were there to deliver a flower arrangement.

If you have confidence in your ability to handle the unexpected, you are more able to stay centered and not fall into the futility of excessive stress about "what if."

Days 2, 5, and 6 of "Communication" in the daily program are concerned with your belief systems.

Recognizing Styles of Coping

In *Peoplemaking*, Virginia Satir, an internationally famous family therapist, states, "Communication is the greatest single factor affecting a person's health and his relationship to others." Satir has found that when people are "under stress" and simultaneously feel that their self-worth is in danger, they tend to respond in one of four styles of communicating. These four styles are placater, blamer, super reasonable, and irrelevant.

These four coping styles are just that: styles; they don't necessarily describe a permanent characteristic or way of acting. How someone acts with one person may be quite different from how he acts with another. Or the situation may make a difference, so that how he acts in his kitchen may be quite different from how he acts in his office. And, of course, he may act differently at one time than another, depending on how he feels.

As caricatures of effective communication qualities, each coping style tends to oversimplify a situation so that one aspect is emphasized and the others ignored. The key elements of any interpersonal situation are one's self, the other person, and the context of the situation (see diagram).

S = One's self

O = The other person

C = The context of
the situation

Each stance is an attempt to conceal the feeling of weakness or imbalance characteristic of stress and is a response to a threat. These attempted deceits do not allow the individual to be congruent. Characteristic words and body postures offer cues for recognizing each of these styles and, consequently, the situations in which people experience stress overload.

74

"Internal dialogues," which are the interpersonal exchanges in a person's own thoughts, reflect feelings of self-worth and the coping style that has been adopted to deal with it.

Stopping a stressful interpersonal situation long enough to acknowledge the threat or stress will often help the person to regain balance and assume a more congruent communication, and reflecting one's own or another's feelings can often have a similar effect.

Responding in one of these coping styles causes you to pay a heavy price, because not being congruent heaps additional stress on the body. *Your body will be most susceptible at its weakest point,* whatever that may be for you. If you typically respond in any one favored style, you will probably experience physical discomfort. Generally, predictable ailments are associated with these four coping styles:

1. The *placater* tends to experience disorders of the gastrointestinal system—nervous stomach, digestive problems, ulcers, colitis. Carried to its ultimate extreme, the placater would commit suicide.

2. The *blamer* tends to experience disorders associated with any tightening of the body—hemorrhoids, high blood pressure, headaches. Carried to its ultimate extreme, the blamer would commit murder.

3. The *super reasonable* tends to experience disorders associated with drying up the body and a rigid posture—skin diseases, inadequate lubrication, stiff neck, bad back. Carried to its ultimate extreme, the super reasonable would become autistic.

4. The *irrelevant* tends to experience disorders associated with the central nervous system. Carried to its ultimate extreme, the irrelevant would become schizophrenic.

To learn more about these coping styles, refer to the accompanying chart.

The Four Most Common Coping Styles*

Coping Style	Characteristic Words	Body Posture	Inside Feelings
1. PLACATER (so the other person doesn't get mad) The other person is the one who counts	AGREE "I am helpless. Whatever you want is okay. I'm just here to make you happy."	Pleading, down on one knee, with furrowed brow reflecting uncertainty, looking to others for solutions.	"I feel like I am a nothing. Without him I'm dead. I am worthless."
2. BLAMER (so the other person will regard you as strong; if he goes away it will be his fault, not yours) I count, not the other person	DISAGREE "I am the boss around here, and don't you forget it! You never do anything right. What's the matter with you?"	One hand on hip while pointing with the other hand, with fierce, angry-looking face.	"I am lonely and unsuccessful."

76

3. SUPER REASONABLE
(pretending the threat is harmless and establishing self-worth by using big words)

The situation counts, not you or me

WITH LITTLE AFFECT "If one were to observe carefully, one might notice the work-worn hands of someone present here."

Stiff body, with eyes toward the ceiling, not making eye contact. Neck is painfully arched, and back is ramrod straight. Looks calm, cool and collected.

"I feel vulnerable."

4. IRRELEVANT
(ignoring the threat, hoping that it will go away)

Nothing counts

DISTRACTING, CHAOTIC. The words make no sense in the situation, come from "left field."

Angular, off balance, in perpetual motion, desperately trying to be noticed.

"Nobody cares about me. There's no place for me."

*Concept of Dr. Virginia Satir

77

When people respond in their coping styles, a dialogue could go like this:

Me: Why don't you ever invite any of our friends over for dinner?   (blaming inquiry)

You: You're right, dear. I never seem to be able to get it all together.   (placating defense)

Me: Certainly it is only a cursory courtesy to reciprocate appropriately when one is the repeated recipient of considerate, hospitable entertaining.   (super reasonable explanation)

You: Oh, honey, you always know the right thing to do. I wish I could be as smart as you.   (placater stalling)

Me: Oh, shut up! Your constant bootlicking makes me sick!   (blaming command) (holding "you" responsible for how "me" feels)

You: Did you notice if the garage door is closed?   (irrelevant response)

It's clear that these two people aren't communicating to each other what they truly think and feel. Instead, it's a combat zone. Are you aware of any increased tension as you follow this dialogue? Does it remind you of any "conversations" you've been involved in? How successful do you think they'll be in getting any resolution on "me's" hidden wish to see people?

Notice that the coping styles can shift with each interaction. Each of us tends to have a favorite style, but we're capable of the entire repertoire. If this dialogue were to continue, the styles could continue to change, as each person desperately grasps for some way to gain acceptance from the other through this distorted communication.

78

Another alternative is possible: to be congruent in your communication. When that happens, context, self, and other *all* count. Then your actions are reflected in what Satir calls "The Five Freedoms."

1. To see and hear what is there
   instead of
   what should be, was, or will be.
2. To say what one feels and thinks
   instead of
   what one should.
3. To feel what one feels
   instead of
   what one ought.
4. To ask for what one wants
   instead of
   always waiting for permission.
5. To take risks in one's own behalf
   instead of
   choosing to be only "secure" and not rock the boat.

When two people engage in congruent communication, they are free to express their thoughts, their feelings, and the feelings that they have about their feelings.* Take, for example, this dialogue between two people who, although feeling overburdened, miss their friends and would like to see them:

Me: It's been a long time since we've had the Millers and the Campbells over for dinner. I know we've both been busy with our work, and I haven't felt up to scheduling the time and effort to plan a dinner party.

(communication is *specific*)

(acknowledging *what is*)

(*how she feels* about what is)

---

* See Days 5 and 7 of "Communication" in the daily program to further explore which of your feelings are acceptable for you to express.

79

You: You're really looking bushed. Let's sit down and talk about it.

(comments on *what he observes*)

(expresses *interest and support*)

Me: I like that. When I get so loaded down with my work that we don't have any time to see people as I'd like, I tend to feel like I'm a poor organizer—even ungrateful, as I'm not returning the invitations extended us.

(*how she feels* about what he said)

(her *feelings about the feelings* that affect her feelings of self-worth)

You: You sound like you wish you could entertain them without it's being a big energy drain. Is that what it is?

(*acknowledges* her wish)

(asks for *feedback*)

Me: Yes, that's it.

You: We've both been working awfully hard recently. I can see where you might feel like you're a poor organizer or ungrateful, because right now you're feeling overloaded.

(acknowledges *her reality*)

(acknowledges her *feelings about the feelings*)

Me: I guess I do tend to put myself down when I'm feeling weary.

(aided by his reflective comments, she is able to *further explore her feelings*)

You: I'd like to see you be especially nice to yourself right now.

(his wish for her)

Me: I realize that I'd like to be able to entertain them as graciously as they do us, and right now that seems like such a big deal. *(further explores her feelings)*

You: What I'm hearing is that you'd like to be the kind of hostess who can take days to prepare for company on Saturday night. Is that what you *are* saying? *(clarifying the issue)* *(asks for feedback)*

Me: Gee, I really want it all, don't I? Having the satisfactions and challenge of work isn't enough for me. I *still* fall into those old traps of wanting to be superwoman. *(has an insight)*

You: It seems to me that part of the problem is wanting to entertain them because you miss not seeing them. Another part is how we do it. Is that how you see it? *(clarifying the issue)* *(asks for feedback)*

Me: You're right. Maybe we could consider doing something on a less burdensome scale. It could still be fun, but just not loaded down with all the preparation time. *(agrees with his perception)* *(with feelings acknowledged and both feeling understood, they then can engage in problem solving)*

How do you feel as you read this dialogue? Are you aware of any tension in your body? Or is there, perhaps, a certain sense of ease and relaxation as you discover how two people who are both "under stress" can relate to each other without resorting to survival coping styles of communication?

Notice how "you," who primarily played the role of a

good listener, frequently checks with "me" for feedback. If he didn't do so, he would be making some assumptions. *Making assumptions about what another means—the feelings behind the words, as well as the words—can lead to enormous and costly misunderstandings.* When you ASSUME, you make an ASS of U and ME.

Another characteristic of the dialogue above is that "me" feels free to ask for what she wants and express how she feels about it. This describes assertive communication. Despite all the flurry of interest in assertiveness training in the last decade, I consistently find that *lack of assertiveness is one of the biggest causes of self-induced stress.*

In my seminars I have known supervisors who didn't feel they had the right to close the door for an hour to attend to desk work, and thus were besieged by constant interruptions. Married couples have come to me for counseling, unaware that they were playing games of "mind reading" in an attempt to anticipate what the other wanted rather than directly stating what they wanted or needed.

It is as if people are reluctant to clearly set their limits or risk asking for what they want for fear of being rejected when they can't be seen as all-giving and all-loving. Sometimes they periodically explode over a relatively small matter, as all the pent-up hostility bursts forth. Keeping it all in, blowing up, or back-stabbing on the part of a passive-aggressive person are guaranteed self-destructive patterns that increase stress for everyone.

When my clients have a tough encounter coming up, I remind them of the possibility of three different "speeches": what they think they will say, what they actually say, and, sometimes in the car driving back alone, what they wish they had said.

Day 4 of "Communication" in the daily program provides more information on assertiveness.

Communication, clearly, is a two-way process, involving both a sender and a receiver. The daily programs will provide a means to become more effective in both roles: learning both how to send more congruent messages and how to be a better listener.

Recommended Reading

Bernhard, Yetta. *Self Care*. Millbrae, Calif.: Celestial Arts, 1975.

Gordon, Thomas. *Parent Effectiveness Training*. New York: McKay, 1970.

Gottman, John; Notarius, Cliff; Gonso, Jonni; and Markhaus, Howard. *A Couple's Guide to Communication*. Champaign, Ill.: Research Press, 1976.

James, Muriel. *Breaking Free: Self-Reparenting for a New Life*. Reading, Mass.: Addison-Wesley, 1981.

Mace, David and Vera. *How to Have a Happy Marriage*. New York: Ace Books, 1977.

Satir, Virginia. *Making Contact*. Millbrae, Calif.: Celestial Arts, 1976.

RELAXATION/OVERVIEW

A familiar scene. Steve finally went to see the doctor—the hard way.

Steve is forty-two years old, is five feet ten inches tall, weighs 188, has been married sixteen years, has a son, Ron, who is fifteen, and two daughters, twelve and ten. Steve is in charge of the in-house print shop at a large corporation. His work is full of ever-constant deadlines, last-minute changes, and rush jobs. In a typical day he may have as many as fifty people bringing in work requests. He has trouble finding and keeping good employees. The technology in his field has improved a great deal, but he finds it a strain to take time off from work to get the necessary training.

Steve was born in the Midwest and grew up on a diet rich in dairy products, red meat, and refined carbohydrates. He played hockey in high school, but since his marriage he hasn't done any regular exercise. He has always thought of himself as being in tiptop shape, remembering his agility and skill as a slim seventeen-year-old hockey player.

Last Saturday morning he decided to shoot a few baskets with Ron, but soon he felt pains in his chest, a new sensation for him. Even though the pains were severe enough to cause him to stop playing, he dismissed them as a momentary peculiarity. He went into the house, had a beer, and flicked on the TV to watch some football. He didn't say anything to his wife, because he didn't want to alarm her. Although she noticed that he appeared strangely preoccupied and withdrawn, she said nothing. Ron felt awkward; he was aware that his parents had some kind of unspoken agreement not to talk about what was bothering Dad. Ron would have liked to know how his dad was feeling, but he didn't know how to bring it up, so he said nothing. The remainder of the weekend was uneventful, and Steve soon forgot the puzzling incident.

The beginning of the work week was hectic, as usual—nothing out of the ordinary. Then on Thursday afternoon, in the middle of an important rush job, the press broke down. Steve couldn't handle the problem himself, and it was too late in the day to get a repair person to come out. It was a mess! The department head called at 4:40 P.M. to say that he was sending over someone to pick up the order, and when Steve told him what had happened, the department head blew his top. Steve adopted his usual posture of "taking it in his stride," but, still, it had gotten to him. Driving home on the congested freeway, he again felt chest pains and had to pull over to the side of the road. By now he was in a cold sweat, trembling, feeling nauseated, and very frightened about what was happening to him. After a little while, the pains subsided, and he resumed driving home.

When he walked in the door, his wife commented that he didn't look well and told him to sit down right away. He asked for a drink "to soothe his nerves," and when she brought the drink he told her what had happened. Both of them, by then, were appropriately alarmed. She called the doctor, who advised her to take Steve to the hospital immediately.

Steve spent four days in the hospital for a complete workup and thorough evaluation. Fortunately, the chest pains proved to be nothing more than that. Steve had been lucky—twice! His doctor cautioned him to slow down and relax, but didn't tell him how to do it.

Steve's chest pains were symptomatic of cardiovascular difficulty, usually due to constricted blood flow in a main artery supplying the heart. The artery is made more narrow due to several causes: a lifelong pattern of consuming the typical American high-fat diet (causing a buildup of arterial plaque and high serum cholesterol), decreasing elasticity in an aging body that isn't countered with regular, vigorous, sustained exercise; and the normal reaction to stress of heightened blood pressure and increased release of chemicals to thicken the blood—the by-now familiar "fight or flight" response. Such chest pains serve as fair warning that drastic changes must be made. If Steve is to turn around what's happening in his life, his very survival depends upon his learning to relax.

Steve was puzzled by his doctor's warning, saying, "But I *do* relax. I read the paper in the morning for an eye-opener, I unwind by watching TV at night, I walk the dog, I play poker with the boys once a week—I even take regular vacations."

These are fine distractions, but they won't help Steve to relax. Relaxation and diversion are very different. When most people think they're relaxing, they're really only taking their minds off their tension for a little while. Watching the evening news on TV or playing cards can in themselves generate a fair amount of tension and anxiety, which actually increases stress. Even vacations, with their break in routine, unpredictability, unfamiliar food and drink, and faster pace, can increase rather than diminish stress.

The relaxation I'm talking about requires an absolutely minimal amount of activity, and is in fact almost as passive as sleep itself. Relaxation produces a pleasant, comfortable state of well-being. This is vital to "recharging your battery," or increasing your superficial adaptive energy, as was discussed in the Introduction. Let's take a look at how it works.

The majority of people who chronically experience stress overload are in the "resistance" stage of the General Adaptation Syndrome (GAS). Rather than responding to any one major stressor, they are constantly assaulted by a number of stressors, which produce a less intense but more prolonged "alarm response." (This certainly describes Steve and the kind of job he has!) Physiologically, their bodies respond with an increased flow of adrenalin and other energizing hormones, higher than normal heart rate, and elevated blood pressure. In this stage, a number of seemingly little things can build up to an intense alarm reaction, a reaction that will feel bigger to someone who is already at a high level of arousal than to someone at a lower level. By practicing relaxation exercises on a regular basis, it is possible to keep the general level of arousal at a low point. This is how it looks on a graph:

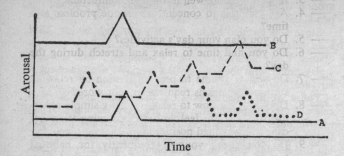

Arousal / Time

Time

A = Person at low arousal level
B = Person at high arousal level
C = Snowballing effect: many little alarms increase until the final alarm seems tremendous
D = Break for relaxation, which brings the increasing arousal level down to a low level

Now that you know how important it is to relax, you may wish to take this self-evaluation.*

How Well Can You Relax?

Answer the following questions by placing a number on the line preceding each one. Select the number that best describes your behavior.

3 = Always
2 = Sometimes
1 = Seldom

—— 1. Are you able to shut out your worries when you go to bed at night?
—— 2. Are you able to take a nap during the day and awaken refreshed?

---

* Sections of this evaluation were adapted from Janet Wessel's *Movement Fundamentals* (New York: Prentice-Hall, 1957), p. 55. Used with permission of the author. Scoring devised by Jackie Schwartz.

—— 3. Is your clothing well fitting and comfortable?
—— 4. Are you able to concentrate on one problem at a time?
—— 5. Do you plan your day's activities?
—— 6. Do you find time to relax and stretch during the day?
—— 7. Do you take time to prevent tension by relieving sustained positions required in your work?
—— 8. Do you know how to relax by doing simple movements when you feel yourself becoming tense because of sustained positions?
—— 9. Do you check yourself frequently for habitual tension habits, such as scowling, clenched fists, tight jaws, hunched shoulders, or pursed lips?
——10. Do you relax these evidences of tension at will when you find them?
——11. Do you find it easy to relax so that you sleep easily and deeply?
——12. Do you know how to release tensions through simple movements so that you can sleep well?
——13. Do you play with such interest that you become completely absorbed in what you are doing?
——14. Do you plan your life so that you can have a change of people, scenery, and thoughts?

Total your point score and enter here:——

A score of 33–42 indicates a high ability to relax.
A score of 24–32 indicates an average ability to relax.
A score of 15–23 indicates a low ability to relax.

Sleep

In the self-evaluation you'll notice how important it is to get a good night's sleep, yet approximately 15 percent of Americans are regularly plagued with some kind of sleep disorder.

Not everyone truly needs eight full hours of sleep a night, but between seven and nine is just about right for most people. Your best guide is to think about how you feel with the amount of sleep you usually get. If you're excessively tired or feel sleepy during the day, you're probably not getting enough sleep. If you regularly get by on less than six hours of sleep, you may be putting too great a strain on your system. "Making up for lost sleep" is a myth. You can't really add hours later to fully compensate for lost sleep because your body has already undergone the experience of operating on depleted reserves.

If you're having trouble sleeping, you may benefit from the suggestions offered in Day 11 of "Relaxation." Here are some other ideas about getting a good night's sleep:

- It's not a good idea to take a nap, as it interrupts the body's natural rhythms of wakefulness and sleep.
- An aid to establishing these rhythms is to set your alarm so that you wake up at the same time each day. Sleeping late on the weekend interferes with this pattern.
- Don't go to bed until you're sleepy. Your bedroom should be associated with sleep and relaxation.
- The bed is not for watching TV, eating, arguing with a bed partner—only for sleep or, of course, sexual activity.
- If you awaken during the night and believe you'll be up for a while, it's a good idea to get out of bed. Again, this is so that your bed is associated with sleep, not tossing and turning.
- Watching TV until the time you choose to go to sleep may prove to be too stimulating. Instead, read a dull book or take a warm bath, as both are sleep inducers.

Keeping a record of your sleeping habits as suggested in Day 11 may provide you with some useful information. Some problems require medical help, and seeing a doctor who specializes in sleep-related problems would be a wise investment.

Biofeedback

Besides offering specific suggestions to enable you to sleep more soundly and naturally, the daily program outlines several different approaches to achieve the desired deep relaxation. One effective approach that is not covered there is biofeedback.

Biofeedback is a learning process measured by a sophisticated electronic instrument, which provides physiological information. This, with practice, will eventually enable you to attain a lower stress level, without instruments, which leads to health maintenance. One machine measures skin temperature. You may recall from the Introduction that during the stress response, your blood is directed to the vital organs, away from the extremities, leaving your hands and feet cold. Therefore, raising the skin temperature of your hands in an indicator of increased relaxation.

Early biofeedback practitioner Elmer Green noted that when a person actively tried to raise the temperature of his skin, it invariably went down. However, when the practitioners introduced autogenic training, using such words as "heavy," "quiet," "relaxed," "serene," "still," "comfortable," and "warm," the person's skin temperature was much more likely to rise. They also found that people began to invent their own visualizations, using words that were personally helpful.

Biofeedback training is one way to produce the relaxed state, with measurably increased skin temperature, increased muscular relaxation, increased alpha brain-wave production, decreased pulse rate, decreased respiratory rate, decreased blood pressure, increased galvanic skin response, and decreased lactic acid level. Biofeedback has been most successful in treating muscle contraction, high blood pressure, migraine headaches, chronic anxiety states, insomnia, and phobias. More moderate success has been reported with gastrointestinal disorders, such as colitis, and Raynaud's syndrome.

Since it would be awkward to tuck a biofeedback machine into a take-home package to accompany this book, I can only refer you to this technique. Qualified biofeedback practitioners may be located at major universities and in most urban centers. The Biofeedback Society of America* publishes a directory, which lists certified practitioners and their areas of specialty, such as high blood pressure, headaches, and neuromuscular reeducation.

Of the techniques that are mentioned in this book, you may find one approach preferable or easier to use than another. At first you may feel somewhat self-conscious as you begin these relaxation techniques, but I encourage you to be patient and nondemanding of yourself. People who

---

* Biofeedback Society of America, 4301 Owens Street, Wheat Ridge, Colorado 80033, (303) 422-8436.

incorporate regular, frequent relaxation procedures into their daily life—*preferably at least twice a day for twenty minutes each*—will achieve maximum results. Taking brief relaxation breaks throughout the day, if only for one or two minutes, interrupts the sustained tension that leads to ever-higher levels of tension. Relaxation has several natural advantages: it doesn't cost anything to obtain, it's simple to use, and it's safe and free of any known negative effects—truly an important positive addiction!

LIFESTYLE MANAGEMENT/ OVERVIEW

> The doctor of the future will give no medicine,
> but will interest his patients in the care of the
> human frame, in diet, and in the cause and pre-
> vention of disease.
>
> —Thomas Edison

By now you may have noticed that all the sections of this book are interrelated. If you become more aware of how you're feeling, you'll find it easier to express your feelings and therefore be more congruent in your communication.

If you begin by communicating more directly, making eye contact, that heightens your awareness of how the other person may be responding.

If you change your diet so that it's more healthful, you put less stress on your system, your body is better able to relax, and the increased energy makes exercise more feasible and appealing.

If you start the other way around by first engaging in an exercise program, you'll notice that you'll be motivated to get rid of excess pounds and eat properly to fuel your activity, and you'll be able to relax more fully because you'll feel a healthful tiredness.

All of these are changes. It's wise to begin a program in which the changes you make in your lifestyle are gradual. You may wish to examine just how many changes you have experienced in your life within the last year. All these "life changes" cause stress, which affect your health. Thomas H. Holmes and Richard Rahe, of the University of Washington School of Medicine, developed the Social Readjustment Rating Scale,* included here as a self-test. It doesn't

---

* T. H. Holmes, and R. H. Rahe, "The Social Readjustment Rating Scale," *Journal of Psychosomatic Research* 11:213–218, 1967. Used with permission of the authors.

matter if the change is positive or negative—*any* change is stressful. Over a period of twenty years, Holmes and Rahe studied diversified groups in the United States and abroad and then ranked certain life changes according to how they affected health. They were able to assign points to each life event, which they called "life change units" (LCUs), ranking them in order of importance. Then they compared the LCU scores of some 5,000 individuals with their respective medical histories. Those who had a high rating on the life-change scale were more likely to contract illness after they had experienced stressful episodes.

One of their studies was of illness patterns among 2,500 Navy officers and enlisted men aboard three cruisers. Here conditions were as controlled as possible: everyone had similar living conditions, the same food, the same work, the opportunities for the same amount of exercise and social interaction. They found that the 30 percent of the men with the highest LCU scores developed nearly 90 percent more first illnesses during the first month of the cruise than the 30 percent with the lowest scores.

Social Readjustment Rating Scale

Circle each event that has occurred within the past year. If one item has been repeated, you may count it more than once.

Life Event	Mean Value
1. Death of spouse	100
2. Divorce	73
3. Marital separation from mate	65
4. Detention in jail or other institution	63
5. Death of a close family member	63
6. Major personal injury or illness	53
7. Marriage	50
8. Being fired at work	47
9. Marital reconciliation with mate	45
10. Retirement from work	45
11. Major change in the health or behavior of a family member	44
12. Pregnancy	40
13. Sexual difficulties	39
14. Gaining a new family member (e.g., through birth, adoption, oldster moving in, etc.)	39

15.	Major business readjustment (e.g., merger, reorganization, bankruptcy, etc.)	
16.	Major change in financial state (e.g., a lot worse off or a lot better off than usual)	38
17.	Death of a close friend	37
18.	Changing to a different line of work	36
19.	Major change in the number of arguments with spouse (e.g., either a lot more or a lot less than usual regarding childrearing, personal habits, etc.)	35
20.	Taking on a mortgage greater than $10,000 (e.g., purchasing home, business, etc.)	31
21.	Foreclosure on a mortgage or loan	30
22.	Major change in responsibilities at work (e.g., promotion, demotion, lateral transfer)	29
23.	Son or daughter leaving home (e.g., marriage, attending college, etc.)	29
24.	In-law troubles	29
25.	Outstanding personal achievement.	28
26.	Spouse beginning or ceasing work outside the home	26
27.	Beginning or ceasing formal schooling	26
28.	Major change in living conditions (e.g., building a new home, remodeling, deterioration of home or neighborhood)	25
29.	Revision of personal habits (dress, manners, associations, etc.)	24
30.	Troubles with the boss	23
31.	Major change in working hours or conditions	20
32.	Change in residence	20
33.	Changing to a new school	20
34.	Major change in usual type and/or amount of recreation	19
35.	Major change in church activities (e.g., a lot more or a lot less than usual)	19
36.	Major change in social activities (e.g., clubs, dancing, movies, visiting, etc.)	18
37.	Taking on a mortgage or loan less than $10,000 (e.g., purchasing a car, TV, freezer, etc.)	17
38.	Major change in sleeping habits (a lot more or a lot less sleep, or change in part of day when asleep)	16
39.	Major change in number of family get-togethers (e.g., a lot more or a lot less than usual)	15

40. Major change in eating habits (a lot more or a
    lot less food intake, or very different meal hours
    or surroundings)   15
41. Vacation   13
42. Christmas   12
43. Minor violations of the law (e.g., traffic tickets,
    jaywalking, disturbing the peace, etc.)   11

Total life change unit values:————————

Here's what your score means:
    150–199 = You have a mild chance of incurring
                   some kind of health change* in the next
                   year
    200–299 = You are a moderate risk
    Over 300 = You are very likely to suffer a major
                   physical or emotional illness

Life-Support Systems

Any one change in your life can affect many of the
items on the scale. If, for instance, you were to accept a
promotion that would require moving to another city, you
could easily run up a high LCU score:

Marital separation from mate (temporary)	65
Major change in financial state	38
Taking on mortgage greater than $10,000	31
Major change in responsibilities at work	29
Outstanding personal achievement	28
Major change in living conditions	25
Change in residence	20
Major change in church activities	19
Major change in social activities	18
Major change in number of family get-togethers	15
Total LCUs	288

Your score indicates that you're moderately susceptible
to a health change. Notice many of the items are related
to the loss of your support system, as you would no longer
be able to have the same amount of contact with your fam-

---

*Holmes and Rahe define a health change to include illness,
surgery, accident, psychiatric disorders, and pregnancy.

ily, neighbors, co-workers, or the people you regularly see in your religious, organizational, social, and professional activities.

Good health and long life are related to a positive and supportive social environment. People who have friends and family they can count on are less subject to stress disorders than those who don't.

These are the findings of a nine-year study by Lisa F. Berkman and S. Leonard Syme entitled "Social Networks, Host Resistance, and Mortality," as reported in the *American Journal of Epidemiology* (1979):

> Every time I found evidence of disrupted social relationships, I found evidence of some sort of negative health outcome. And the range of disease outcomes is very broad indeed. For example, people with interrupted social ties exhibit more depression, unhappiness, and loss of morale, more complications of pregnancy, higher mortality rates for many diseases, including heart disease and cancer, higher morbidity rates for such illnesses as gastrointestinal upset, skin problems, arthritis, and headaches.
>
> On the other hand, people who have a close-knit network of intimate personal ties with other people seem to be able to avoid disease, maintain higher levels of health, and in general to deal more successfully with life's difficulties than people who lack such social support systems.

I know the vital importance of my own support system. Much of the work I do as both psychotherapist and management consultant is of the solo variety. But because I need contact with knowledgable, supportive peers, I've created for myself the kind of support I know I need. Four years ago I formed a support group comprised of women in diversified professions. Most of the women in the group either work independently or are at the top of their organizations, having few peers with whom they can share their feelings and experiences, and often are the only women in male-dominated fields. We meet on a monthly basis to share our hopes and fears, our self-doubts, our failures and successes. It's a place where we are free to try out something new and receive feedback. We benefit through sharing our struggles, sometimes learning vicariously what pitfalls to avoid if we should find ourselves in a similar situation. Both personal and professional concerns are relevant. Certainly, whatever happens at work affects our home life, and whatever happens at home affects our work.

Knowing how vital my support group is to me, my husband formed a support group comprised of male friends and friends of friends. They meet every two weeks, rotating the meetings at different members' homes. Although they don't have any set agenda, their discussions have included their feelings about success or lack of success, spending time alone, work-related and personal problems, personal goals, and their multiple roles—husbands, ex-husbands, lovers, fathers, stepfathers, brothers, sons, men in the work force, community members. Their contact with each other is generally not limited to the biweekly sessions, as they also take bike rides and weekend hiking trips together, among other activities. They are as close as brothers.

The experience that both my husband and I have with our support groups is rare. Very few people have initiated steps to provide such support for themselves or to maintain their friendships.

I'm aware of two patterns that seem to prevent people from getting the support they need from others. The first occurs when a couple first gets married and the man tends to drop his men friends. Since most of his women friends are women whom he had once gone out with, they, too, are dropped. His new wife becomes his best friend, the person in whom he makes his total emotional investment. Women, on the other hand, tend to keep their women friends. In counseling sessions, women confide that they wish their husbands had some friends of their own. They complain that "most of *our* friends are *my* friends." Typically, the wives provide the emotional content in the marriage.

The second pattern is that as people become more involved with their work, they tend to drop their friendships. They don't seem to consider the time spent in those relationships as productive as time spent on work. This is especially true of the Type A personality, who neglects the building and nurturing of intimate relationships.

99

Type A/Type B

Ah, yes, the ever-present Type A personality. Cardiologists Meyer Friedman and Ray Rosenman identified the Type A personality, establishing a link between heart disease and certain behavior. In *Type A Behavior and Your Heart*, they defined the Type A personality as "an action-emotion complex that can be observed in any person who is *aggressively* involved in a *chronic, incessant struggle to achieve more and more in less and less time,* and, if required to do so, against the opposing efforts of other things or other persons."

In contrast, they identified the Type B personality as one "rarely harried by desires to obtain a wildly increasing number of things or participate in an endlessly growing series of events in an ever decreasing amount of time." Type B's are calmer, more patient, and less hurried.

Dividing human behavior into just these types is arbitrarily simple. Actually, at different times people tend to be more or less of Type A or B. The Type A's are three times more likely to develop heart disease than Type B's. (You may recall that we identified the Type A personality as a Major Risk Factor in the overview on "Exercise.") Friedman and Rosenman estimate that 50 percent of urban Americans exhibit Type A behavior most of the time.

The Type A's feel compelled to act that way because they think it will help them advance professionally, and to a degree they're right; the Type A does usually occupy the higher managerial positions. However, it is the Type B who reaches the very highest echelons of business because he is better at setting priorities, making selections, focusing on one thing at a time, using his creativity, engaging in problem solving, and establishing better relationships with people. Type B is also less competitive and has less free-floating hostility.

As my colleague Beverly Kaye has pointed out in *Up Is Not the Only Way*, our value systems have changed somewhat in the last decade, so that not *everyone* believes that climbing the corporate ladder is the only indicator of performance reward. Employees are seeking innovative styles and types of work, such as flextime, so that they can be free to pursue other interests. An increased emphasis on

100

wellness and holistic living has helped to modify some Type A personalities. Supervisors are beginning to recognize the importance of career-development programs, in which employees are counseled about their opportunities for professional growth and personal satisfaction. This may include lateral moves and even moving down, because occasionally someone who has accepted a promotion and is then dissatisfied may be better off in his former job, at which he excelled.

Parents tend to foster Type A behavior by urging their children to do something productive instead of just sitting around daydreaming or reading. Because they may be uncomfortable just sitting still and relaxing, they don't like to see that in their children, either. The competitiveness found in most school classrooms and in most sports and games reinforces Type A behavior, too.

To find out which type you are, you may wish to complete the self-test "How Cardiac Prone Are You?" in Appendix B.

Undoubtedly, we need to take a giant leap toward practicing preventive medicine, as advocated by Thomas Edison so long ago. This would be a great benefit to Americans, who spend over $120 billion every year on health care—three-quarters of that amount during the last year of their lives! Too many of us seem to prefer to continue our patterns of negative addictions and then pay for intricate surgery, costly medical procedures, and medication rather than seriously evaluate what we're doing to our bodies and adopt good self-care practices. We can't truly expect a doctor to restore good health in a few visits after years of violating basic wellness practices. If you want to find out where you stand, you'll be interested in the self-evaluation chart entitled "Rate Your Risk of Heart Attack or Stroke."*

The chart is based on factors the American Heart Association has identified as most decisive in determining a person's risk of heart attack or stroke. Adapted with permission from one prepared by the Cardio-Metrics organiza-

---

* From *The Complete Book of Running* by James Fixx (New York: Random House, 1977), pp. 228–229. Used with permission of the author, originally adapted with permission from one prepared by the Cardio-Metrics organization in New York City.

	Heredity	Blood Pressure	Diabetic	Smoking	Weight	Cholesterol	Exercise	Emotional Stress	Age	Sex and Build
6	Three or more relatives who had heart attacks before age 60 (parents & siblings only)	High blood pressure not controlled by medication	Diabetic with complications (circulation, kidneys, eyes)	More than 40 cigarettes daily	More than 50 lbs. overweight	Over 281	Complete lack of exercise	Intense problems, can't cope, see a psychiatrist	Over 60	Male, very stocky
5	Two relatives who had heart attacks before age 60	High blood pressure partly controlled by medication	Diabetic on insulin—no complications	21-39 cigarettes daily	36-50 lbs. overweight	250-280	Sedentary job, light recreational exercise	Constantly need pills or drink for stress	51-60	Male, fairly stocky
4	One relative who had a heart attack before age 60	Persistent mild high blood pressure, untreated	High sugar controlled by tablets	6-20 cigarettes daily	21-35 lbs. overweight	231-255	Sedentary job, moderately active recreation	Take pills or drink for stress on occasion	41-50	Male, average build
3	Two or more relatives who had heart attacks after age 60	High blood pressure only when upset	High sugar controlled by diet	Fewer than 5 cigarettes daily	6-20 lbs. overweight	206-230 (or don't know)	Sedentary job, very active in recreation	Moderate business or personal pressures	31-40	Female after menopause
2	One relative who had a heart attack after age 60	Normal blood pressure (or don't know)	Normal blood sugar (or don't know)	Cigars or pipe only	Up to 5 lbs. overweight	181-205	Moderately active in job and recreation	Rare business or personal pressure	21-30	Male, thin build
1	No heart disease in family	Low blood pressure	Low blood sugar	Nonuser or stopped permanently	More than 5 lbs. underweight	180 or below	Very active physically in job and recreation	No real business or personal pressures	10-20	Female still menstruating
Your Score										
										Total

10-20 points - Low risk
21-40 points - Moderate risk
41-60 points - High risk

From The Complete Book of Running by James Fixx

tion in New York City, it will give you a reliable estimate of the danger you personally face.

No chart can be an infallible predictor of health. It does, however, reflect current scientific research and is therefore a useful guide. Exercise, weight, and smoking are habit patterns that are within your control. Heredity is something you can't do anything about.

I suggest you examine those areas where you can effect some change, paying less attention to those over which you have no control.

Steps to Relaxation

To attain a more relaxed, less pressured way of life, it's helpful to keep in mind these ABC's of Stress Management, as formulated by my colleague Sam Farry.

A is for Awareness. With awareness, pay attention to your own early-warning symptoms. Notice what's happening within you and in your environment. As an analogy, assume that you have a well-engineered automobile that begins to malfunction. When the red warning light comes on, you stop immediately, pinpointing the source of the problem. Because you take prompt action to have it repaired, the problem stays relatively minor and the cost is limited to that initial problem. But, typically, that's not what happens when you first feel the early warnings of stress overload. Instead, you bargain with yourself, believing that you can relax once this hectic period is over. Worse, you may ignore the symptoms altogether, taking some medication to obliterate the feelings so that you can continue at your breakneck pace. That's how the nervous stomach becomes a peptic ulcer, or the chest pains blossom into a full-scale heart attack.

B is for Balance. Stress is a state of being out of balance with yourself or with your environment. The balance can be both physical and mental, and includes your own and others' needs, capabilities, actions, and resources at any given moment. You need to restore your body to a place of balance when you experience a distress symptom. Holistic healing, medical care, or both may be required.

C is for Choice. Take a look at your lifestyle. People who feel they can't influence the course of their lives often experience excessive stress. Choosing to live more fully and

103

healthily may be a better way of asserting yourself in an active and involved participation with life.

A, B, C. It sounds so simple. You know you have a limited number of resources, that you're not going to live forever. What quality of life do you want for yourself? What priorities in your everyday work and your everyday life can you set so that you will feel fewer demands?

You have the opportunity to examine those activities you regularly engage in to determine just how satisfying they are to you, and, if necessary, to substitute more life-nourishing practices. You may wish to question, for example, the value of how much time you spend watching television.

Over 100 million Americans watch television as a regular, daily practice, spending an average of five hours a day in this hypnotic activity. In a darkened room, they sit in a comfortable chair, unaware of their bodies, not talking to anyone. There is no other activity in which the eyes don't move; even at a movie, the size of the screen requires eye movement.

Watching television removes people from real life. Instead, they experience life vicariously, through whatever is delivered on the tube. It renders the viewers passive. It is one way to go through life that isn't painful. Some people say they are addicted to watching television, finding it "comforting," "familiar," "good company." They turn it on "just because it's there" or "for company," even if they don't have the sound loud enough to pay full attention. You are free to choose how you want to spend your life. What will give you the greatest satisfactions?

The lifestyle sections of the daily program contain information and recommendations about reducing stress in critical areas that don't fit neatly into any of the other five categories. How to begin to develop regular contact with supportive friends, guidelines for becoming more of a Type B personality, and overall lifestyle habits are examined. The emphasis is on developing what William Glasser has called positive addictions in his book of that title. A positive addiction is one that you enter into voluntarily, engage in regularly and frequently, and feel guilty if you don't do. Instead of the typical, negative addictions with which most of us are all too familiar—taking a drink to relax, overeating to dull anxiety or loneliness, watching too much television, smoking too much, avoiding pain or tension through pills—positive addictions provide life-giving alternatives.

You already know about one of the most potent positive addictions: regular, vigorous, sustained exercise. Frequent contact with nature, regularly seeing supportive friends, practicing affirmations, engaging in periodic planning and goal setting, utilizing effective time-management methods, and practicing a positive mental outlook can also be positive addictions. These are covered in the daily program.

DAY 1

AWARENESS DAY 1/ HOW DO I LIMIT MYSELF?

Here's a puzzle for you. Below are several sets of nine dots, one big set and three smaller ones. The smaller ones are for you to practice on; when you think you've got it, complete the bigger one.

Without lifting your pencil from the paper, connect the nine dots by making four straight lines that go through every dot only once. *Spend at least three minutes in attempting to solve the problem*, and answer the questions that follow as you work on it. The time you take to write answers to the questions is in addition to the three minutes of problem solving.

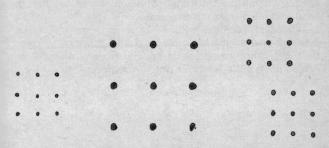

1. As you explore different possible solutions, what are you aware of feeling?
2. Do you notice any tension in any part of your body?
3. In what part of your body do you feel the tension? Is this a familiar response for you?
4. What is your inner voice saying? What messages are you giving yourself?

5. How do those messages affect your ability to solve the problem?
6. Do you find that you're sending yourself more negative messages as it takes you longer than you had expected to complete the puzzle?
7. Are you aware of becoming increasingly tense the longer it takes?
8. Are you calling yourself such "bad names" as "dumb," "incompetent," "uncreative"?

Now that you've spent at least three minutes attempting to solve the puzzle, and have answered the questions above to get more in touch with what was happening to you during this process, you may wish to answer this question:

What are you doing to limit yourself?

Ponder this question. Then go back and reread the directions and spend another two minutes working on the puzzle. Has anything changed for you? Do you see any new possibilities?

The answer to the puzzle is in Appendix C. As tempting as it may be to flip to that page, allow yourself the experience of trying to solve the puzzle in the manner suggested. If you don't, you probably won't fully experience your typical responses to a frustrating situation. Be in touch with what you learn from this experience.

Whenever you find yourself in a situation where you hear yourself saying "It can't be done," think of the nine dots. What are you doing to add restrictions where there are none? *What boundaries can you push back to get what you want?*

NUTRITION DAY 1/
BUT I EAT LIKE A BIRD

Do you know how much food you actually eat in a day? Few of us do, as we tend to remember only our main meals or, perhaps, only the main dishes of the meals. If you're concerned about changing your eating habits, one way to approach this major effort is in a spirit of discovery about just what you do eat.

This isn't the time when you have to start making wholesale changes in your eating—simply find out *what you eat, when you eat, and what's happening and how you feel while you eat.* No telling what you might learn about yourself!

To keep track of what you eat, I suggest you go to the stationery store and get a small (5 by 7 inches) spiral notebook containing ruled pages to use as your Food Awareness Log.

Set up the log in this format:

1. A ½-inch column for *time of day.*
2. A 1½-inch column for *food*, where you'll list *everything* you eat, drink, or otherwise consume, including chewing gum, prescription drugs, and patent medicines. Indicate the quantity consumed, such as 2 slices of rye toast, 6 oz. breast of chicken with skin, 2 T catsup, 6 small chocolate chip cookies, 8 oz. whole milk, 2 T Maolox.
3. Another 1½-inch column for *activity*, where you'll record what you were doing while you ate and with whom, if anyone, you were doing it. For instance, were you reading the paper, watching TV, having lunch with a friend, at a business meeting, at your desk, in your car, at the movies with your spouse?
4. Finally, another 1½-inch column for *feelings,*

where you'll note how you were feeling while you were eating.

After you've started keeping your log, it will begin to look like this:

Food Awareness Log			
Time	Food	Activity	Feelings
5:30 p.m.	1 cup peanuts 2 daiquiris	with Beverly & Barry after work	felt tense & vulnerable, needed to unwind
7:45	2 cups green salad ½ lb. hamburger	watched TV	needed to take off the buzz from the drinks,
	1 small baked potato 2 sourdough rolls	alone	made myself a good solid meal
10:30	¾ cup choc. ice cream 2 T. choc sauce	Lee came home, wanted company	felt over-indulgent; happy to share my day

You may want to make an agreement, called a "self-contract," with yourself, something like this:

> Each day I'll record *everything* I consume, noting what time of day, with whom, doing what, and how I felt at the time. I will keep this record for a period of seven days. I can eat anything I want. Nothing is forbidden. I can choose how much and which foods I want to eat.

It's a good idea to create a reward for yourself, and you might want to think about what kinds of nonfood rewards would please you. A small reward for recording each day's food and a bigger reward at the end of the week could be nice motivators for this recordkeeping discovery process.

EXERCISE DAY 1/ READY OR NOT?

The echoing alert in the children's game of Hide and Seek is "Ready or not, here I come!" Here that alerting call can be a threat to your health if you don't make adequate preparation. In the overview of "Exercise" you were advised of the hazards of beginning an exercise program without getting ready for it, and it was mentioned that many people walk less than two and a half miles per day.

How can you find out how much you walk in a day? One way is to become aware of the distance and keep a record, which then becomes your daily Activity Log. Divide a notebook page into two columns of equal width, with a ½-inch column at the right. The left column is where you record your *activity*, the right column is where you note your *reflections on exercising*—what you felt and thought about engaging in exercise that day—and the narrow column at the right is for the *time of day*.

Activity Log		
Activity	Reflections	Time
Drove to	Could have walked the 3 blocks, but	12:40 p.m.
restaurant	no one else was walking	
Staff meeting	Didn't climb two flights of	3:30 p.m.
in conference room	stairs — maybe I'll walk after dinner	

As with the Food Awareness Log, for a full week go through your day from the time you get up to the time you go to sleep and write down your actual exercise activities (or lack thereof), how you felt about it, and what thoughts occurred to you.

If you wish, you can combine the Food Awareness and the Activity Logs by keeping them on facing pages in your spiral notebook. It would look something like this:

Food Awareness and Activity Log						
Time	Food	Activity	Feelings	Activity	Reflections	Time
3:15 p.m.	herbal tea	coffee break with Lisa	anxious about my work	walked 4 blocks to coffee shop	felt good to be outside	3:15 p.m.
5:45 p.m.	club soda	stopped at Joe's for a drink	able to relax without alcohol felt great	swam 6 laps	time cut short because of drink	7:00 p.m.
8:15 p.m.	vege soup	read paper with dinner	refreshed, not too hungry after my swim	walked the dog 2 blocks	felt energized from my swim	9:45 p.m.

Remember the excuses for not starting an exercise program listed at the beginning of the overview of "Exercise"? People can be astonishingly creative when it comes to making up excuses. Now is the time to stop making excuses and to explore what you can do to get more exercise, and the Activity Log can help. It's for your eyes only—consider it as an exploratory field trip into what makes you tick. Try not to substitute your own critical inner voice for that of your doctor or another authority, however; just be honest with yourself and find out what really is happening.

Another less constantly attentive way to get an idea of how active you are is to obtain a reliable pedometer, which can record how much you walk in a day. When clipped onto your belt, a pedometer will keep track of your distance as long as you wear it, and it's a useful way to obtain a beginning measurement of how much ground you're covering right now. Again, you need make no effort

114

at this point to increase the distance; simply record it for seven days, total each day's distance, and divide by seven in order to get your daily average of distance covered. (Pedometers can be purchased at most sporting-goods stores.)

Both of these methods have advantages, and they can both be utilized, if you wish. The Activity Log will provide you with information about opportunities taken (and avoided) for exercise and what you thought and felt about these opportunities. The pedometer will give you hard facts about how active (or inactive) you are. If you do choose to begin an exercise program, a pedometer is a good modest investment, as you'll be able to chart your increasing distance as you become more fit.

COMMUNICATION DAY 1/
YOUR TRUE FRIEND

"How are you feeling?"
"Fine," is the usual response.
Do you know how you're feeling right now?
Are you aware of any tension anywhere in your body?
What emotions are you aware of?

If you're like a lot of people, you probably aren't aware of the wide range of emotions you may be experiencing. One way to begin to know yourself better is to keep a journal or a diary.

Make your selection today, and buy everything you'll need to start your journal, including colored pens for emphasis. Decide now what time today you will make an entry in your journal for this day.

You have lots of choices when it comes to deciding on the format of your journal. It can be a simple 8½-by-11-inch spiral notebook with either blank or lined pages. Or it can be a bound book like those used for keeping official records, again with either lined or blank pages. Or it can simply be loose sheets of paper that are kept together in a folder, which from time to time you'll gather together, perhaps in a looseleaf notebook.

The advantage of ruled paper is obvious—to give you guidelines as you write. However, the blank-page approach offers some nice advantages, too. You're free to use the page in any way you wish. If you want to write small and close together, you can. If you feel like writing large, boldly, and expansively, you can do that, too. Best of all, the blank page invites your nonverbal messages, so that you can express yourself with different-colored pencils or inks.

I prefer a journal with blank pages, as I find it frees me from feeling that I have to be neat and legible, which I associate with writing on lined paper in school.

116

To begin with, use the divided page approach described below. Feel free to change to another system that may suit you better whenever you wish.

One way to begin is to fold a page in half vertically. On the left side, write down *what happened* that you want to record. On the right side, write down *how you felt* about what happened.

At first you may have three or four paragraphs about what happened and only a few lines about how you felt about it. But, since keeping a journal encourages you to become more aware of your feelings, after a while you may notice that the ratio is reversed. Then what happened may take up only a paragraph and how you felt about it may require four or five paragraphs. You may find that you have several conflicting feelings about the same event or that you need to make a decision.

A journal is an available resource that you can use as often and as regularly as you wish. It's a good idea to record the time of day, date, and even your location as you write. I find it helpful to start my journal entry by scanning my body and noting what are my bodily sensations at that time. For instance, I might begin:

> This day has been too packed to go unnoticed. So many feelings about what all that's happened, I hardly know where to start. The noise from the party next door doesn't intrude, now that I'm alone with my journal. The warm glow from the fire soothes me, and I feel my left side getting warmer. I'm aware of some tension in my right shoulder area. My left foot is tucked under me, and it feels like it's asleep, and as I start to think about what happened earlier, I get goosebumps.

Recommended Reading

Capacchione, Lucia. *The Creative Journal*. Athens, Ohio: Swallow Press, 1979.

Progoff, Ira. *At a Journal Workshop*. New York: Dialogue House, 1975.

Simons, George F. *Keeping Your Personal Journal*. New York: Paulist Press, 1978.

RELAXATION DAY 1/ *YOU'VE ALWAYS GOT IT WITH YOU (PART 1)*

The most powerful, immediate tool in enabling you to relax is one you always have with you. It's colorless, weightless, and (usually) soundless and odorless. It doesn't cost anything to obtain, but you need to take care of it so that its supply isn't needlessly diminished.

Perhaps you've solved the puzzle by now and recognize that this wonderful aid is your breathing. By learning to control your breathing, you can change your blood pressure and your heart rate so that you can induce a state of calm upon command, thus cleansing and revitalizing your body. Because it is such a vital tool, several breathing exercises are given for Days 1 and 2 of "Relaxation."

Basic Relaxing Breath Exercise

Become aware of your breathing right now. As you breathe in, push out your belly gently, keeping your shoulders level and your chest relatively motionless. I call this "belly breathing." Be aware of the breath as it moves further down in your chest as you inhale through your nose and then let the breath out through your mouth. Inhale and exhale. You have plenty of time. Exhale and inhale. Feel yourself relax as your breathing becomes deeper and slower, expanding your chest to the side and in front. Inhale and exhale. You may wish to alter your breathing so that you breathe in through your nose to a count of four and breathe out through your open mouth to a count of eight. Exhale and inhale. Continue slow, deep breaths, allowing the gentle nourishing breath to rid your body of any tension. If you're aware of any place in your body that feels tense, direct your breathing to that place to ease away the tension. Feel your body letting go, letting go of the tension as your breath heals you, relaxes you.

Alternate-Nostril Breathing

Place your right hand over your nose so that your right thumb rests lightly against your right nostril, your index and third fingers are together on your forehead, between your eyes, your ring finger rests lightly against your left nostril, and your little finger rests between your left nostril and your upper lip. You may wish to increase your relaxation by closing your eyes. Notice the calming effect of your fingers resting lightly on your forehead. Exhale slowly and deeply through both nostrils. Press your right nostril closed with your thumb and slowly inhale a deep breath through your left nostril to a count of eight. Press your left nostril closed, which means that both of your nostrils are momentarily closed, and hold the nourishing breath in your lungs for another count of eight. Open only your right nostril, and exhale completely through your right nostril for a count of eight. Now inhale through your right nostril to a count of eight, keeping your left nostril closed. Hold your breath again for a count of eight, keeping both nostrils closed, and exhale fully through your left nostril for a count of eight. Repeat three times, noticing that, as you breathe in, your breath fills more of your lungs. Each time you exhale, your body becomes more relaxed, and a warm relaxation comes over your whole body.

LIFESTYLE DAY 1/ YOU *DO* HAVE ENOUGH TIME

So you think you don't have enough time? That's the most commonly given excuse for neglecting to do the exercises and activities in this book. Guess what? *You have all the time you will ever have right now—it's just a matter of how you choose to use it.* Think of the whole scheme of things, and you'll recognize that the quality of your life is determined by the state of your health.

> When health is absent, wisdom cannot reveal itself, art cannot manifest, strength cannot fight, wealth becomes useless, and intelligence cannot be applied.
> —Herophilus,
> physician to Alexander the Great

Simply, if you wish to change your lifestyle so that it promotes wellness, you'll need to schedule some time to make it happen. I've learned that I must schedule my exercise first thing in the morning, or else I'll allow something "more important" to interfere. Here are some fundamental points about time and energy management.

A date book can be your biggest asset. I find it useful to keep my "to do or not to do" lists in a small bound book. If I'm thinking of something that's a possible activity, I write it down. I'm free *not* to do it, but by putting it in writing I unburden my mind. Many months later I can completely reconstruct a day, remembering just how I felt when I was doing what. *Write down everything you want to do in a day.* If you set aside fifteen minutes at the end of your (work) day to do this, you can develop a tentative plan for the next day. Select a specific time during the day that suits you, and use it as a regular time for planning. Don't worry about whether you're mixing personal and business items. It's still *you* who must do it.

After you've written everything down, set your priorities—*what simply must be done that day?* Does everything on the list have to be done by you? Can you delegate? Can you shift some of the tasks to another day?

If you're really feeling pressed for time, *estimate how long each activity will take.* You may quickly determine that it's not humanly possible to accomplish everything on that list. I do this when I find I'm pacing and hardly breathing because I'm so anxious about taking care of everything that has to be done. Whenever I hear myself saying "I don't have time," I take fifteen minutes to write down what I feel I must do. Once it's on paper, I find I can get some perspective, and my breathing improves.

Schedule what must be done, allowing time for the unexpected. When do you feel most productive? Are you a "morning person" or an "evening person"? Schedule your most creative work requirements at your peak time.

Look over your lists. *How would you categorize your activities?* Are you spending most of your time on low-priority tasks and busy work?

Your personal effectiveness and satisfaction rest on your ability to control your own time. To do this you need to know just what you would like to accomplish in your lifetime. How important are the family, social, community, spiritual, financial, and personal-growth parts of your life? Repeatedly I find that people who experience a great deal of stress neglect other areas of their lives in order to focus on their careers, thus becoming workaholics. I suggest you identify what you want in your life by putting down your goals on paper.* Then schedule how you might make it happen.

I advise my clients to schedule appointments with themselves. Many are so caught up in giving to others that they tend to neglect themselves. I encourage them to think creatively of that free spirit locked within them that they'd like to release. They may select a name for that part, perhaps choosing to make an appointment with "Ariel."

---

* The "What Would It Be Like" exercise in Day 10 of "Awareness" and "Five Years from Now" exercise in Day 12 of "Lifestyle" are a good start for this process.

No one else can know what is truly important to you. Only you are in the position to say "yes" to those things you really want and to say "no" to those things that drain your life energy. No one else will make it happen *for* you. So ask yourself, "Am I worth it?"

Recommended Reading

Assagioli, Roberto. *The Act of Will*. New York: Viking, 1973.

Bliss, Edwin. *Getting Things Done*. New York: Bantam, 1976.

Greenwald, Harold. *Direct Decision Therapy*. San Diego: EDITS, 1973.

Lakein, Alan. *How to Get Control of Your Time and Your Life*. New York: Signet, 1973.

MacKenzie, Alec. *The Time Trap*. New York: McGraw-Hill, 1975.

DAY 2

AWARENESS DAY 2/
KNOW YOURSELF

The overview of "Awareness" gave you a preview of the Relaxation Log. Today is the first of four days in which you will note your own indicators of and responses to stress. The first half of the Relaxation Log includes "Sources of Stress" and "Common Physiological Indicators," portions that are particularly helpful in determining which areas need more attention. Most people are more alert to the performance of their automobiles than they are to that of their own bodies.

These first two sections of the Log* are reprinted below. On the left side of the items is a checklist on which you can note the *intensity* of that item; on the right side is a checklist on which you can note the *frequency*.

If you wish, you may respond to the first six items (separation, deadlines, noise, financial concerns, overcrowding, and relocating) in terms of whether they are problems at home or at work. Instead of simply using a checkmark for frequency or intensity, use a "W" for work, an "H" for home, and a "B" for both.

The last six items under "Sources of Stress" (smoking, alcohol, drugs, weight problem, handicap, illness or personal injury) may be checked in terms of whether they are problems for you or for another important person in your life, such as your spouse, partner, parent, or child. Use an "S" for self, an "O" for other, and a "B" for both.

Using the suggestions above, complete this part of the Relaxation Log using today as a typical day. If today happens not to be a work day for you, then use your last work

---

* From *The Relaxation Log* by Jackie Schwartz (Kasriel Productions, 1908 Benecia Avenue, Los Angeles, CA 90025), 1978. Copyright by Jackie Schwartz.

Intensity					Sources of Stress	Frequency				
1	2	3	4	5		1	2	3	4	5
					Separation					
					Deadlines					
					Noise					
					Financial concerns					
					Overcrowding					
					Relocating					
					Change in job responsibilities					
					Recent death					
					Divorce					
					Traffic					
					Trouble at work					
					Trouble at home					
					Current events					
					Change in living conditions					
					Worry too much					
					Outstanding personal achievement					
					Gaining a new family member					
					Loneliness					
					Boredom					
					Smoking					
					Alcohol					
					Drugs					
					Weight problem					
					Handicap					
					Illness or personal injury					

Intensity					Common Physiological Indicators	Frequency				
1	2	3	4	5		1	2	3	4	5
					Muscular tension					
					Digestive difficulties					
					Skin eruptions					
					Sleeping difficulties					
					Stomach pains					
					Grinding of teeth					
					Circulatory difficulties					
					Headache					
					Continued physical pain					
					Sexual difficulties					
					Excessive sweating					
					Chest pains					
					Difficulty in breathing					
					Depression					
					Speech difficulties					
					High blood pressure					
					Hyperactivity					
					Increased irritability					
					Absence or irregularity of menstrual period					
					Nervous mannerisms					

day as the one on which you'll base your responses in the Log.

The Relaxation Log (Part I)

Place a checkmark under the appropriate number in the Intensity and Frequency columns.

Intensity	*Frequency*
1 = None	1 = Never
2 = Very little	2 = Very seldom
3 = Moderate	3 = Occasionally
4 = Fairly severe	4 = Fairly often
5 = Extremely strong	5 = Almost always

What patterns emerge as you look over these checkmarks?

Which are sources of stress, or "stressors," over which you have no control?

What can you do about those stressors over which you do have some control?

What needs to be changed? What can be changed? (Remember the nine dots!)

What price do you pay for reacting in your usual manner to your sources of stress? How does it show up in your body?

NUTRITION DAY 2/
CALORIES DO COUNT

In the overview of "Nutrition," you read about the importance of calories. There's no getting away from it: if you want to control your weight, you need to know how many calories you consume and how many you need in order to maintain your weight.

The first step is to find out your caloric intake. This knowledge will enable you to make choices about how to "spend" your daily allotment of calories, based on how many calories you expend in your daily activities. It's very simple. If you take in fewer calories than you burn up, you'll lose weight.

If you don't already own one, get a calorie counter. Supermarket checkout stands carry pocket-size ones, and many cookbooks contain them, sometimes even stating the caloric content per portion of a recipe. Now, armed with your calorie counter, you can review your Food Awareness Log to determine the caloric value of the food you've been eating. I suggest that you enter the calorie count in a different-colored ink.

Check the section on diet and health at your local bookstore—you'll see that there are almost as many books on specialized diets as there are cookbooks, which says something about America's preoccupation with food. From some of the diet and exercise books, you can get an estimate of how many calories your body needs, based on your activity level and age.

You may be interested to browse through some of the books describing healthy diets with your newly acquired knowledge. Finding a sensible and effective program for permanent weight control that incorporates the principles of stress-free eating takes considerable knowledge. Refer again to the overview of "Nutrition" so that you can incorporate healthy foods into your program.

Above all, be patient. You didn't put on those extra pounds overnight, so it's expecting too much to lose them in a short period of time. Repeated experience indicates that rapid weight losses are seldom maintained. After all, what you're most interested in is changing your lifestyle in several dimensions so that you'll be letting go of stress. Just as you wouldn't expect to suddenly be able to practice stress-free communication without a lot of trial and error, don't expect to launch full-blown into an austere diet. Gradualism is the answer.

EXERCISE DAY 2/
"NO EXERCISE"
EXERCISE

If you've started an Activity Log, you may have already made some interesting discoveries. You may find that you actually get less exercise than you had thought. If that's the case, you may want to consider what I call "no exercise" exercise.

Many of us think of exercise as something that requires special clothing or equipment, scheduling a certain time every day, and so on. All that is true for the kind of exercise that will benefit you the most, but it doesn't have to be all or nothing at all.

"No exercise" exercise simply means being creative in figuring out ways to get your body moving more often during the day.

Let me tell you about a client I'll call Margie, a thirty-three-year-old office worker who is married and has two children, ages eight and five. Margie lives in the suburbs and must drive forty minutes to work every day. Once a week she attends an evening meeting near her office, which means that she has a two-and-a-half-hour "break" before the meeting starts. Usually she regards this as "time to kill" and goes shopping in a department store for nothing in particular or browses through a bookstore.

Margie's day starts at 6:30 A.M., when she gets up, gets dressed, prepares breakfast for the family, and makes lunches for herself and the children. Margie regards taking time for exercise as just another demand on her already limited time. (She's not yet ready to acknowledge how much her energy would be increased by a regular exercise program!) We discussed what she could do with "no exercise" exercise, and this is what she devised.

As she drives to work in commuter traffic, she keeps her muscles loose through shoulder rolls and other exer-

131

cises to alleviate tension in her neck muscles. Every time she comes to a red light, she uses that as a cue to strengthen her abdominal muscles by sucking in her abdomen and holding for a count of ten. When she finds herself becoming anxious about how long it's taking her to get to work, she uses a look at her watch as a cue to do deep breathing, which enables her to relax, thereby short-circuiting the cycle of increasing tension.

When she finally nears her office building, Margie parks a fair distance from the entrance so that she is compelled to walk. At first, that was only a slightly more distant part of the parking lot, but as her ability to exercise more increased through regular practice, she began parking several blocks away. Once she enters the office building, she makes a pact with herself to use the stairs instead of the elevator at least once out of every three opportunities. (That frequency may increase as she becomes more fit.) Instead of always picking up the "intercom" line or phoning someone in an office four or five doors away, she makes those contacts in person at least two out of every five opportunities. (More room for improvement here, too, if she wishes!)

Lunchtime used to mean a short walk down the hall to the employees' lunchroom with her brown bag where she sat with co-workers in a smoke-filled room talking about office politics—hardly relaxing conversation! Now she chooses instead to take her brown bag out of the building to find a quiet place to eat, allowing at least twenty minutes of her hour's break for a brisk walk. She sometimes uses that time as an opportunity to explore different neighborhoods near where she works.

On those days when she has two and a half hours between her work day and her meeting each week, she now has lunch at a restaurant, making that her main meal of the day, and eats something very light in the evening, leaving her time to indulge in some joyful, active pursuit. She may go roller-skating, folk dancing, or ice-skating, or she may go to a gym near her office for a swim, to use a stationary bike, or participate in a jogging group or jazzercise class. If it's still light, her options are increased. Some of these activities may require a shower afterward, but that's possible within her time limit. (Remember the nine dots!) It's too tempting to rule out something before you consider some of the possibilities.

How many of Margie's "no exercise" exercises could you engage in?

How do you feel about these kinds of activities as a possibility for you?

What "yes, but's" do you find yourself raising as "good reasons" why such possibilities for more exercise won't work for you?

When was the last time you walked to the mailbox a block away to mail a letter? Or chose to take the stairs up two flights rather than use the elevator? The choice is yours.

COMMUNICATION DAY 2/
BELIEVING WILL
MAKE IT SO

Time was when everyone was convinced that the world was flat, or that a four-minute mile was impossible. Just because these beliefs were widely held didn't mean that everyone agreed with them, and some went on to challenge these so-called truths.

The same principle applies to you. You can either increase or decrease the amount of stress you experience, depending on what you believe and the stories you tell yourself. Do any of the following declarations sound familiar?

> "This traffic infuriates me. I'll never be able to get there on time, and Tom will be upset with me."

> "I can't find anything to wear. Everything I have looks terrible on me."

> "I can't stand all these interruptions. I'll never get my work done."

Such negative thinking almost guarantees that your dire predictions will come true. But how would it be if, instead, you acknowledged what is going on and gave yourself a vote of confidence? What if your thinking was more like this:

> "Even with this heavy traffic [inadequate wardrobe, unexpected interruptions], I can use a relaxation technique to stay calm, and I can adjust my plans, like getting off the freeway and calling Tom to say that I'll be late [selecting the best possible outfit, readjusting my schedule]—so that I know that I have done the best I can."

134

Think of a time recently when you realized you were becoming quite upset. Perhaps you were aware of some unpleasant physical symptoms as well, such as a headache, upset stomach, or elevated blood pressure. What were you telling yourself that might have increased your anxiety? Were you calling yourself names that made you feel worse, like "you slob" or "you no-good"?

For two weeks, keep a record of each upsetting incident you experience, including how you interpreted what happened, what story you told yourself, how you acted, and how your body responded. Be especially aware of the times you made predictive statements, such as "I'll never get it right." This could serve as a basis for changing what you say to yourself. Just as you can make yourself sick with worry, you can also help yourself to relax by using your thoughts to your advantage.

RELAXATION DAY 2/ YOU'VE ALWAYS GOT IT WITH YOU (PART II)

Here are some more breathing exercises that will enable you to relax wherever you are in only a few moments.

Controlled Sigh

Have you ever noticed how people sigh when they're automatically releasing their tension? Here's a breathing exercise you can do that's like a controlled sigh. Breathe in through your nose, pushing out your belly, to a count of ten. Hold your breath for a count of ten. Then, forcefully and suddenly, let out all your breath through your open mouth. It's okay to make noise. Wait ten seconds and then repeat two more times. Wait thirty seconds before repeating the entire sequence of three.

Progressively Deeper Breathing

Breathe in through your nose to a count of four, pushing out your belly, and breathe out through your mouth to a count of eight. Breathe in through your nose to a count of eight, breathing out through your mouth to a count of twelve. Breathe in to a count of twelve, and breathe out to a count of twenty. Be aware of how readily you relax as your breathing nourishes every part of your body. When you exhale, your body becomes more and more relaxed. You'll feel how this exercise can lower your blood pressure in only a few moments.

Efficiency Walk

When you're in a situation in which you're rushed, feeling crowded, aware of how tense your body is, and wish you could do something about it all, this is a good exercise to enable you to look efficient while, in actuality, you're controlling your breathing and obtaining some instant relaxation. Some people think they look even more efficient if they carry a manila folder in one hand as they quickly step through this one! Do whatever you need to do, but remember that your body's regulating system will take care of you better if you aren't burdened with anything, even a piece of paper. The first requirement is that you have some open space, such as a corridor or a parking lot. Begin walking at a very brisk pace, and breathe in through your nose, pushing out your belly, to a count of six steps. Hold your breath for a count of six steps, and then exhale through your open mouth for a count of six steps. This exercise helps you cover a lot of ground quickly, look like you're in charge, and relax your body as you control your breathing.

LIFESTYLE DAY 2/
ON BECOMING TYPE B

To become more of a Type B personality, I suggest the following:

1. Avoid doing more than one thing at a time.
2. Slow down your pace of walking, talking, and eating. Take time to smell the flowers. Develop your capability to listen with interest, and stop talking so quickly, so emphatically, so much. Put down your fork between bites occasionally.
3. Organize your day to eliminate unnecessary deadlines. Instead of procrastinating until the very last minute, schedule your work so that it's done without panic, building in time for the unexpected.
4. "Bunch" your calls. If you have a secretary or an answering service, your calls can be screened and you can return them all at one time, instead of having constant interruptions.
5. Leave enough time between activities to minimize overlap.
6. Allow enough time so that you don't have to rush to get somewhere, arising earlier if necessary.
7. Set priorities. Instead of handling everything due to insecurity and competitiveness, determine what's really important. Learn to delegate, and stop trying to prove yourself, even with trivia.
8. Learn to say "no." Eliminate as many activities as possible that drain you. Unless it contributes to your socioeconomic well-being, drop it. Say "no" to new opportunities or responsibilities if they would overload or rush your day. This means knowing your priorities!
9. Make time each day to relax, meditate, and exer-

cise. Avoid the workaholic syndrome and allow time for pleasures totally unrelated to your work. Spend some time each week, too, doing things you've "been meaning to do," such as calling an old friend, playing the piano, doing a maintenance project. Exercise acts as a safety valve for your free-floating hostility.

10. Make time for rituals, myths, and traditions. A holiday dinner, a visit to a museum, a Sunday walk in the park, reading a book you don't want to skim—all these activities nourish your social and spiritual side.

11. Make your midday break a *break*. Don't use that time to do more work. Take time to walk around the block, browse in a bookstore, or window-shop. Schedule a lunch with a friend one day a week.

12. Learn to live with unfinished tasks.

13. Work in a place that is not chronically high-pressured and chaotic. Keep your environment orderly and esthetically pleasing.

14. Establish life goals. Find out what you want to accomplish in your life, on and off the job. Put your goals in writing and review them at least once every three months. Your birthday is a good time to write and review your life goals. (It's a good time, too, to review your financial situation and your will!)

Recommended Reading

Friedman, Meyer, and Rosenman, Ray. *Type A Behavior and Your Heart*. New York: Knopf, 1974.

DAY 3

AWARENESS DAY 3/
LEMONS OR LEMONADE?

Looking back over the stressors you've checked on your Relaxation Log, you may see that certain situations give rise to the same stressors each time. For instance, if you have to drive to work every day in heavy traffic, you have some expectation of what it will be like and are prepared for a certain number of unknowns that might interfere with your time schedule. Over a period of time, you will have adopted certain ways of coping with this stressor. You may be interested in discovering additional ways of coping with it, but for now this is no big problem for you.

Looking now at the stressors you've checked in the "Sources of Stress" segment of the Relaxation Log, determine which people in your life regularly cause you distress. Which ones are corrosive like lemons?

Are they really so bad in themselves, or is it how you react and interact with them?

What can you do to change the relationship so that it's more satisfying for you?

If this is a person you can't avoid, how can you respond differently so that it's not so stressful for you?

Are there certain people with whom you stay in contact for reasons that are no longer valid?

What do you want from each "lemon"?

Do you feel free to ask for what you want?

Are you willing to re-evaluate and possibly terminate the relationship if it's clear that you will not get what you want?

How high a price are you willing to pay, in terms of your own distress, to stay in an unsatisfactory relationship—in either your professional or personal life?

NUTRITION DAY 3/
SOMEHOW I JUST FOUND MYSELF EATING

If you've been keeping your Food Awareness Log, as suggested on Day 1, you're now in a good position to recognize some of the situations you respond to by eating certain foods.

Do you find that you tend to eat the same kinds of food when you're with certain people? Will these foods help you attain a high level of wellness?

Are there certain events in your week that prompt you to eat the same food each time, such as having a rich dessert whenever you eat at that "great little French restaurant down the street"?

Apart from the dining area, are there certain rooms in your home or office, or certain areas in a room, where you subconsciously expect to have something to eat? For example, an easy chair in the living room where you sit while you watch TV and have a cup of coffee and dessert. Another example is the employees' lounge.

If your analysis of the Food Awareness Log reveals that you have developed patterns of unconscious eating that aren't in your best interest, you should become extremely aware of those situations as cues for eating. Then you'll need to retrain your responses so that they're not automatic. Once you do that, you'll have a *choice* as to whether or not you wish to eat. I'm not saying you can't have popcorn at the movies any more. What I am saying is that you'll be more in control of your food intake if you're able to actively choose what you want to eat. It's the unconscious eating that leads to poor eating habits and unhealthy food. When you simply respond rather than choose, you're not taking charge of your dietary needs of wellness.

Let's say that you're in the habit of going to the refrigerator when you first come home, regardless of how hungry you are or what time of day or night it is. You usually rummage through the refrigerator until you find something that will satisfy you, perhaps put something together at the kitchen counter by the sink, and then, still standing up, devour your find. In this case, your environmental cue is that when you come home you expect to eat something—immediately, and with minimal preparation.

You could modify this pattern in this way. When you first come home and head for the refrigerator, make a pact with yourself that you can still eat whatever you choose, but instead of simply throwing it together and eating it standing up, you will put the food on a plate (rather than eating it with your hands or on a paper towel), put the plate on a placemat at the table, and sit down to eat. This significant change requires you to be very conscious of what you're doing. Further, it builds self-respect, as it's a way of saying to yourself that you are worth the time and trouble it takes to make eating a pleasant experience.

Another unconscious eating habit is to eat while reading or watching TV. If you want to do this, at least make a point of looking at the food with each bite you take. Blindly shoveling in food while your eyes are fixed elsewhere makes you less aware of how much or how fast you eat and what the food looks and tastes like. This pattern—doing two things at once, eating very fast—is associated with the Type A personality. Slowing down and focusing on the one thing you are doing will help reduce tension.

Many experts believe that modifying your eating habits, called behavior modification, is an essential step toward permanent weight control. Fortunately, some excellent publications are available to help you become more knowledgable and able to break poor eating habits.

Recommended Reading

Arensen, Gloria. *How to Stop Playing the Weighting Game.* Los Angeles: Transformation Publications, 1978.

Mahoney, Michael and Kathryn. *Permanent Weight Control: A Total Solution to the Dieter's Dilemma.* New York: Norton, 1978.

Stuart, Richard B., and Davis, Barbara. *Slim Chance in a Fat World: Behavioral Control of Obesity.* Champaign, Ill: Research Press, 1972.

EXERCISE DAY 3/ WINDOW-SHOPPING

In the overview of "Exercise" there were guidlines about proper clothing for exercising and the importance of getting good shoes for running. Now it's time to visit a sporting-goods store, or a store that specializes in attire for runners, to examine shoes, socks, and other clothing. Yes, even socks! Cotton socks absorb moisture, and nylon socks reduce friction; some people wear one pair of each. Other joggers wear no socks at all.

You can get by on just about any clothing, old or new, that is comfortable and appropriate. Those splashy jogging warm-up suits are attractive but not essential. Their purpose is to keep your body warm while you do warm-up exercises until your body heat is raised by the level of activity. If you're running in cold weather, it's wise to wear a woolen watch cap and mittens to conserve body heat.

Today your goal is simply to find out what is commercially available. Talk to the salespeople about their preferences and suggestions (clerks in stores specializing in equipment for runners are usually runners themselves and are most knowledgable). They may even know about fitness programs for beginners. Ask about any "fun runs" that might be coming up. These are noncompetitive runs for people interested in fitness, often sponsored by these specialty stores or by the local YMCA, to encourage people to take part in running to attain high-level wellness. People of all ages participate in these runs, which are characterized by a high spirit of camaraderie and mutual support.

If you visit a sporting-goods store, you may wish to take a look at the stationary bicycles to see if something like that might suit your needs. They are most popular in those parts of the country where winter weather inhibits outdoor exercising. Some come with a bookrack so that you can read while you pedal. Some people place them in front of their television sets so that TV viewing becomes an active rather than a sedentary activity—at least as long as they keep pedaling.

Find out what you need to get started on an exercise program. Continue to keep your Activity Log.

COMMUNICATIONS
DAY 3/
WHADJASAY?

If it's been a long time since you felt that someone truly listened to you, you may wish to consider the physical aspects of your communication patterns, as noted by Virginia Satir.

How often do you find yourself calling from one room to another, talking to someone who may not be giving you her full attention? Or maybe she's quite nearby but is concentrating on the newspaper she's reading or what she's doing at the workbench, the kitchen counter, the typewriter, or under the hood of the car. Just because she isn't looking at you doesn't keep you from speaking to her as if she were giving you her full attention. So you speak to her, and she replies "over the shoulder," perhaps without even looking up for a moment, still concentrating on what she's doing.

It's likely that she'll respond to something altogether different than what you were talking about, because she hasn't made enough contact with you to find out the meaning of your words.

How do you feel when you think that what you have to say isn't important enough for the other person to make an effort to really listen to you?

How much of your feelings about this do you share with the other person?

On the other hand, how do you feel when *you're* involved in a task and someone yells at you from another room to request information or tell you something important?

If you feel divided, what would it be like if you told the other person to wait until you could give him your full attention?

Too much "over the shoulder" communication contributes to unnecessary tension, because people have to strain to understand the message.

The next time you have something to say to someone, I suggest you follow these guidelines to increase the potential for clear, meaningful communication.

1. Position yourself so that you're facing each other squarely, preferably at no more than arm's length.
2. If you're of different heights, do whatever is necessary so that you are both at eye level, such as sitting down together or kneeling to talk with a child.
3. Look the other person in the eye when you speak to him. Making and keeping this eye contact is sometimes difficult for people who aren't accustomed to it, but you may know several people who seem to be comfortable looking right at you while they're talking to you.

When care is taken about the physical aspects of a conversation, two people are more likely to communicate effectively.

RELAXATION DAY 3/
MELT AWAY
YOUR TENSION

Many people aren't aware of the amount of tension they experience most of the time because they never fully relax. This exercise is designed to contrast how you feel when you exaggerate tensing your muscles with how you feel when you relax them. This method works exceedingly well in enabling you to achieve full body relaxation.

I've recorded this method on tape, as many people find it helpful to listen to someone else guiding them through it, rather than having to remember what comes next. You can record the directions on tape to achieve a similar effect. The exercise takes ten to fifteen minutes, but allow yourself plenty of time.

Loosen your belt and remove your shoes so that you have full freedom of movement and are not bothered by your clothing.

Lie down on your back with your legs uncrossed, your neck supported by a cervical roll pillow, a pillow under your knees, and your arms at your sides, not touching your body. (If you wish, you may make a substitute for a cervical roll pillow by folding a bath towel in half vertically and rolling it up to make a roll no more than five inches in diameter.) Close your eyes and take several deep breaths. Each time you exhale, notice how much more relaxed you become. Then breathe normally.

Beginning with your feet, curl your toes tightly, hold for a count of five, then relax. Repeat. Splay your toes, separating them from each other, hold for a count of five, then relax. Repeat. Then proceed throughout your entire body, from the feet up, in the same manner: identify some motion you wish to exaggerate, make the muscles tense, hold for a count of five, then relax and repeat, developing a continuous rhythm.

150

Point your feet away from you
Thrust your heel away from you
Tighten your kneecaps
Make a fist
Spread your fingers
Tighten your upper arms
Squeeze your buttocks together
Tighten your sphincter muscles
Suck in your abdomen
Push out your abdomen
Expand your chest
Tighten your shoulders
Make your neck shorter and fatter
Stretch your neck long and thin
Open your mouth wide
Clench your teeth
Press your tongue against the roof of your mouth
Smile hard
Purse your lips
Wrinkle up your nose as if you smelled something foul
Close your eyes very tight
Raise your eyebrows high in a questioning look
Frown fiercely, bringing your eyebrows down low over your eyes and close together in the middle of your forehead

Allow the feelings of relaxation to flow throughout your entire body. Your jaw may drop open, and that's all right. Be aware of the improved blood flow throughout your body as each part receives attention.

After you've done this exercise several times, you'll notice that while you're going through it your breathing may become slow, deep, and relaxed, in tune with the rhythm of the exercise. Many people fall asleep doing this, and it's an excellent way to unwind after a stressful day, especially if you anticipate having trouble getting to sleep. If you do fall asleep, your own inner timer will awaken you when you need to get up. You may wish to tell yourself this as you begin the exercise.

LIFESTYLE DAY 3/
PEOPLE NEED PEOPLE

When you were a child, you probably had a group of friends with whom you could go out and play. Do you have people in your life now with whom you can "go out and play"? Here's how you can find out.

Make a big circle in the middle of a large sheet of unruled paper and write your name in it. As quickly as you can, write down the names of other people in your life with whom you feel a strong bond, circling each name. These are the people who have "been there" for you, from whom you'd like a hug, with whom you'd like to share a meal, and from whom you'd enjoy receiving a letter or a phone call. You may wish to jog your memory by referring to your address book or your Christmas-card list. Think, too, of people with whom you went to school, used to work, or shared an important event or time in your life, such as an old buddy from the service. Think of the social, political, professional, and religious groups you belong to and the people you have grown close to in those associations. Your names will include people whom you'd like to get to know better as well as old friends.

How do you feel as you look over your own personal support network? You may be aware of people with whom you would like to make contact, and perhaps there are some people toward whom you feel a great deal of appreciation or affection, which, until now, you haven't expressed. The time to make some changes is *now.*

DAY 4

AWARENESS DAY 4/ WHAT'S YOUR REACTION?

Until now you've become acquainted only with the "Sources of Stress" and "Common Physiological Indicators" segments of the Relaxation Log. What you do to alleviate stress is just as important, so we'll now explore the "Common Stress Mediators" section of the log.*

On the left side of the items is a checklist on which you can note the *quality* of that experience; on the right side is a checklist on which you can note the *frequency*.

Now look at Day 2 of "Awareness," in which you checked your stressors and how your body reacts to stress. After reviewing that day, complete the following checklist to see how many of the common ways of alleviating stress you choose for yourself.

What are you aware of as you look over this checklist? How satisfying were your choices?

Now with a different-colored pencil, go over this checklist and note which mediators you typically use. Be sure to mark the "quality" section in order to determine how satisfying the experience was.

If you find a discrepancy between what you did on Day 2 and what you usually do, what was different about Day 2?

Are there other choices you could have made to diminish your tension on that day? What kept you from selecting them?

If there are other choices, what can you do to make sure you alleviate your stress in your preferred style next time?

Are there some choices you never or rarely make that open up new possibilities for you?

---

* From *The Relaxation Log* by Jackie Schwartz (Kasriel Productions, 1908 Benecia Avenue, Los Angeles, CA 90025), 1978. Copyright by Jackie Schwartz.

THE RELAXATION LOG (Part II)

Place a checkmark under the appropriate number in the Quality and Intensity columns.

Quality
1 = Unacceptable
2 = Minimal
3 = Acceptable
4 = Superior
5 = Outstanding

Frequency
1 = Never or rarely
2 = Seldom
3 = Occasionally
4 = Fairly often
5 = Extremely often

Common Stress Mediators	Quality (1 2 3 4 5)	Frequency (1 2 3 4 5)
Chewing gum		
Taking a stretch break		
Focused breathing		
Brisk walk		
Grooming		
Music		
Routine tasks		
Stream-of-consciousness writing		
Meditation/yoga/prayer		
Exercise		
Hot bath/jacuzzi/sauna/steam		
Nap/deep relaxation		
Working with hands		
Cosmetic improvement		
Physical labor or workout		
Unilateral rage release		
Contact with nature		
Gardening		
Massage		
Contact with friend(s)		
Entertainment/social interaction		
Sexual activity		
Counseling		

Do you find yourself saying, "Yes, but . . ." as you expand upon your answers to these questions?

What can you do to get what you want for yourself?

You may wish to experiment with new ways of alleviating your stress, using the items listed as a starting point for exploration. People who have used the Relaxation Log have been most inventive in letting it help them create new alternatives. As an example, one of my clients, an insurance executive, was reminded of how much she enjoyed her "contact with nature." Instead of her morning coffee break, she began taking advantage of those fifteen minutes for a brisk walk around her huge plant facility, taking in the sights and sounds of the birds and trees. She returned to her work with renewed freshness and a clearer perspective.

What three new mediators do you wish to experiment with?

NUTRITION DAY 4/
A "RICH DIET"
CAN KILL YOU

Do you know what rich foods are a regular part of your diet? Do you know which of the foods you eat are high in cholesterol? Look at your Food Awareness Log over the past three days and, using Barbara Kraus' *Dictionary of Sodium, Fats, and Cholesterol*, find out the cholesterol content of the food you've been eating.

Select one meal a day where you can substitute foods with less cholesterol. For breakfast, for example, instead of bacon and eggs, white toast and butter, a glass of orange juice, and a cup of coffee, you could select something like the following:

Toasted English muffin, with only a small portion of your usual amount of butter.
PLUS
Low-fat cottage cheese, which you could eat atop your muffin. If you like, you can sprinkle the cottage cheese with nutmeg or cinnamon, or both, and broil it.
OR
Sourdough or seven-grain pancakes, cooked in very little oil (or in a pan sprayed with an oil-free lubricant) and sweetened with undiluted orange-juice concentrate.

OR
Unsweetened cereal (Grape Nuts and Shredded Wheat are two) to which you add fresh fruit and non-fat milk or unflavored yogurt.
OR
Oatmeal or other whole-grain hot cereal to which you add raisins or other dried fruit for sweetening.
AND
Substitute fresh fruit for the orange juice (half a grape-

fruit or a whole orange has the same amount of calories and Vitamin C, and also provides bulk and the satisfaction of slower eating).

Cutting back on coffee is recommended, and will be discussed further in Day 11. This is only a partial list, but it may be enough to get you started.

EXERCISE DAY 4/ TELL ME WHAT IT'S LIKE

Today is a fine time to find out what kinds of organized exercise programs are available. Exercising with a group of other similarly motivated people, with guidance and support, will increase your enjoyment of whatever activity you select. Being able to exercise on your own may be an ultimate goal, but it's awfully hard for most people to muster the proper discipline and make the necessary commitment at the beginning.

Perhaps someone you know and respect is following a good fitness program. Many people who take good care of themselves are only too happy—even persuasively so—to share their methods. Think about the people you know who might fit this description, including people at work, at home, in your neighborhood, in religious, social, or cultural groups you belong to. Select three persons and ask each of them the following questions:

What kind of fitness program do you engage in?
How many days per week?
How long each day?
What facilities do you use?
Do you exercise with others or alone?
How strenuously do you exercise?
What is your current resting heart rate?
What was it before you started a fitness program?
Do you do warm-up and cooling-down exercises?
Do you get any additional exercise (lifting weights, playing racquetball, swimming)?
What kinds of supervision, instruction, or guidance do you receive?
What kind of training, experience, and knowledge characterize those providing guidance?

How much does your program cost?
What benefits do you feel you get out of it?

I wouldn't be surprised if you find out much more than just the answers to these questions. People who take good care of themselves may be all too eager to let you know, too, of the other kinds of benefits, apparently unrelated to exercise, that fitness has for them. Besides the obvious ones of better food choices, better sleeping, and greater enjoyment of sexuality, some people report a remarkably increased ability to solve problems and be more creative.

COMMUNICATION DAY 4/
I AM WORTH IT

Being assertive means that you are able to express your thoughts and feelings directly, spontaneously, and honestly. You feel good about yourself, because you know "I am worth it." And you feel good about other people, too, respecting their rights, thoughts, and feelings. When you act assertively, you're able to express something positive *or* negative and still maintain your dignity and have good feelings about what happened.

Think of a time when you did not act assertively. The following checklist * may alert you to the situations in your life when, instead of being assertive, you were aggressive, passive, or passive-aggressive. Check the items that tend to cause you to behave nonassertively.

HOW ASSERTIVE ARE YOU?

1. Who has made you feel passive or nonassertive?
   —a spouse? a lover?
   —children?
   —a relative?
   —a friend?
   —an employer? an employee?
   —a teacher? a doctor? a police officer?
   —a salesclerk? a waiter or waitress?
   —an acquaintance?
   —other: —————
2. When have you felt nonassertive, especially if you ask for:

---

* From *The Assertive Woman* by Stanlee Phelps and Nancy Austin (San Luis Obispo, Calif.: Impact Publishers, 1975), pp. 52–53. Used with permission of the authors.

LIFESTYLE DAY 4/
FORTY HOURS A WEEK

In the introduction to *Working: People Talk About What They Do All Day and How They Feel About It*, Studs Terkel describes his book this way: "It is, above all (or beneath all), about daily humiliations. To survive the day is triumph enough for the walking wounded among the great many of us."

Without any doubt, the kind of work you do and how you feel about it affects every part of your life. In my role as a consultant to various organizations, I have found stress on the job is often linked to lack of interpersonal support, Type A behavior, poor health, and an unsatisfying social life. People lose their spirit as they accept or create limitations in their work life. They may love the challenge of the work but, somewhere, recognize that their very essence is being snuffed out. My picture of a middle manager is a shock absorber holding an umbrella. The manager needs to absorb all the troubles of the people who report to her and, at the same time, shield them from the flak coming down from her boss.

Some jobs are certainly more stressful than others, but all share the potential to cause the stressors below. If you'd like to see how you score on job stress, you may wish to complete the "How Stressful Is Your Work?" questionnaire (Appendix D).

For now, consider these four divisions of job stressors, as categorized by colleague Robert W. Hanna:

1. Job Role: how you fit with the job, role conflict, role ambiguity, expectations.
2. Job Tasks: satisfactions, performance, evaluation, competence, interruptions, authority, responsibility (workload, alertness) for people or things.

3. Job Environment: superiors, subordinates, peer relationships, relationships with other units, physical environment, structure.
4. Organizational Environment: suppliers, customers/service recipients, competing organizations, community, government.

Now that you've considered the above stressors, identify those that currently affect you. Write them down and describe how they affect you. (How do you react physically? How do you react emotionally? What are your thoughts? What is your behavior?) This is a good time to enlist your problem-solving skills to find out where you go from here.

Since job stress is a result of your work or the way you're managed on the job, you may wish to see what you can do with your job itself—the supervision, the support you need, the environment. You may even want to discuss this segment or the job-stress questionnaire with your supervisor. Knowing that unnecessary stress is very costly to an organization, your supervisor may be motivated to initiate some in-house training to pinpoint sources of stress in the organization and develop alternatives that can boost morale, creativity, and productivity.

If this is unsatisfactory or no changes are possible, you'll need to develop your own methods to cope with stress more effectively, using the techniques emphasized in this book.

DAY 5

AWARENESS DAY 5/ I'M GONNA CHANGE MY WAY OF LIVIN'

The last segment of the Relaxation Log covers behavioral changes you can make to decrease tension and increase enjoyment in your life. It consists of two parts: the first will help you plan your activities; the second will help you make behavioral changes.

Planning your activities on a regular basis is essential to combating the "Oh, I never have enough time" lament.* Here simply note that the Relaxation Log recognizes the importance of planning and presents a daily checklist:

Plan:
Tomorrow's goals
For special occasions
Days off
Reviewing long-range goals

The second section includes these behavioral changes.

BEHAVIORAL CHANGES

On a scale of 1 to 10, with 10 being the most difficult or the most needed, rate yourself according to how you typically see yourself in the following areas:

I have difficulty
—being more assertive
—being able to "be myself"

---

* The importance of planning and specific guidelines are presented on Days 1, 7, and 12, of "Lifestyle" and on Day 10 of "Awareness."

—making decisions
—expressing anger
—maximizing my capabilities
—finishing "unfinished business"
—being on time

I need more time for
—myself
—friends
—family
—social stimulation
—learning/expansiveness

Look again at Day 2 of "Awareness" and, once again, review that particular day. With a different-colored pencil, rate yourself on the scale above according to what your difficulties or needs were on that day.

What are you aware of as you look over this checklist?

If you find a discrepancy between what you did on Day 2 and how you typically see yourself, what was different about Day 2?

How are you limiting yourself by what you fear may be others' reactions to your new behavior?

What self-image do you feel you must maintain in order to feel good about yourself?

Is it working for you now?

If it's not working for you now, what personal costs do you suffer as a result of hanging on to it?

Can you see yourself free of those old restrictions about what is "right and proper" for you?

How do you feel about that "new you" as you think of yourself that way?

NUTRITION DAY 5/ "WHITE DEATH" NUMBER ONE

Looking over your Food Awareness Log, do you notice some time during the day when you regularly have a high-sugar food? It could be at your coffee break, if you add two teaspoons of sugar to your tea or coffee or usually have a doughnut or other pastry. Or maybe it's after dinner, when you might have a piece of pie or some other sweet dessert.

Think about some one time during your typical day when you know you're probably going to take in some sugar. Remember your desire to become a healthier person and sugar's link with bad health.

Select one food that's high in sugar and substitute a piece of fresh fruit as a natural sweetener.

If you can't stand the idea of drinking your coffee without sugar, cut back from two teaspoons to one; a 50 percent decrease in that one area diminishes the toll of sugar on the body.

EXERCISE DAY 5/
WHAT'S NEW UNDER THE SUN?

Now that you've talked to some people about their exercise programs, it's time to find out what else may be available. You may wish to visit two or three health clubs to find out what they have to offer, and by all means be sure to visit your local YMCA or YWCA, which have a well-deserved outstanding reputation for fitness programs under careful supervision. Before you join anything, inquire about obtaining a visitor's pass so that you can use the facilities, get an idea of the leadership, and become acquainted with the people who are attracted to these facilities.

This is one time when paying more for something is not necessarily an indicator of quality. High-priced memberships may include services you'll never use. So be sure of what you want and then shop around. Some of the questions asked on Day 3 may be applicable here, too. Additionally, you might inquire about how the membership money is targeted. Does it go back into improving the facilities, providing personnel with further training, providing scholarships for those unable to pay, and/or providing educational offerings for its members, such as instruction on stress reduction, prenatal fitness, and cardiopulmonary resuscitation?

You might also inquire about

- the peak hours of attendance
- how many people use the facilities at any one time (this information will let you know if you'll have to wait for a locker or a shower when you want one)
- on what basis maintenance is performed (as needed or scheduled regularly)
- how members make their requests or needs known

- who has control over how funds are spent
- what their plans are for expanding their operations
- if they have any group program for company membership

The answers to these questions and your own personal observations will enable you to make a wise selection. You'll be able to determine by their facilities and personnel whether their primary orientation is toward cardiovascular fitness or personal appearance.

COMMUNICATION DAY 5/
FREE AT LAST

How would you characterize your growing-up years? If you had an ideal home environment, you were part of an intact family with two loving parents who provided the most emotionally nourishing atmosphere imaginable. Communication was open and honest, and family members were free to talk about their feelings, wishes, fears, dreams, and doubts with each other. No one had to pretend to be anything she wasn't. From the youngest family member to the oldest, every person knew that his views and feelings would be listened to and respected. You freely expressed affection among yourselves with an abundance of caring, touching, and holding. When things didn't go well, conflicts were brought out into the open and resolved, and the issue was put to rest.

If this describes your early years, congratulate yourself. You are rare indeed! More likely your parents wanted you to have the very best and benefit from the riches and rewards they never had as children but, unfortunately, a gap existed between their intentions and your reality. The scenario above may have been their dream, too, but somehow daily pressures or other influences may have intervened to rewrite the script. Since most parents know about parenting only from their own experiences growing up, their main determination is often "not to raise my children as I was raised."

Out of their own needs for survival, when your parents felt frustrated, helpless, angry, desperate or embittered, they may have yelled at you or called you names, some of the most popular of which are "crazy," "dirty," "stupid," "sick," "weak," "lazy," "sad," and "immature."*

Since you were determined to have your parents' love, you may have done your best to "prove" that the names they called you didn't fit. For instance, if you were frequently called weak or stupid, you may be seen today as quite strong and bright. If you were called sick and lazy, you may be seen as healthy and energetic. Or maybe you agreed with your parents, thus becoming something you originally weren't.

The problem arises when you work extremely hard to become something you're not as a result of an image associated with the way you were characterized—the names you were called—as a child. All of us are capable of acting out any of those names at some time in our lives. And yet, not being free to acknowledge that you may have some of those characteristics is just as much a prison. It's as if those old voices were still in your head, ready to humiliate you if you let down your guard.

Worse, if someone in your present life implies or calls you one of those names, your self-esteem is endangered. At that early time in your life when you first heard those names, you probably felt unlovable. So now, if someone touches that still sensitive nerve your self-worth takes a nose-dive, and you may have no idea what's happening.

Reread that list of names above, and if you have others that aren't on the list, include them, too. Can you accept these characteristics as occasionally true parts of yourself? Which are the names that make you feel unlovable? Who in your present life still triggers that old response? How do you usually respond? With your new knowledge, how can you respond?

* Thanks to Virginia Satir for this concept.

RELAXATION DAY 5/ MY OWN SPECIAL PLACE

This is an exercise that you will probably want to read through first; then you can either record it on tape or have a friend read it to you as you go through it. Begin by getting yourself comfortable, relaxing your body through "belly breathing," and clearing your mind of "mind chatter." Allow yourself plenty of time, and don't hurry the deepening relaxation.

With your eyes closed, picture yourself walking alone through a beautiful, fragrant garden, with the gentle sunlight warming your body. Your body is protected from the sun's harmful rays. You are walking at a comfortable pace, taking plenty of time to gaze at and smell the lovely flowers that are blooming everywhere. Perhaps it's been a long time since you've taken the time to feast your senses in this way. As you walk through the garden, you notice a large building ahead. The building seems very quiet, peaceful, and inviting.

You enter the building and go down a long corridor. No one seems to be around, and it seems like it's awaiting your discovery. Even though you are curious, you feel calm and relaxed. The corridor is lined with many doors of different shapes, sizes, and colors. It's a most unusual place indeed. You may open any door you wish, but first you need to pick the door that most appeals to you. Now that you've selected the door to open, see yourself turning the door handle, about to enter the room. The room can be any size you want it to be.

When you first open the door, you notice that the floor is covered with the finest, most luxurious, deepest-pile carpeting you can imagine. It is any color you want it to be. As you enter the room, your feet gently sink into the deep carpeting. You've never before known such plush softness.

Then you look at the four walls of the room. What do you see? If there are windows, what do you see through the windows? You can see anything you want to see. You could even see scenes that don't make sense, like a waterfall emptying into a small tropical pond through one window, a sparkling-bright winter snow scene high in the mountains through another, and liquid amber trees of brilliant hues as their leaves change in the fall through still another. You can make the room and what you see in it anything you want. Select scenes that are the most relaxing to you. Listen to the sounds you hear in your own room.

Now you can bring into your room anything that has special significance in relaxing you. It could be a comfortable afghan or pillow, some favorite books, music or artwork, a relaxing chair, a familiar tea cup, a letter from a friend, favorite photographs. Be aware of all the events, things, and people in your life that have nourished you, and bring to your room any reminders of them that you want near you.

Look around your room, your own special place, and be aware of how relaxed and peaceful you feel among your treasures. Notice how quiet, deep, and nourishing your breathing is as you enjoy your special place. You can stay here for as long as you wish. Whenever you are ready, open your eyes and come back to your reality, knowing that you can return to your special place any time you feel tense or anxious. It is exclusively yours, and you can make it any way you wish so that it totally relaxes and nourishes you.

LIFESTYLE DAY 5/
IT'S ALWAYS THERE

When is the last time you lay under a tree and noticed the contrast of the green leaves against the blue sky or how the limbs branched out and intertwined?

When is the last time you walked barefoot in the grass or the sand and were aware of the texture against the bottom of your feet?

When is the last time you sat still in a park, with your eyes closed, and listened to the songs of the birds?

Being in contact with nature is a vital need that we too often neglect. Even though the opportunity for that contact is all around us, sometimes we think of it only as a weekend or vacation activity.

I suggest that you creatively determine how you can have some daily contact with nature. One dear friend of mine has positioned a mirror in her bedroom so that it catches the winter sunrise, reflecting it onto her bed. Certainly the popularity of house plants attests to our need to be in contact with living things. Gigot, my French sheepdog, demands my attention from time to time as I write these words, pressing his large, cuddly head into my lap. I give in and pet him. Sometimes he wants me to take him outside. It is as if his is the ultimate wisdom, because I return to write with a fresh perspective.

Expand your thinking to make daily contact with nature a reality for you. The truth is, it's always there. We simply have to take the time to notice it and, consequently, be softened and rejuvenated by it.

DAY 6

AWARENESS DAY 6/
MY MANY FACES

Day 5's exercise asked you to examine your self-image—that picture you carry of yourself. Here's another way of looking at how this works.

Below are three "selves." The first self is "How I see myself." The second self is "How other people see me." The third is "How I would like others to see me."

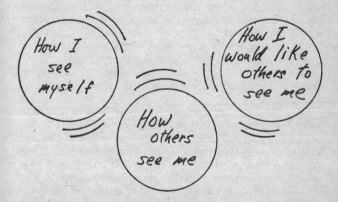

Take a moment and jot down on a piece of paper "How I see myself." Allow yourself at least three minutes to write down as many adjectives as you can about yourself.

Now take a second piece of paper and write "How other people see me," keeping in mind a particular group of people as you write. Feel free to repeat adjectives used in the first list. Again, allow yourself at least three minutes to put down as many adjectives as you can. (If there are several important and very separate groups of people in your life—

for instance, your work associates, your religious group, your tennis buddies—you may wish to make a separate list for each.)

Finally, take a third piece of paper and write "How I would like others to see me." Again, repeat adjectives if they're appropriate. This time, too, take at least three minutes to write down your response.

Put the three (or more) lists side by side, and think of them as the three circles in the diagram. Circle the adjectives that appear on all three lists.

Does that account for most of the adjectives, or are there a significant number that are not shared among the lists?

What do these discrepancies mean to you?

How do you feel about the discrepancies?

Are you aware of any tension as you think about the discrepancies?

Think of each of these lists as being in movement, at times overlapping, at times separate and distant from each other. The more they overlap, sharing the same adjectives and the same views of the self, the less tension you will experience. The more distant they are, with differences among these three selves, the more tension and "pulled apart" you will feel.

Are you aware of any changes you would choose to make to decrease the distance among your selves?

How do you feel as you contemplate making those changes in order to become more of the same person in all three circles?

Do you experience any change in your level of tension as you think about what that would be like for you?

This is a tough exercise to do on your own, and you may wish to use this time to set up an appointment with someone to be your guide and timekeeper. Of course, you have no obligation to share with that person the contents of your lists or the process you go through in answering the questions. But if you *do* choose to share this confidential information, you'd automatically reduce the distance between your self and how that other person sees you. You'd be making your humanness more accessible, and therefore creating the possibility of a meaningful connection.

NUTRITION DAY 6/ "WHITE DEATH" NUMBER TWO

The next time you automatically reach for the salt-shaker, pause a moment. See if there isn't another seasoning that would be just as flavorful, such as lemon juice or herbs. If you cook for yourself, you can add them during the preparation.

Select a food that you ordinarily eat prepared with salt, or to which you add salt at the table—meat, poultry, fish, or vegetables. For once, substitute another seasoning for the salt. For example you may wish to season your chicken with rosemary and your tomatoes with basil.

You may remember from the overview of "Nutrition" that adding salt to foods is an acquired taste. Over time you can learn to give up that habit and, for the sake of your good health, replace it with a more beneficial practice.

If you truly crave the flavor of salt, potassium-chloride salt substitutes are available.

EXERCISE DAY 6/
THE BEST EXERCISE
YOU CAN GET

What's the exercise most doctors recommend? Walking! Why walking, you may wonder. Simply because, of all exercise, it is the most readily available and requires the least preparation or equipment—and most of us are already doing it to some extent, so it's just a matter of doing it some more. You may recall that Margie, the office worker described on Day 2, devised a way to increase her exercise through walking by methodically parking her car farther and farther from her office building.

Walking is one of the few exercises that is good for all parts of the body. If you let your arms swing loosely and get good movement in your spine, you allow your muscles to move naturally, smoothly. In order to have that freedom of movement, you should not carry anything. A purse, camera, or tote bag slung over a shoulder automatically puts you off-balance. If you must carry something, use a small daypack that fits over both shoulders to better distribute the weight.

Let your foot land on the heel and roll down the outside of the foot, and push off with your toes. The more vigorously you swing your arms, the greater the cardiovascular benefit. The extra energy required to do this will help raise your heart rate. Pritikin says that your upper torso should be as tired as your lower torso after you've walked energetically, swinging your arms vigorously.

If you've been keeping your Activity Log, you have an idea of how much you walk in a day. Today take a walk in your neighborhood using the style of walking described above—nothing in your hands, swinging your arms vigorously. Walk just as long as you feel comfortable, but use this style and keep up a brisk pace.

If your neighborhood isn't the type that invites you to

184

walk comfortably and regularly, you may wish to consider other places where you can walk. Whenever I run at the high school track, I share it with people who are walking; easily one-fifth of those on the track are walkers, some in small groups, others alone. A dear friend of mine regularly takes her morning constitutional at a block-long city pocket park nestled in a residential area. She has measured the distance by driving around that block and can compute how far she walks.

You may choose to develop a schedule that will permit you to reach a goal of walking briskly for one mile twice a day. If you do decide you want to make walking your regular exercise, invest in a good pair of jogging shoes. If you don't choose to buy jogging shoes, wear low-heeled shoes with good arch supports and make sure your shoes aren't run down at the heels. Improper shoes will contribute to excessive fatigue and back strain.

To achieve maximum benefit, you need to walk regularly and briskly, and steadily increasing either your distance or your time, to ensure maximal cardiovascular benefit.

COMMUNICATION DAY 6/
A BEDTIME RITUAL

That critical time just before you go to sleep is an opportunity for an activity that can make you feel better about yourself. The brain's receptivity to positive messages may at that time influence dreaming.* Unfortunately, too many of us use those last thoughts to go over a "laundry list" of the things we must do the next day or to rehash something we don't feel good about.

Instead, I suggest you use this technique. When you're ready to go to sleep tonight, think of a situation in which you felt very good about yourself. It could be an incident in which you behaved in an assertive, caring manner or in which you used your expertise on a problem that was therefore more easily resolved. Or it could be a situation in which, instead of becoming exasperated and yelling, you were able to put things into perspective and remain calm by using a brief relaxation technique. There doesn't have to be any tangible product—just something you feel good about.

Does any situation come to your mind right now? If it does, fine. Mentally hang on to it for later. If nothing occurs to you, you may have to dig a little.

When you think of the situation, imagine yourself again in the actual scene. Think of all the life experiences, knowledge, and personal attributes that are *you* and that enable you to feel good about yourself. Congratulate yourself on your continuing journey of self-exploration, learning, and self-improvement. This openness to learning is essential to finding a more rewarding life. Be appreciative of

---

* Another powerful activity at this time is Affirmations, in Day 10 of "Lifestyle."

186

the fact that you're able to take the time to pursue a healthier, more fulfilling lifestyle.

I wouldn't be surprised if you find this a difficult exercise to do, but if you're willing to stick with it you may make some interesting discoveries. It's almost as if there's some unwritten rule in this society that it's wrong to love ourselves or to think good thoughts about ourselves. I find that we're so accustomed to putting ourselves down that we have a hard time thinking of situations when our goodness and positive attributes prevailed. That contributes to a lowered opinion of ourselves, making us susceptible to self-induced stress.

I find this technique helpful when I'm with complaining friends who characteristically bemoan their inadequacies or disappointments: they can tell me anything they want to about their shortcomings—*provided that* they also tell me something good about themselves.

RELAXATION DAY 6/ RUB THE TENSION AWAY

Today you'll learn another method to relax yourself simply and quickly. It takes only two or three minutes and can be combined with other stretching exercises or relaxation techniques to reach a deeper state of relaxation.

Release any tension that you may be aware of. You may wish to loosen your clothing, remove your shoes, and unfasten your belt. If you're sitting down and your legs are crossed, start by putting your feet flat on the floor. Allow your legs to relax so that your knees fall away from each other. Let your arms lie comfortably in your lap. You may already feel some relaxation from the tightness. If you can afford to close your eyes, so much the better. Notice how much more relaxed you are with your eyes closed.

Now, with your fingers, rub your temples in a slow circular motion, using gentle pressure. Allow plenty of time. Feel the relaxation come. Your body is getting more and more relaxed. Experience the aliveness of the increased blood flow to your head.

Now let your head drop forward so that your chin is on your chest. Then, ever so slowly, rotate your head to the right, as if to look over your right shoulder. Then reverse the rotation, slowly moving your head to the left, as if to look over your left shoulder. Keep your shoulders level and your body straight, moving only your head and neck. Repeat three times. (This is Beginning Position No. 1 for relieving neck pain in Day 8 of "Exercise.")

Notice how relaxed you are after these simple movements.

LIFESTYLE DAY 6/
SEVEN SIGNIFICANT HABITS

Here's a simple tried-and-true formula. You can make a vital improvement in your health by practicing all seven of these favorable health habits:

1. *Eat a good breakfast.* It should consist of fruit or juice, protein, fiber, and a slow-burning carbohydrate. You ought to consume 25 to 30 percent of your daily calories at breakfast.
2. *Don't eat between meals.* Snacks generally lack food value and provide mostly sugar, fat, and calories. Snacking is often an indication of poor diet habits and a lack of regular, balanced meals. If you eat smaller meals, however, and have *healthy* snacks, fine.
3. *Get seven to eight hours of sleep each night.* Unless you regularly sleep other than seven to eight hours and feel no ill effects, sleeping less is often an indication of extreme stress and sleeping more may indicate depression. Either may be a symptom of a physical problem.
4. *Keep within a few pounds of your recommended ideal weight.* Since tables of average weight reflect the general population's excess weight, you may wish to have a skinfold test, which shows how much of your weight is fat.
5. *Exercise regularly.* Exercise for a minimum of twenty minutes a day at least three times a week, getting your heartbeat to within 70 to 85 percent of its maximum rate.
6. *Don't smoke.* If you've stopped smoking, you may have reversed some of the damage to your cardiovascular system through a vigorous exercise pro-

gram and a diet high in fiber and unprocessed foods. However, the damage to your lungs may be irreversible.

7. *Drink moderately or not at all.* Abstainers can congratulate themselves on this one, although it's been shown that a glass of white wine with dinner may alleviate stress and diminish cholesterol.

How many of these seven health habits do you practice? If you don't practice many of them and you're young, you may not notice any ill effects yet, but your bad habits will catch up with you.

Based on research with almost 7,000 people over a course of several years, as reported in *Preventive Medicine* in 1972, Nedra B. Belloc and Lester Breslow found the following:

> In every age group, those who reported all seven favorable health habits had, on the average, better physical health than those who reported six. With one minor exception there was a consistent progression toward better health at each age as the number of good health practices increased.
>
> The average physical-health status of those over 75 who followed all of the good health practices was about the same as those of 35 to 44 who followed fewer than three. . . . These data are consistent with the idea . . . that a lifetime of good health practices produces good health and extends the period for relatively good physical health status by some 30 years.

How healthy a life do you choose for yourself? What changes will you have to make in your daily habits to make that happen?

DAY 7

AWARENESS DAY 7/ *EVERYBODY IS DIFFERENT*

By now you have a pretty good idea of how you *typically* respond to stress and how that relates to your reactions on one particular day. How about those other people in your life who are close to you? How do they respond to stress?

One person might appear very calm and controlled, while someone else might get very agitated and nervous. One might have trouble sleeping, and another can't get enough sleep. One might have diarrhea, another constipation. And so on.

It's valuable to know how the people close to you respond to stress so that you don't falsely assume that their reactions will be similar to yours. If you know what's happening, you're in a position to be supportive when they need it. And vice versa.

Below is a sentence-completion exercise I designed to enable people to find out these things—about themselves and about others. You may wish to complete it yourself and then have someone close to you complete statements 2 and 3 for you. That way you'll have an idea of how well the other person knows you and your typical response patterns. You can then do the same with the other person.

This kind of information could be helpful in achieving better results with a work team *if* there's high trust and mutual respect and caring.

1. My biggest fear about stress is . . .
2. When I'm experiencing an overload of stress,
   on the inside I feel . . .
   on the outside I show . . .
   people respond to me by . . .
3. I would like people to respond to me by . . .

4. I would be embarrassed if people knew that when I'm experiencing stress overload, I . . .
5. The people I live with respond to stress overload by . . .
6. The people I work with respond to stress overload by . . .

Selected responses to this instrument are included in Appendix E, "How People React to Stress Overload," compiled from members of professional organizations, students in graduate schools of business, people in the helping professions, and executives in different fields from all over the United States enrolled in courses on Managing Executive Stress.

NUTRITION DAY 7/
SIMPLER IS NOT BETTER

In the overview of "Nutrition," you learned of the advantages of complex carbohydrates over simple carbohydrates.

Looking at your Food Awareness Log, you may notice that some of your food intake consists of the very simple carbohydrates that you now know are not beneficial. Following are two suggestions to increase your consumption of complex carbohydrates. Try one or both of them, or something similar of your own choosing.

The next time you're in a restaurant, instead of ordering mashed potatoes, which might come from a box and contain additives as well as potatoes, order a baked potato. It's a perfectly healthy, filling food. When you're offered either butter or sour cream and chives, try it with just the chives. You can well afford to pass up the cholesterol, fat, and calories of butter or sour cream.

Or, instead of a canned soup for lunch, take the time to prepare a bountiful fresh green salad. Flavor it with lemon juice instead of a bottled dressing high in oil. Oil-free dressings are commercially available, but, unfortunately, they usually contain additives.

EXERCISE DAY 7/
HOW HARD IS
HARD ENOUGH?

Exercising isn't really effective unless your pulse rate is increased so that your heart gets a good workout. Since the heart is a muscle, it will be stronger and more resilient if it is well exercised. Most people, however, are afraid of over-extending themselves, fearing that they may work their hearts too hard.

Find out your Resting Heart Rate (RHR) by taking your pulse first thing in the morning before you are stimulated and before you get out of bed. When you first open your eyes, use a timer with an indicator for seconds and take your pulse by placing your fingers on the carotid artery (in your neck) or on your wrist and count for ten seconds. Then multiply by 6 to find out your RHR.

The RHR is an indicator of individual differences, and it reflects how fit you are. If you are not fit (overweight, out of shape, a smoker or a drinker), more heartbeats per minute are required to nourish the body. The more fit you are, the lower your RHR.

Here's the formula so that you can figure what's right for you.

220 minus your age = your Maximum Heart Rate (MHR)
minus your Resting Heart Rate (RHR) = K (constant)

Let's say that you're a forty-year-old lap swimmer. Your formula would look like this:

220 − 40 = 180 (MHR) − 60 (RHR) = 120 (K)

To increase your volume of oxygen consumption (VO^2), it's best to work the heart at 75 percent of its maximum rate; this is called the Working Heart Rate (WHR). If the heart isn't working at a minimum of 70 percent of the MHR, the exercise isn't vigorous enough for improved cardiovascular functioning. Since 85 percent of the MHR is the upper limit for safety, don't exceed this figure for the first few months.

Using our forty-year-old swimmer as an example, here's how he would calculate his limits.

Percentage of WHR	RHR + (% of WHR x K)	One Minute	Ten Seconds
70% minimum WHR	60 + (.70 x 120) = 144		24
75% ideal WHR	60 + (.75 x 120) = 150		25
85% maximum WHR	60 + (.85 x 120) = 162		27
100% = Capacity WHR		180	30

Take your pulse rate when you finish exercising and see how you do. It's wise to take it a second time—two minutes after exercising—to find out your Recovery Heart Rate, which should be near the rate at which your heart ordinarily functions. Your Recovery Heart Rate may vary from day to day, according to how you feel. If you have a cold or you didn't get much sleep the night before, your Recovery Heart Rate will be higher.

As your heart gets stronger, you'll need to work it harder by increasing either the time you spend exercising or the effort you expend during exercise to achieve the same WHR. For instance, when a fifty-year-old friend of mine first started running, she felt like she was going to die after thirty seconds. Respecting her body and knowing that it needs time to build up after being sedentary, she gradually increased the time she spent running, at first by fifteen-second increments. Ultimately she reached her goal of being able to run for thirty minutes. She made the commitment to herself to run, and she went through the proper warm-up and cooling-down exercises each time, keeping track of her Working Heart Rate and her Recovery Heart Rate. She didn't think it was silly to do warm-up exercises for so short a time of running; she knew she was changing her lifestyle, and the stretching exercises were good for keeping her body limber and increasing her blood flow. She wasn't concerned that people might scoff at her humble beginning, because she knew what was possible if she stuck to it.

Now that you've taken your RHR, you can decide what commitment you are willing to make toward increasing your exercise.

COMMUNICATION DAY 7/
YOU ARE A RAINBOW

Over and over again in my counseling practice I meet people who seem to lack joy and true pleasure in their lives. They function within a rather narrow band of "everything's fine" or "I'm okay," rarely experiencing any big highs or dealing with any major lows in their emotional spectrum. Perhaps they've suffered some sadness and pain earlier in their lives—the death of a parent, the loss of a love relationship, betrayal by a friend, humiliation by a teacher—that has contributed to their building a wall around themselves to keep them from feeling.

Then they may seek counseling because nothing in their lives seems to really matter. They live in a rather predictable manner, taking only relatively safe risks, if any. In general, they shun anything that has a strong emotional content, concerning themselves with such leisure activities as playing cards or watching TV situation comedies—something relatively mindless, requiring no personal disclosure by anyone, just something to get them through the day or night.

What they fail to recognize is that by eliminating the pain in their lives, they eliminate the joy as well. Cutting off one part of your emotions leads to cutting off other, desirable emotions.

Look over this list of feelings.

accepted	bored
affectionate	competitive
afraid	confused
angry	defensive
anxious	disappointed
attracted	free
betrayed	frustrated

grief	rejected
guilty	repulsed
helpless	respect
hopeful	sad
hurt	satisfied
inferior	sexual
jealous	shy
joyful	superior
lonely	suspicious
loving	trusting
powerful	weak

Do certain emotions stand out as acceptable to you? Are others repugnant or unacceptable for you to feel? When you think of people who are in touch with all these feelings, what kind of a person comes to mind? How does that person talk, act, move, and communicate with others? What about that person is attractive to you? Could you see yourself being in touch with all your feelings? How do you feel right now as you think about this?

Being a whole person means being in touch with all the feelings you have as well as knowing that they are yours and that they are all acceptable. You are capable of experiencing all the feelings listed above. Your emotions comprise a rainbow of possibilities, some dark and heavy, others brilliantly glowing. Being in touch with how you feel is a critical first step in getting to know just who you are. Knowing the range of your feelings and being sensitive to subtle changes or conflicting emotions serves to alert you to what is going on in your body, sensitizing you to the first signs of stress overload.

Acknowledging your feelings does not mean you have to act upon them. You may feel furious with someone, but that doesn't mean you have to *do* something furious. Simply acknowledge what's going on within you, and you may or may not choose to give an "I message" to reveal your feelings.

RELAXATION DAY 7/
LAUGH AND THE WORLD LAUGHS WITH YOU

When's the last time you had a good belly laugh? How about a hearty chuckle? People experiencing stress overload often become so tense and determined that they forget the relaxation that can come with laughter. If they can delight in their sense of humor, they can improve their physical as well as their psychological health. Hearty laughter provides an emotional release while it reduces tension.

Probably the best-known documentation of the healing power of laughter is found in Norman Cousins' account of his bout with a life-threatening illness, *Anatomy of an Illness*. He speculated that if you can make yourself sick with worry, then it should follow that you can make yourself well with laughter. He included something to make him laugh as part of his unorthodox daily healing regimen, and found that he felt better and slept better. Later he supported his hypothesis with laboratory tests, which showed that laughter releases endorphins and enhances the body's ability to fight the disease: "I made the joyous discovery that ten minutes of genuine belly laughter had an anesthetic effect and would give me at least two hours of pain-free sleep."

Cousins used humorous films, including the Marx Brothers and "Candid Camera" TV shows, and humor books, including E. B. and Katherine White's *Subtreasury of American Humor* and Max Eastman's *The Enjoyment of Laughter*. He also suggests the humorous writings of Stephen Leacock, Ogden Nash, James Thurber, and Ludwig Bemelmans.

What kinds of things that make you laugh can you introduce into your life on a regular basis? Decide upon doing something today that will make you laugh out loud. It might be a trip to the zoo, a pet store, a children's playground, a park, or a library. Or you might want to do something physical, like ice-skating or roller-skating, if those are activities you don't know how to do. Feel free to do something you might label as "silly."

Rediscover the joy of play, too. Too early, adults lose the pleasure from play once they expect their activities to yield a product. We tend to take ourselves too seriously. Enjoy the meditative rhythm as you enjoy swinging on a park swing. Make patterns in the sand, knowing how temporary they can be. Put soapy water in a bowl and blow soap bubbles through a straw. You can even share the bowl with a friend who's blowing on another straw.

If you can laugh over it, that's what counts.

LIFESTYLE DAY 7/
WHERE IS IT?

Can you see the top of your desk?

When does your car next need a lube and oil change?

How much money did you pay in late charges last year?

Who did you stand up because you forgot an appointment?

Disorganization creates untold stress for those who choose to live their lives in a chaotic manner. Once caught up in the mess, it seems impossible to get out from under it. They know that it will take some time to get organized, and because they're busy people they simply add more clutter instead of taking the time to sort things out. Only when the cost is high enough, either in dollars, personal disappointment, or frustration, might they be motivated to tackle the problem. Fortunately, some excellent books are available as guides. Here are a few basic suggestions.

1. Buy a pocket-size appointment calendar. This date book can become your most precious tool, if you use it wisely and carry it with you.
   a. Record all appointments, with follow-up phone numbers. That way, if you're stuck somewhere, you can call.
   b. Record your expenses and the purpose of your meetings.
   c. Note tasks to be done and set your priorities.
   d. Note whom you want to call, see, or write.
   e. Write reminder notes to yourself. If you promise to return a book to someone, note the return date. If someone has promised to deliver something to you, make a note of when you should follow up.

f. Note due dates for bills, taxes, travel deposits, etc.

g. Note important occasions on an annual basis, such as birthdays, anniversaries, and holidays. Allow yourself adequate lead time for those occasions you wish to honor, such as sending a card three days before a birthday.

h. Record routine activities: exercise, how much you weigh, daily level of stress (on a 1-to-10 scale), number of sales calls made, etc. This is an excellent idea for any activity you wish to monitor.

2. Buy some self-sticking notes. Available from stationery stores, these waxed-back notes come in different sizes and can be used in many different ways. When you get directions to go somewhere, write them on one of these and place it in your date book for the appropriate day; then, when you get ready to drive there, stick it on the dashboard of your car. Use them freely as reminder notes, especially for recurrent activities, like "pay bills" or "fertilize plants," and simply relocate them in your date book from month to month.

3. Sort your mail as it arrives into these four files:
   A. Things to do, which could be segregated as to "urgent," "this week," "pending," and "reading."
   b. To file.
   c. Your spouse's or lover's name (if you have one) for anything you need to discuss with her.
   d. Financial, for bills, taxes, etc.
   When your mail arrives, open it where you keep these files and sort everything immediately or discard it. If you have a "hmmm pile"—that is, if you think "hmmm, that's interesting, and some day it may be useful"—throw it out.

4. Set up a filing system with manila folders and labels. A typical set of files for the home might include Automobile, Entertaining, Fashion, Financial, Health, Holidays, Household, Medical, Personal Correspondence, Property, Restaurants/Entertainment, Taxes, Tradesmen (plumbers, etc.), Warranties and Guarantees. If you have a lot of warranties and guarantees, you may wish to

keep them in an accordion file under the appropriate letter.

5. Organize the rest of your living environment accordingly. Take one room at a time, one section of each room at a time, and set aside a maximum of two hours at a time to clean up and clear out. Don't get overeager and try to do it all in one day. That's too overwhelming!

Once you've attained the degree of order and cleanliness you desire, you're likely to feel less fragmented, burdened, and harassed. Maintaining your surroundings to your liking is much easier and swifter once you have a system and learn to follow it regularly.

Recommended Reading

Moskowitz, Robert A. *How to Organize Your Work and Your Life*. New York: Doubleday, 1981.

Wilson, Stephanie. *Getting Organized*. New York: Warner, 1979.

DAY 8

AWARENESS DAY 8/
THE BIGGER PICTURE

In the overview of "Awareness," you learned that a "system" can be defined as an interrelated group of people or things that, together, make up a whole.

Your work team is a system. It consists of people and things that, together, get the job done. If a machine is "down" on Line 3, then everyone who works on that line is stressed. If the boss asks for a special status report on your team's work project, the pressure of that subsystem (the boss) causes increased demand for performance from everyone else in the system. If your company receives a major contract as a result of a proposal submitted several months ago, everyone connected with that project is affected.

Having completed the exercises in Day 6, you now know a little about how the individuals in your work team respond to stress overload. Think about how your organization responds to stress overload. What are the characteristic ways it responds?

What style does management adopt as the organization experiences more stress?

What are the costs to the organization, in both monetary and human terms? (For instance, increased turnover, higher absenteeism, decreased productivity, poor morale.)

Are any alliances formed among subgroups as a result of stress? If so, how are they affected by increased stress in the organization?

What new role, if any, are you aware of for yourself as part of the organization when it experiences stress overload?

Are you aware of any increased tension as you review these characteristic responses?

Where do you experience this tension in your body?

What alternatives can you imagine for creating a more humanistic system in your workplace?

NUTRITION DAY 8/
FINS AND FEATHERS
ARE FINE

How many times a week do you have red meat? If you ordinarily have it five times a week, cut back to three times a week, and you'll significantly reduce your intake of saturated fat and cholesterol. Substitute chicken, turkey, or fish for red meat at those two meals, and you've a bargain on protein along with fewer calories, no saturated fats, and much lower cholesterol. Remember, however, to remove the skin and all visible fat from poultry.

EXERCISE DAY 8/
FOR THAT PAIN
IN THE NECK

Many people find that tension is expressed in their bodies as a pain in the neck, sometimes associated with headaches. The neck and shoulders easily become tense, and this tension can be aggravated by an improper sleeping position, carrying a shoulder bag, poor posture, and what seems to be a present-day epidemic—whiplash.

These exercises are designed to alleviate neck and shoulder strain, to make those muscles looser. These, like all other exercises, should be done only to the degree to which you are comfortable. Don't strain, and don't bounce, jerk, or make sudden movements. Your objective is simply to get the muscles moving and increase the blood flow so that they become looser and better nourished with oxygen. Slow, gentle movements best accomplish this. You may notice that, without any apparent effort on your part, you're able to rotate your head farther with increased repetition. Closing your eyes increases relaxation.

Head Rotation

Stand comfortably or sit in a straight-backed chair, with your head and body erect. This is Beginning Position No. 1. Now slowly rotate your head to the right, as if to look over your right shoulder. Then reverse the rotation, slowly moving your head to the left, as if to look over your left shoulder. Avoid any temptation to raise your shoulder as your chin nears. Keep your shoulders level and your body straight, moving only your head and neck. Repeat seven times.

Head Nods

Assume Beginning Position No. 1. Nod your head so that you slowly bring your chin toward your chest and then reverse the direction by letting your head go back, raising your chin in the air. Simply allow your head to fall forward on your chest; don't force it. Do the same when your head goes back, letting gravity do the work. Repeat seven times. *If you're recovering from a whiplash injury, don't do this exercise.*

Ear to Shoulder

Again in Beginning Position No. 1, keep your head directed forward and slowly rotate your head so that your right ear approaches your right shoulder. Don't raise your shoulder to meet your ear; instead, just allow your ear to move toward your shoulder. Then reverse direction, allowing your left ear to move toward your left shoulder, keeping your head directed forward. Once again, allow gravity to take over. Repeat seven times.

Modified Head Roll

In Beginning Position No. 1, allow your chin to fall forward on your chest, and then slowly rotate your head to the right until your chin is over your right shoulder, keeping your chin close to your body. Then reverse direction, allowing your chin to glide along your chest back down the front of your chest and up toward your left shoulder, stopping when your chin is over your left shoulder. Repeat seven times. (Note: The popular version of the Head Roll is to allow your head to slowly rotate in a complete circle, which compresses the cervical vertebrae. This is not recommended.)

These last three exercises are aided by gravity. You may notice that your head feels heavier and that it takes less effort on your part to move it, as gravity assists a slow, rhythmical movement.

COMMUNICATION DAY 8/
AT THE NEXT GAS STATION

Picture this scene. You're driving to drop off a package at the home of a friend who has recently moved to a newly developed section of the city. The directions you have aren't very good, but you're confident that you'll be able to find the place. You figure it should take you between ten and fifteen minutes to get there. After ten minutes, you're having trouble finding the street names. Fifteen minutes pass, and none of the markers he told you about have appeared.

What do you do now? How do you feel? How would you rate your level of self-confidence at this point? Are you willing to stop and ask for help at the next gas station?

If yes, then give yourself a gold star for not being burdened with feeling that you must forever maintain an image of being the ever-confident, strong, silent type.

Think of the times you've carried something that's too heavy for you. Or persisted at puzzling over a problem that is clearly beyond your capabilities. Or worked on a job with your two hands when three hands would have made it much easier. Or continued working on something when you weren't feeling well because it was your job and you didn't want to be seen as irresponsible. Does this sound familiar? If these incidents describe you, then think for a moment of what would have happened if, first, you had recognized that you could have used some help and, second, had been bold enough to ask for help?

Being able to ask for help when you need it is an extremely effective aid in eliminating unnecessary stress. For too many people, this is a very difficult thing to do. They feel like failures if they have to admit they don't know something or if they can't do something they think they should do—or that they think others expect them to do. So,

214

rather than admit their need for help, they proceed as if they know what they're doing, sometimes to everyone's peril.

Almost everyone can benefit by more freely being able to ask for help when necessary. I'm not saying that you have to be a complainer, a whiner, or weak and ineffectual. I am saying this: Imagine three situations that could occur in the next two days in which you would feel like you were in over your head, you weren't able to complete a job as you'd like, or you didn't have all the information you needed, and imagine yourself *asking for help*. (It could be as simple as requesting assistance in selecting an appropriate restaurant where you can take some visiting big shots.) After you select the three incidents, think of who can be your resource people. How do you feel as you anticipate asking for their help? What do you expect will be their response? If one of them were to say "no," how would that affect your willingness to make other requests for help?

I find that people are generally very eager to help when they feel that what they have to offer will be appreciated. Asking them for help is almost a gift, as it provides them with an opportunity to show off their talent, knowledge, skill, or strength. You may be surprised at how warmly people will regard you if they believe you don't have all the answers all the time. It allows them to feel that they can be of some importance in your life.

RELAXATION DAY 8/
FIND YOUR CENTER

People have been meditating for over 2,000 years, but only recently have scientific studies demonstrated the extreme effectiveness of meditation as a way of combating stress. Meditation does not have to be cultic or religious in nature. If you meditate regularly you'll be able to induce a state that is the exact opposite (physiologically and psychologically) of the "fight or flight" response. During meditation you lower your blood pressure and heart rate, slow your breathing, decrease your consumption of oxygen, and change your brain waves to produce more alpha and theta waves, which are characteristic of more relaxed and creative states.

These changes can affect your whole life. The meditator has an increased emotional and psychological stability and a greater capacity to cope with the pressures of everyday life. The calm and restorative nature of meditation exceeds that of sleep and dreaming. In fact, one of the things that meditators often notice is their decreased need for sleep.

There is no one right way to meditate! Meditation can be achieved through many different techniques, and only two are given here. Pick one you like and stay with it for three or four weeks, spending at least fifteen minutes each day. I suggest that you get up early in the morning to make that extra fifteen minutes available to you. It's better to meditate every day for fifteen minutes than twice a week for an hour.

Here are some guidelines for meditating:*

---

* From *You're in Charge: A Guide to Becoming Your Own Therapist* by Janette Rainwater (Los Angeles: Guild of Tutors Press, 1979), 139–143. Used with permission of the author.

1. Select a place where you can meditate without being disturbed. If necessary, take the phone off the hook and shut out intruders with a warning notice.
2. Sit on the floor in a "classic meditative position" or in a chair. If you sit in a chair, have your feet flat on the floor with your hands in your lap. The "classic meditative position" may be uncomfortable for people in this culture. Here you sit on the floor, back straight with hands resting on your thighs, palms up. Your legs are either crossed or parallel, with your feet tucked under your buttocks.
3. Say to yourself "I intend to set aside my emotions and my problems for this period of time."
4. Close your eyes.
5. Notice that you have judgments, expectations, and fantasies of what this will be like, and then set them aside so that you can experience what *is*.
6. Relax any tightness in your body, including your face and jaw.
7. Regulate your breath. Breathing through both nostrils, see how many counts are required for your incoming breath. Let your stomach expand as you begin to inhale. Then allow the same count for your exhaling breath. Hold yourself motionless for an instant or two before beginning to exhale. Let your breath be gentle and quiet. When your breathing seems even, start your meditation technique (either one of the following).

Breath Mindfulness

Observe, describe, and label your breathing. "I am breathing in a long breath. My abdomen is rising, now my chest. Now there's a gap. Now the breath is leaving," etc. In this technique you do not attempt to change your breathing, you just notice how it is. Go with the flow. Particularly notice the gaps between the breaths, the one between the incoming and outgoing and the other between the outgoing and the incoming. At these times you are most in your center.

When a thought comes in, don't fight it, just acknowledge it, give it a label, and set it aside where you can find it another time if you wish.

217

What's Going On at My Nostrils

Very simply, notice the air going in and out at the point where it enters or leaves your nostrils. Don't notice the gaps between breaths or whether your tummy is pushing out. That's not part of this exercise, much as your bored mind might like to try to enlarge the scope. It's as if you're noticing people going through a revolving door. "Here's one coming in, here's another going out." You don't pay any attention to where the breath goes when it enters the body or what happens to it when it leaves. Just keep your attention focused at the tip of your nostrils and notice what's happening there. Again, when a thought comes in, acknowledge it and put it aside.

LIFESTYLE DAY 8/
SOAR OR SUFFOCATE?

I find that many of my clients cause themselves unnecessary stress by ignoring the banquet that life has to offer. Rather than seize the opportunity to try something new, they stick with what is safe and familiar. Maybe they believe old messages about being too fat (conservative, minority, educated) to try anything like that. Above all, they feel, they would rather avoid making a fool of themselves or run the risk of failure. By choosing to avoid a risk, they deprive themselves of the experience of trying and learning what can come from that.

My colleague Adele Scheele calls this "Experiencing Doing."

Experiencing Doing is a testing and stretching over time of our boundaries of possibility, a continuing discovery of new aspects of ourselves. It is also the cultivation of an attitude toward life, one that propels us into experience rather than withdrawing us from it.

We act, experiment, practice, and create occasions for developing and exhibiting skills that had not otherwise been available to us. We take what we have to start with and we learn to make something of it, something more than we imagined to be possible at the beginning.

You will reduce fear of doing only by doing, by building a repertoire of experiences as a base of support for every new life adventure. *They will give you new perspective and understanding of who you are and how you want to move.** (Emphasis added.)

Adele Scheele, *Skills for Success* (New York: Ballantine, 1980), pp. 35–42. Used with permission of the author.

"Okay," you may be thinking, "but where do I start?" I suggest you do the following.

Think of three people you admire, people who seem to be truly enjoying life, with plenty of time for themselves in addition to the outer trappings of success. You don't have to know them very well. Tell them that you'd like to interview them for an hour about some of the choices they've made in their lives. You may want to tell them that you're engaged in a self-improvement program, and that this interview could provide you with some new insights.

Then, in the interview, ask them how they arrived at the place they are today. What led to what, and what kinds of experiences—either flops or successes—contributed to their being able to take the risks to ask for what they want and to vigorously embrace what life has to offer? How did they get the support they needed? What were their resources? Who inspired them? What discouraged them and how did they handle it? When did they get the feeling that they knew they could do it? What frightens them now? What new adventures or challenges excite them now? What experiences in their lives do they wish their children could have?

You recognize, of course, that the very fact of your calling and asking for the interview is taking a risk. Are you willing to allow yourself that exciting possibility?

> It is not death that is the source of all man's evils, but rather the fear of death.
>
> —Epictetus

DAY 9

AWARENESS DAY 9/
ON THE HOME FRONT

Just as the work team is a system, so is the family. The family consists of people who have identifiable roles and responsibilities that are interconnected with others in the system. If one of the family members is unable to perform his roles and responsibilities—due to illness, absence, or personal overload—the whole family system is stressed.

The same kinds of concerns arise in examining the family experiencing stress overload. What are the characteristic ways your family responds to stress overload?

What styles do the authority figures adopt as the family experiences more stress? (The authority figures could be parents, grandparents, those in charge of caring for younger children, or an absent parent who is providing child support.)

Are any new alliances formed among family members when the family system experiences stress overload? If so, how do they respond to the increased stress?

What new role, if any, are you aware of for yourself as part of your family when it's experiencing stress overload?

Are you aware of any increased tension as you answer these questions?

Where do you experience this tension in your body?

How would you like things to be different?

NUTRITION DAY 9/
HOW MUCH PROTEIN?

How much protein do you consume in a day? From what sources—animal or vegetable? If, like most Americans, you have eggs for breakfast, a meat sandwich or a hamburger for lunch, cheese to snack on, and more animal protein for dinner, you're probably getting more than 16 percent of your calories in protein.

Add up your total calories for the day. Then add up the number of calories of protein. Divide the latter by the former, and you'll get the percentage of protein you consumed that day. If it's more than 16 percent, it's time to substitute whole grains, vegetables, or fruit.

EXERCISE DAY 9/
RELAXING
YOUR SHOULDERS

To obtain relief from shoulder tightness, it's a good idea to begin with Day 8's exercises for neck pain. Since the neck and shoulders share some of the same muscles, you may wish to use every exercise available to ease their tightness.

These exercises will loosen up your shoulder muscles. When my shoulder muscles are tight, they feel like a solid wall of muscle, and I find these particularly helpful in making me experience them as separate muscles working together. Remember, slow, gentle stretching!

Shoulder Rotations

Stand comfortably or sit with your body erect in a chair, keeping your eyes forward. This is Beginning Position No. 2. Now raise both shoulders simultaneously toward your ears, as if to hunch them against the cold, and slowly rotate them in a circle, first backward for seven revolutions, then forward for seven revolutions.

Elbow Pull

From Beginning Position No. 2, raise your left arm straight up and then allow your arm to bend at the elbow so that your forearm is behind your head and your palm rests on the midline of your back, just below your neck. Grasp your left elbow with your right hand and gently, gently pull your left elbow toward your right arm. Hold for a count of ten. Then reverse, pulling your right elbow toward your left arm. Hold for a count of ten.

Posture Clasp

The first time you do this one, you'll probably need to use a handkerchief, a small towel, or some other sturdy piece of fabric. Holding the handkerchief in your left hand and in the same beginning position, again raise your left arm straight up and allow your arm to bend at the elbow so that your forearm is behind your head and your palm is near the midline of your back, just below your neck. With your right arm by your side, bend it at the elbow, place it behind your back, and grasp the end of the handkerchief, gently pulling so that your muscles are slightly stretched. Hold for a count of ten. Then reverse, with your left hand pulling down on the handkerchief held in your right hand. Again, hold for a count of ten. As you become more limber, you may be able to interlock your fingers to achieve this stretch. You may notice that you're more limber on one side than on the other. The years women have spent fastening brassieres in the back make them better prepared than men for this exercise.

Clasped Hands

Stand comfortably with your feet shoulder-width apart. With your arms behind your back, clasp your hands together and bend forward at the waist, keeping your knees straight and your upper torso parallel with the floor. Keep your eyes straight ahead, which means rotating your head backward as you bend forward, thrusting your chin forward. (If you're recovering from a whiplash injury, keep your eyes on the floor.) Keeping your elbows straight, slowly raise your arms above your body. Hold for a count of ten. If you're unable to bend the full 90 degrees required to make your upper torso parallel with the floor, it may be because your hamstrings (the rear upper-leg muscles) are too tight, causing pain in your buttocks or the back of your thighs. Women accustomed to wearing high heels will probably have tightened hamstrings.

COMMUNICATION DAY 9/
YOU DID WHAT?

If everyone always did everything we wanted in exactly the way we wanted it, we wouldn't have any reason to be critical. Wouldn't that be awfully dull and predictable?

Instead, the reality that we live with is that, from time to time, others will act in ways that displease us. Being able to say how we feel about this is essential to our good health. Yet some supervisors actually anguish about conducting a performance review, and some parents avoid disciplining their children. You may ease self-induced stress if you practice giving constructive criticism. Offering criticism is not the same thing as blaming.

This technique, presented by my colleague Margie Joehnck, fosters an encounter of equality, which demonstrates both parties' concern for self and respect for self-esteem. Both people share information, each is heard by the other, and, most important, power is used to raise the issue, not to impose a solution. Sample monologues are included.

1. Set a time and place to talk. "I want to discuss with you an issue that concerns both of us. When and where would be a good place to do this?" Agree on a time and place. Allow yourselves enough time and make sure you'll have complete privacy.
2. State your intentions and expectations for the outcome of this meeting. Once you've met as planned, say something like "I intend to raise an issue about a certain way we're working together. I hope we can join together to create a solution that will be agreeable to you as well as to me."
3. State the event. "Remember when . . ." (use de-

scriptive terms about a specific behavior. Wait for acknowledgment.)

4. State your feelings about the event and end your statement with a question. "When you . . . , I felt. . . . I felt that way because I wanted. . . . How were you feeling?"

5. Explore all relevant information (facts, interpretations, feelings) concerning the event. "I'd like to tell you my view of what happened, and I want to hear your side, too." (Avoid the strong temptation to go for solutions now!)

6. Repeat your partner's view of the event. "Okay, let me see if I understand your statements. What you're saying is . . ." (Continue until partners agree that they have been understood.)

7. Explore solutions that would satisfy both parties. "Maybe now that I understand what you were thinking and feeling, and you understand me, we can explore some ways to solve this kind of thing in the future." "What might I do differently?" "Here's what you could do to help me." (Think of lots of alternatives here. Don't just stop at one or two.)

8. Offer fair-exchange proposals. "Okay, I'll do this for you in the future if you'll do what I want you to in exchange."

9. Test for agreement and commitment. "Do you really think we can carry out this bargain? What will we do if someone breaks his/her half of the agreement?"

This outline is a guide from which you can depart in your own individualized style and language. It's important to acknowledge that, in every conflict, both parties contribute to the problem. Having the courage and skill to face issues as soon as they occur will aid in their resolution.

RELAXATION DAY 9/
MY WORDS RELAX ME

Autogenics training is a method of inducing a deep state of relaxation that is effective in treating various physiological disorders and useful in reducing fatigue, irritability, and general anxiety. It's also very helpful in reducing or eliminating sleeping disorders.

First, select a quiet place where you won't be disturbed. The room should be at a comfortable temperature with the lights turned down low. You may choose to sit in a comfortable chair, with your back, neck, and arms supported, or to lie down with a pillow under your knees and a cervical roll pillow or towel substitute under your neck. Your legs should be parallel and relaxed, not crossed. You may wish to take off your shoes and loosen any tight clothing.

Begin by scanning your body for any areas of tension. "Breathe into" that tense spot, allowing the tension to disappear. Close your eyes and relax by doing "belly breathing." Say to yourself, "When I open my eyes, I will feel refreshed and alert. I don't have to worry about falling asleep. If I should fall asleep I will awaken when my own internal timer alerts me."

Repeat each phrase to yourself two times, pausing five seconds between each repetition. Take plenty of time, going through this process at least once, and preferably twice, a day. Focus all your attention on that one part of your body as you say the phrase, visualizing it and feeling it relax.

Start with your right foot, saying "My right foot is heavy, warm, and relaxed." After pausing for five seconds, repeat that phrase. Then move on to "My right calf is heavy, warm, and relaxed." Pause for five seconds, and repeat. Continue in this fashion with:

My right thigh
My right leg
My left foot
My left calf
My left thigh
My left leg
Both my legs are heavy, warm, and relaxed.

My right hand
My right forearm
My right upper arm
My right arm
My left hand
My left forearm
My left upper arm
My left arm
Both my arms are heavy, warm, and relaxed.

My buttocks
My pelvic area
My lower back
My abdomen
My solar plexus
My chest
My shoulders
My neck
My head
My whole body is heavy, warm, and relaxed.

Once you have gained skill in relaxing yourself with this method, you may use this briefer version. Again, repeat each phrase twice, allowing five seconds between repetitions.

My legs are heavy, warm, and relaxed.
My arms are heavy, warm, and relaxed.
My trunk is heavy, warm, and relaxed.
My whole body is heavy, warm, and relaxed.

You may wish to intersperse these phrases with the others.

My thoughts are focused inward and I am at ease.
I feel an inner quiet.

I feel serene and still.
My mind is quiet.

If you have any special concerns or targeted areas of tension, such as congested sinuses or a concern about smoking or overeating, after you have completed the above scan, you may add appropriate phrases.

My sinuses are relaxed, clear, and open.
Smoking is something I can live without.
I am satisfied with small portions.

LIFESTYLE DAY 9/
I LOVE MYSELF

I know there are aspects about myself that puzzle me,
and other aspects that I do not know.
But as long as I am friendly and loving to myself,
I can courageously and hopefully look for
the solutions to the puzzles and for
ways to find out more about me.*
—Virginia Satir

Let these words roll off your tongue: I love myself. How does that feel? Do you find that you speak them in hushed tones, for fear of being overheard? Or are you recalling old voices in your head telling you not to be too brash or vain, as you will certainly head for a fall? How do you feel about saying these words out loud, as if you really meant them, even if other people are around? I suggest you do just that.

Repeatedly in my counseling practice I find people expect a great deal, even perfection, from themselves. They are agonizingly self-critical. When I ask them, "How do you love yourself?" they draw a blank. Then they become intrigued with this neglected side of themselves and set out to discover how they can love themselves. I generally ask them to do two things. Here's the first one.

I suggest you write yourself a love letter. No one else has to see it, if you wish. You are to tell yourself all the attributes you cherish about yourself, the things that really please, comfort, and excite you. You may be aware of the tendency to "yes, but," such as "You are a very generous person, but you let people take advantage of your generosity." Drop the second half. Include only the qualities you admire, as you would in a true love letter.

When I sat down and wrote my own love letter to myself, I chose the most elegant stationery I could find. I was worth the best. I made only the original, no copies, and then I addressed an envelope to myself and stamped it. I entrusted my letter, emphasizing that it was my only copy, to a dear friend with the request that she mail it back to me at some unspecified time. It came a few months later, amid the usual bills, advertisements, and mass mailings, brightening my day and my week. I liked the idea so much that I kept it for a while and then entrusted it to another friend in another city, repeating the process. They have been inspired to do the same. I rarely have my letter in my hands more than a few weeks, as it's such a true delight to receive it.

You may choose to write your letter and keep it safely tucked away where you can read it whenever you like, or you might like to ask a friend to mail it to you, as I did.

The second suggestion I have is that you ask three friends for a "letter of recommendation." No, it's not for a job. It's because you're engaged in a self-improvement program, and this is a part of it. Ask them to write what they value about you, the qualities that attract them as friends.

I suggest that you read these letters—your own and those from your friends—when you're feeling low. Know that you are lovable and capable, and allow the letters to reflect what a wonderful person you are.

DAY 10

AWARENESS DAY 10/ *WHAT WOULD IT BE LIKE?*

Unless we're confronted with some tough decisions, we rarely need to evaluate what is important in our lives. Most of us are creatures of habit and spend our days pretty much as we spent the ones before, seldom questioning the wisdom of our choices.

Every once in a while, a situation arises that forces us to examine what we want for ourselves. For instance, you may be offered a promotion within the company, necessitating a move to a city 2,000 miles away. Only when you think about what you'd be gaining and what you'd be giving up do you realize the importance of some of the things—places and relationships—that are nourishing to you at present.

The same is true, of course, in terms of relationships. If you have the opportunity to spend your life with someone you care about, again you need to evaluate what you'd gain and what you'd give up. At the other end, if you're thinking about ending a relationship, you need to examine how you'll benefit or how you'll suffer if you stay in it. Too often people prefer the pain of the familiar to risking excitement of the unknown.

This soul-searching does not come easy. Neither does this next exercise in awareness. Because it's a tough one, I suggest that you enlist a friend as timekeeper and question asker to guide you through it. You should allow two minutes per question for each of the first four questions and four minutes for the last question. Write down your responses as fast as you can within that time. You don't have to feel obligated to share your responses with your friend.

However, a nice adaptation of this exercise is to do it with a group of trusting friends. Have someone take the leadership role and the rest of you will write down your responses at the same time. You could then choose either to

237

keep your responses to yourselves, or to share them with one other person or with the group at large. The sharing provides an opportunity to find out your similarities and differences, usually with the realization that you are not alone.

Your guide begins reading here.

You have just been visited by a magical genie who bequeaths you $1 million and guarantees you good health.

1. What would you do if you found out you had only *six months* to live?
2. What would you do if you found out you had only *one month* to live?
3. What would you do if you found out you had only *one week* to live?
4. What would you do if you found out you had only *one day* to live?
5. What would you do if you found out you were *immortal*?

Be in touch with your feelings as you answer these questions.

Do you find that some parts of your life that you value highly in your responses are, in daily practice, rather neglected?

How important is money in the whole scheme of things?

How important is your good health?

What changes do you choose to make in order to create a more satisfying life for yourself?

When do you plan to start making some of those changes?

What do you have to do to make those changes possible?

How do you feel as you imagine yourself having made those changes?

NUTRITION DAY 10/ MILK IS NOT GOOD FOR EVERY BODY

Many of us grew up thinking that milk, one of the four basic food groups, was good for us. For a while, in fact, the dairy industry's slogan was "Milk is good for every body." But the Food and Drug Administration admonished the dairy industry to refrain from using that slogan, as it's not always so.

Are you one of the people who doesn't digest lactose? If so, you may wish to limit your intake to fermented milk or low-fat natural yogurt. If you take acidopholus tablets, available from health-food stores, before you drink milk, they will assist in its digestion. This is also a wise precaution for sensitive people before they eat any foods in a milk or cream sauce or that are made with milk.

Try an experiment. See if omitting milk from your diet for a day makes any difference in how you feel. Instead of adding milk to your cereal, subsitute low-fat yogurt or apple or orange juice. You might feel better.

EXERCISE DAY 10/ STRENGTHENING YOUR LOWER BACK (Part I)

Perhaps you're one of the more than 7 million people in this country who suffer from chronic back pain. Here are some simple exercises to strengthen your lower back, that most vulnerable area where many people experience pain. Respect the basic guideline of engaging in slow, deliberate movements, with no sudden jerks.

Knee-Chest

Lie on your back on a firm surface, without a pillow under your head, with your legs parallel to each other and your arms by your side. This is Beginning Position No. 3. (If you wish, you may use a cervical roll pillow or towel substitute.) Bend your legs at a 55 degree angle and, keeping your left foot planted firmly on the floor straight ahead, bring your right leg up, keeping it fully bent and the knee directed toward your armpit. Grasp your leg close to your chest, placing your hands behind your knee and around your thigh. (Putting pressure on the upper calf or the knee itself causes undue strain on the knee.) Bring your knee toward your armpit; don't raise your shoulders toward your knee. Hold for a count of ten. Repeat with your left leg, again holding for a count of ten. You may also wish to do this exercise in the standing position.

Single Leg Raise

Lying on your back in Beginning Position No. 3, bend your left leg at a 55-degree angle and keep the right leg straight. Slowly raise your right leg, keeping it straight, until you make a 30-degree angle. Hold for a count of five, and then slowly allow the leg to return to the floor. Repeat with your left leg. Raising your leg more than 30 degrees will decrease the effectiveness of strengthening your muscles. This exercise is especially good for strengthening your hip-flexing (iliopsoas) muscle.

Sit-ups

Sit-ups can be done according to the varying amount of strength required. Here are only three possible varieties. Lying on your back in Beginning Position No. 3, bend your knees at a 55-degree angle and keep your feet planted straight ahead. (1) With your arms alongside your body, slowly curl up your upper torso by raising your head and stretching your arms toward your ankles, and then slowly recline into your starting position. Your middle back should stay in contact with the floor, as you raise only your head and shoulders, keeping your chin near your chest. Repeat ten times. (2) Fold your arms across your chest and slowly curl up your upper body by raising your head and upper torso slightly, feeling the pull in your abdominal muscles, and then slowly lower your upper torso back to the floor. Repeat ten times. (3) Interlock your fingers behind your head, with your forearms alongside your ears, and your elbows facing forward. Then, alternating legs, raise one bent leg at a time toward the opposing elbow as you raise your head and shoulders. Touch your right elbow to your left knee, your left elbow to your right knee, setting up a rhythmical pattern of rotating your body and strengthening your abdominal muscles. For extra stretch, thrust your heels forward as you bring your bent leg to your chest. Repeat twenty times.

Back Stretch

Kneel on the floor with your legs parallel to each other, close together, tucked under you with your buttocks resting upon your ankles. Bend forward at the waist, allowing your arms to stretch out at full length in front of you, with your upper arms alongside your head. Rest your forearms comfortably on the floor in front of you and let your hands relax. Your forehead will be resting on the floor, and your nose will be between your knees. Your weight has shifted so that your buttocks are slightly elevated and there is no pressure on your ankles. Let your ankles and feet relax, forming a modified circle as they splay out. You may hold this relaxing position for as long as you wish.

See Appendix F for "Hints for Avoiding Back Strain."

Recommended Reading

Friedmann, Lawrence W., and Galton, Lawrence. *Freedom from Backaches*. New York: Pocket Books, 1976.

Lettvin, Maggie. *Maggie's Back Book*. New York: Houghton Mifflin, 1977.

Rush, Anne Kent. *The Basic Back Book*. New York: Summit, 1979.

COMMUNICATION
DAY 10/
I COUNT

Sentences that say something about how you feel, think, or act can best be received by others as a clear communication from you if you begin your sentence with "I." This may sound self-evident, but the sad truth is that many people hide their responsibility for their own thoughts and feelings behind words like "we," "they," "my wife and I," "our company's policy is," and so on.

A sentence that begins with "I" is called an "I message" and has the distinct advantage of reducing the likelihood of an argument. For instance, saying "I feel warm" is a simple statement of how you feel, in contrast with the evaluative statement, "It's warm in here," which encourages everyone to either agree or disagree with you.

Similarly, saying "I am disappointed and angry that you kept me waiting" reveals your transparent feelings, in contrast to "You can never be on time," which is guaranteed to heighten strong feelings. The "I message" provides the listener with an opportunity to respond to how you feel at that moment, making a connection possible. If you give blaming criticism, the listener first has to deal with being attacked, which creates further distance.

Here's an exercise for you to do in a spirit of adventure with a friend. Sitting opposite each other, feet flat on the floor and within arms' reach, begin a dialogue in this stylized way: Each of you begin your sentences with "we." No matter what you want to say, be creative and begin your sentences with "we" *for three minutes*.

Then go on to the next phase, when you begin your sentences with "it." As much as you may long to deviate from the constraint of only starting your sentences with "it," stick to it for three minutes.

The next phase of the dialogue is to start your sentences

with "you," again for three minutes. Be aware of any tension in your body as you keep up this dialogue.

When that three-minute segment is over, start your sentences with "they."

After the required three minutes, shift to the last phase, starting your sentences with "I." Be aware of any change in your tension now that you're able to talk with "I." You may wish to make this final segment last for *five minutes*.

What were the limitations of each pronoun? What were the advantages? How able were you to express what mattered to you in each segment? What did you discover about yourself during this exercise?

RELAXATION DAY 10/ HEALING HANDS

Receiving a massage is one of the most relaxing pleasures possible for most people to experience. Our skin is the largest organ of our bodies, and it requires nourishment through caresses, touch, and cuddling. Sadly, this need often goes unrecognized.

How often do you touch or are you touched by friends or family members? When was the last time you had a massage?

Decide today how you will go about getting a massage. If you don't have a spouse, lover, or friend to massage you, you can still enjoy the pleasures of massaging yourself.

Bookstores offer many guides to massage, with detailed instructions on how to rub, knead, and squeeze the body to provide an assortment of sensory experiences. If you're giving the massage, you should feel free to do whatever feels good to you.

As the recipient of a massage, you will enjoy the experience more if you keep your eyes closed, focus your thoughts on your breathing, and become aware of each part of your body as it is being touched. Concentrate only on what's happening at that particular moment, and enjoy the feelings. Feel free to say what you like or don't like.

A massage is less artificial if the recipient is nude, unrestrained by clothing, but if you're not comfortable with that, wear whatever you like. It's often enjoyable for both the giver and the receiver of the massage to be nude. Both derive pleasure from the giving of a massage, and it's not essential that you reverse roles. Knowing that you are doing what is right for you at that time, which may be only to receive the massage, is your best guideline.

LIFESTYLE DAY 10/
AFFIRMATION OF LIFE

How you think about yourself and your life strongly affects how much stress you experience. You know that negative thinking tends to bring negative results.* Thinking positively is a vital first step. Using affirmations is an even more powerful tool. An affirmation is a positive thought that you consciously choose to immerse in your consciousness to produce a desired result. Through the repetition of affirmations, your mind will create your desired goals.

To give you an idea, here are some sample affirmations:

I, ———— (your name), deserve and get the best in life.

I, ————, ask for what I want.

I, ————, choose my own reality and I choose to tell myself positive stories about my experience.

I, ————, express myself both positively and negatively.

I, ————, share my thoughts and feelings with others in such a way that they appreciate my honesty and caring.

I, ————, deserve a partner who loves me and treats me well.

I, ————, am a cheerful person.

I, ————, make time for what is important to *me*.

I, ————, appreciate individual differences.

I, ————, enjoy taking new risks.

I, ————, take care of my body so it will serve me well.

I, ————, am free to relax without feeling guilty.

I, ————, know that people are basically good.

---

* This is also discussed in Day 2 of "Communication."

I, ———, choose when I will be a good listener.

I, ———, am free to discuss my self-doubts, fears, and fantasies with people close to me.

I, ———, am content to be with my own thoughts and feelings.

I, ———, consciously choose what I drink and eat.

I, ———, reward myself for my proud moments.

I, ———, am always open to new learnings.

I, ———, am free to discuss all aspects of my sexuality with my partner.

I, ———, am courageous—willing to move through my barriers of fear, ignorance, and anger so that my centered self can emerge.

I, ———, am very self-accepting.

Here's how to use affirmations:

1. Think of an area in your life that you would like to change.
2. Write an affirmation, starting with "I, ——— (your name)," stating the goal in a positive, present-tense statement.
3. Start with one or two a day.
4. Write each affirmation ten or twenty times on a sheet of paper, leaving a space to the right for "responses."
5. As you write down the affirmation on the left, put down on the right whatever occurs to you—any thoughts, doubts, fears, qualifiers, considerations, or beliefs. Keep repeating the affirmation, observing how the responses on the right change.
6. Write affirmations in this way just before going to sleep.
7. Once you've worked through each affirmation, make a list of your affirmations or, better yet, make a tape recording, which you can play before you go to sleep or while you're driving. You may also wish to post your affirmations around the house or in your date book where you'll see them.

Here's an example from the affirmations listed above:

I, Karen, am content to be with my own thoughts and feelings.

No, I can't sit still for a moment.

I, Karen, am content to be with my own thoughts and feelings.

It's not productive.

I, Karen, am content to be with my own thoughts and feelings.

People will think I'm lazy.

I, Karen, am content to be with my own thoughts and feelings.

That's no way to be successful in life.

I, Karen, am content to be with my own thoughts and feelings.

I feel guilty because it's not right.

I, Karen, am content to be with my own thoughts and feelings.

I get panicky when I think about it.

I, Karen, am content to be with my own thoughts and feelings.

I wish I could believe this.

I, Karen, am content to be with my own thoughts and feelings.

That would be a scary thing for me to do.

I, Karen, am content to be with my own thoughts and feelings.

I don't know if I could do it.

I, Karen, am content to be with my own thoughts and feelings.

Maybe I could give it a try.

I, Karen, am content to be with my own thoughts and feelings.

Maybe.

What's happening here is that the repetition enables the subconscious to bring to the surface all the negative thoughts and feelings from your past. You can then discover what has kept you from reaching your goal. You may consciously want to change, but until the old conflicts are resolved, you're stuck. Repeating the affirmation will simultaneously make an impression on your mind and erase the old thought pattern, producing permanent—and desirable—changes in your life.

Recommended Reading
Ray, Sondra *I Deserve Love*. Millbrae, Calif.: Celestial Arts, 1976.

DAY 11

AWARENESS DAY 11/
WHO'S THERE?

What does another person who's important to you—a partner, spouse, parent, or child—look and act like when he feels lonely, angry, exuberant, sad, sexually aroused, disappointed, joyful, or hurt? Like most people, you probably know the answer to that question better than if I were to ask you how *you* look and act under the same circumstances.

Very often, people go through their lives "tuned in" to pleasing others, sensing their moods and wishes, perhaps knowing them better than they know themselves. If they center their lives around trying to please others, attempting to minimize conflict and not arouse anyone's anger, they may do so at the expense of leaving their own needs unmet, even unrecognized.

This is an opportunity for you to get to know who you are, what some of your wishes, needs, and desires are. I suggest that you set up a tape recorder and sit in a comfortable position in front of a mirror that is no more than six inches from your face. Using your eyes as a camera, simply take in who that person is and what that person looks like. Don't be caught up in judgments about this wrinkle or that imperfection. Instead, talk into the tape machine and record what you see. Take at least five minutes to go through this process.

After this initial getting to know that person in the mirror, be bold enough to inquire as to how that person feels about her life. Have a dialogue in which you play interviewer and the person in the mirror responds to your questions. Your questions could include the following:

- What does she really treasure about herself?
- What does she want for herself?
- How is she feeling right now?

251

After your dialogue is over, listen to the tape recording. What do you notice during the observation process and during the dialogue? Does your voice change? What are the feelings behind the words?

What has this process been like for you and her? Would you be willing to do it again?

Since you and she are always changing, there's no predicting what her responses would be at another time. She is your friend, your very best friend. Do not betray her. Listen to her counsel, to her needs, and honor them.

NUTRITION DAY 11/
HOW ABOUT A CUP OF COFFEE FOR A PICKUP?

"Sit down, have a cup of coffee, and relax"—how often you've heard those words spoken by well-meaning friends. Few people realize just how impossible it is to do that. In the overview on "Nutrition," you read of coffee's negative effects upon the body. The "pickup" you get with coffee is a jolt of adrenalin—just what you *don't* need to help relaxation!

If you're typical of most people, you probably have six to twelve cups of coffee per day. Analyze just when you drink coffee: at meals, at your desk, at meetings, at a coffee break. Cut down your coffee consumption by one-third, aiming for a maximum of two cups a day if you feel you *must* have coffee. Take a thiamin supplement to compensate.

Better yet, substitute noncaffeine herbal teas, such as chamomile or linden tea, but beware—even some herbal teas contain caffeine! In this area, too, you'll need to become a knowledgable consumer. You might also like hot carob drink, which is a natural flavor similar to chocolate. See how you like it without sugar, flavored with a drop of vanilla extract.

EXERCISE DAY 11/ STRENGTHENING YOUR LOWER BACK (Part II)

Here are some more exercises to strengthen your abdominal (psoas) muscles, which therefore strengthen your lower back.

Riding a Bicycle

Sit on the front edge of a straight-backed chair with your feet on the floor in front of you. Grip the sides of the chair with your hands, with your thumbs near your buttocks. Keeping your spine erect, raise your feet approximately eight inches off the floor and make a forward circular motion with your feet, keeping your toes flexed toward you, as if you were riding a bicycle. Then reverse, "backpedaling" your bicycle. Build up your number of repetitions to twenty-five in each direction.

The Squeeze

Still sitting in a straight-backed chair with your spine erect, lean back slightly and grip the front edge of the chair at the corners. Quickly lift both knees high toward your chest. As your knees come up, move your upper body slightly forward to create a squeezing action. Return your feet to the floor and straighten your spine. Repeat. Develop a quick rhythm, building up your number of repetitions to twenty. Remember to exhale as you squeeze, inhale as you return to starting position.

Squaw Sit-ups

Lie down flat on your back on the floor. Bring your legs up so that your feet are tucked under your calves (if you were sitting up, you'd be in a cross-legged or "squaw" position). Place your hands behind your head (not your neck!). Keep your chin near your chest and curl up your shoulders, raising them only a few inches off the floor. The beauty of this exercise is that it's very difficult to raise your body any more than the necessary few inches to strengthen the psoas muscles. You *can* do it, but the crossed legs act as a natural interference.

More exercises to strengthen the back are given in Appendix F.

COMMUNICATION
DAY 11/
I AM RESPONSIBLE

"She won't let me."

"You make me nervous."

"I must get some new shoes."

"I couldn't help it—he made me do it."

"I can't go to the office party."

"Why can't you make me happy?"

These statements or ones like them are heard all too often. They have one thing in common: they characterize you as a helpless victim who has no power over your own life. Statements like these don't allow you to take responsibility for your own feelings, thoughts, and actions.

Let's look more closely at "She won't let me" and "I couldn't help it—he made me do it." Certainly, from time to time, our choices are limited in particular situations. What's often overlooked, though, is that we usually have at least three choices, many more than the forced choice of an "either/or" alternative, which most people settle for. Here you need to fully examine all possible alternatives. Be creative in pushing for additional solutions. At what personal cost do you choose an unattractive option? How much power and influence do you truly bring to the situation? Are you avoiding responsibility for your own actions by playing a helpless role? Think about the worst thing that can happen. Personal growth can come about through testing old limits. It may be unsettling to anticipate, maybe even to experience, but sometimes when you do what you know is best for you, the other person is relieved at no longer having to be the one "in control."

Now let's look at "You make me nervous" and "Why can't you make me happy?" You and you alone are responsible for how you feel. No one can make you feel anything. You choose to feel the way you do. If, for instance, your spouse is not really watching TV but restlessly clicking from one channel to another, and you find that irritating, you have several choices. You can say how you feel, making an "I" statement; you can use the irritation as a cue to engage in something that relaxes you, such as "belly breathing"; or you can leave the room. In all three of these responses you're being honest with yourself about what is going on with you, not playing helpless with "that annoys me." *It* doesn't annoy you—you allow *yourself* to feel annoyed.

Finally, let's look at "I must get some new shoes" and "I can't go to the office party." "Can't" means "not able," and you may be perfectly physically capable of going. Phrased in a more accurate way, each of these is a simple matter of choice. "I choose to" or "I would like to get some new shoes" and "I don't choose to" or "I don't wish to go to the office party" are accurate statements—and how much more revealing and responsible they are! Saying "must" and "can't" inappropriately tends to characterize you as someone who is locked into rigid patterns.

Become aware of your speech patterns and those of others close to you, noting how often you or they use these words or phrases. What benefit do you get from feeling like a victim? What benefit do you get from feeling that you're locked into a plan, which is indicated by using the word "must"?

RELAXATION DAY 11/
PLEASANT DREAMS

Getting a good night's sleep is vital to increasing your ability to cope with stress effectively. Yet stress seems to be the main villain in preventing you from getting the sleep you need. At some time, almost everyone will experience difficulty in sleeping. As discussed in the overview of "Relaxation," problems in sleeping—insomnia, waking up too early, waking up in the middle of the night—are generally regarded as symptoms, not as a disease. Therefore, the cure is not a pill, as was discussed in the overview of "Nutrition."

If you have trouble sleeping, you may wish to keep a record of your sleep patterns for two weeks. Note what time you went to bed each night, what time it was if you awoke and were awake for more than ten minutes, and what time you awakened in the morning. If you take naps, mark them down, too.

For two weeks, set aside a certain time each day to answer these questions:

1. How long did it take to fall asleep?
2. How often did you wake up?
3. How much total sleep did you get in twenty-four hours?
4. What time did you awaken in the morning?
5. What were you thinking about as you went to sleep?
6. Was yesterday a particularly stressful day?
7. Did you get any vigorous exercise yesterday morning?
8. Was today a day you were anxious about?
9. How did you feel when you woke up in the morning?

10. Did you feel alert throughout the day?
11. Were you tired last evening?
12. Were you tired when you went to bed?
13. Did you have any caffeine, sugar, or starches within four hours of bedtime?
14. Did you overeat at dinner?
15. Did you intentionally relax yourself at bedtime?

After keeping your sleep record for two weeks, see if you can discover any patterns that help or hinder your sleeping.

What helps one person get to sleep may not help another, so you may wish to experiment with different methods to find one that works well for you. Following are two methods that require you to focus your mind on an intellectual challenge.

One of my clients suggested this one: think of a category, any category—vegetables, countries, birds, colors, etc.—and go through the alphabet from A to Z, naming one item in the category each time you exhale. For instance, A is for asparagus, B is for broccoli, C is for cauliflower, etc. You may find that your breathing becomes deeper and slower as you consciously need more time to think up a word for the next letter. I like this one because of the constant variety.

Another more common method is simply counting backward from 100 with each breath. You can make it more absorbing by counting backward in three's—100, 97, 94, 91, etc.

Specific exercises in this book—the progressive relaxation of "Melt Away the Tension" in Day 3 and the autogenic training of "My Words Relax Me" in Day 9—are excellent aids for sleep induction. The breathing exercises are good, too, for focusing the mind and getting into a relaxed state.

You can use a tape recorder that turns itself off to listen to prerecorded relaxation tapes or carefully selected music, such as Halpern's *Spectrum Suite,* designed to induce relaxation, or Bach's *Goldberg Variations,* which were written for an insomniac patron.

Recommended Reading and Listening

Coates, Thomas J., and Thoresen, Carl E. *How to Sleep Better: A Drug-Free Program for Overcoming Insomnia*. Englewood Cliffs, N.J.: Prentice-Hall/Spectrum, 1977.

Goldberg, Philip, and Kaufman, Daniel. *Natural Sleep: How to Get Your Share*. Emmaus, Pa.: Rodale Press, 1978.

Halpern, Steven. "Spectrum Suite" and other musical relaxation recordings. Available from Halpern Sounds, 620 Taylor Way, #14, Belmont, CA 94002.

Schwartz, Jackie. "Relaxation: Relief from Tension" audio cassette tapes of progressive relaxation. Available from Kasriel Productions, 1908 Benecia Avenue, Los Angeles, CA 90025.

Recommended Reading and Traders, by Gerald Thomas McCaul. Boston: Little, Brown.
Dr. J. Firpo. *Growth for Greenness*. Mountain Lake Village, Calif.: Prentice-Hall, Spring 1973.
Outdoor Plans and Anchors, Dural, Kevin, New City, N.J.: Arrowright, Research Press 1978.
[illegible] *Soho, and other chemical colors.*
Available from Dr. Alice Swenden 320-2302.

LIFESTYLE DAY 11/
WHO'S INDISPENSABLE?

Do you feel like you're indispensable? If so, you're probably heaping additional responsibilities onto your overtaxed schedule, as you feel that no one can help you. This is one of the most common feelings expressed in the training I conduct with industry personnel. People often feel trapped and overwhelmed.

A participant in one of my training sessions was an ex-Army colonel, a self-described "cardiac cripple," who shared with the group this bit of wisdom: "Next time you're convinced how indispensable you are, I suggest you immerse your hand in a bucket of water. Notice the hole it leaves when you pull it out."

It's time to delegate. Answer these questions:

1. Have I taken all the vacations due me in the past five years?
2. Am I usually behind in my work?
3. Do I habitually come into the office when it's closed?
4. Do the people who report to me consistently make recommendations to me?
5. Are decisions made at the lowest level at which all information is available?
6. Do the people who report to me know how much authority they have?
7. How many times have I overruled them in the past month?
8. Do I grant the people who report to me the right to be wrong?
9. Can I count on someone "minding the store" if I'm sick?

261

10. Do I work longer hours than those reporting to me?

Review your answers to these questions, using them as a basis for an action plan. You may wish to set up an assignment sheet like the one below.

		Assignment Sheet				
Date	In Charge	Job	Checkpoints			Due Date
7-24	Norton	capital improvements report			7-30	8-3
7-26	Stan	videotape sales meeting		8-3	8-10	8-18
7-26	Reva	coordinate colloquium	8-12	8-20	9-10	9-19
7-28	Karen	coordinate departmental goals	8-5	8-12	8-25	9-5

This assignment sheet contains the important addition of dates for checkpoints, which are agreed upon between the two parties. They provide an opportunity for each of you to share concerns, obtain additional information if needed, and remain focused on the task. I have found that just knowing such an assignment sheet is being kept tends to motivate people to be more responsible.

Delegation does not have to be limited to the workplace. Think of other people in your life who can help you feel less overwhelmed. You might consider hiring someone to perform services that are time-consuming but don't necessarily require decisions on your part, such as routine errands and household-maintenance tasks. Young people with new driver's licenses are often eager to do such work.

Recommended Reading
Steinmetz, Lawrence L. *The Art and Skill of Delegation.* Reading, Mass.: Addison-Wesley, 1976.

DAY 12

AWARENESS DAY 12/
THE BLIND MEN AND
THE ELEPHANT

Remember the high school psychology exercise where an "accident" is staged before a class and the witnesses are caught up in their own interpretation of what "really happened," with few, if any, being able to re-create the scene? We all have "internal agendas"—our own feelings, perceptual filters, and expectations—to deal with, even though we may be reluctant to admit their importance.

Because of these internal agendas, we aren't able to see the whole picture, as the whole picture means taking into account everything and everyone who is a part of that picture. That means everyone's feelings, motivations, perceptions, and so on—an impossible task!

Recall the Indian legend of the six blind men and the elephant. They all had heard about elephants but had never encountered one. One felt the animal's side, and he described the elephant as smooth like a wall. The second felt its trunk, and he said it was like a snake. The third blind man felt its tusks, and he said it was sharp like a spear. The fourth blind man felt its leg, describing it as tall like a tree. The fifth blind man felt its ear, saying the elephant was wide like a fan. The sixth blind man felt its tail, describing the animal as skinny like a rope. Each was sure he was right.

Who was right? Certainly, all of them were right. *They all had their own truths*. The rajah advised them that they had too little evidence and that they would have to put all the parts together to get the whole picture. The same applies to our lives. There's no such thing as "the one right way" or "*the* truth." Many truths exist.

Think of a recent incident in which you "knew" that your story was the "true story" and the other person was wrong. Are you willing to re-examine that experience from another perspective, allowing that the other person had a different and, for him, equally accurate and truthful version of what happened?

What happens inside you as you consider this possibility? Are you aware of any change in your body, any change in your tension?

Do you insist on maintaining that your story was the "true story"? Are you aware of any tension as you maintain your position? How do you benefit by hanging on to the one "true story"?

NUTRITION DAY 12/
WHAT YOU DON'T KNOW CAN HURT YOU

In the overview of "Nutrition," you read about the false sense of protection most of us have about the FDA and the GRAS (Generally Recognized as Safe) list. Now it's time for you to become a private investigator in your own behalf to discover just what you're eating.

You can begin your investigation in your own kitchen. Go through the cupboards and the refrigerator and read the labels on the foods you've already purchased. Make a list of all the ingredients *identified* on the labels that are not food. You might place checkmarks beside those that are repeated.

How does your chemical feast look to you? Who has benefited by these additions to your foods—you (the consumer) or the food processor? Do you wish to continue to put those substances into your body? Do you know the effect of all those added ingredients? Are you willing to find out just what impact they can have on you?

On your next trip to the supermarket, read the labels of the processed foods you buy. Unless the label says something like "absolutely no preservatives or artificial ingredients added" (and "unsweetened" or "no sugar added" is a help, too), you may be getting a lot more than you know about. Unfortunately, to obtain foods so labeled, it's often necessary to locate a source, such as a health-food store, that sells unpolluted foods.

The next time you're in a restaurant, ask the waiter or waitress if MSG is used in preparing the food. Since it's in most common seasoning salts and most prepared sauces, both of which restaurants commonly use, you'll be hard-pressed to find restaurant food that isn't polluted, too. Ethnic and better-quality restaurants that make their own sauces and soups are more likely to use only pure ingredients in their food preparation. Unfortunately, for most dishes, that will include salt and sugar, which chefs tend to believe are necessary in order to make food palatable to the American consumer.

Recommended Reading

Hunter, Beatrice Trum. *Fact/Book on Food Additives and Your Health*. New Canaan, Conn.: Keats, 1972.

Verrett, Jacqueline, and Carper, Jean. *Eating May Be Hazardous to Your Health*. New York: Doubleday/Anchor, 1975.

EXERCISE DAY 12/
STRETCH AWAY YOUR TENSION (Part I)

Since most of us lead sedentary lives, it's easy for our bodies to virtually get stuck in one position. That's when it's helpful to engage in some simple stretching exercises to get your body moving again. What's important is to break the sustained tension of sitting for hours at your desk or watching TV. Here are some exercises that fill that bill.

Picking Grapes

Stand comfortably and raise your hands above your head. Stretching one side at a time from your fingertips to your toes, reach for the ceiling; stretch as far as you comfortably can, rocking from one foot to the other as you reach. Pretend you're picking grapes from an overhead vine and you have to stretch your whole body to get the grapes. Keep your eyes directed forward, and don't raise your head to look toward the ceiling. The rhythm you set in motion will almost be like slow dancing as your weight shifts from the toes to one foot to the other with each stretch and your body is free to change direction. Feel the gentle pull under your arm and at the side of your torso as you slightly arch your body to one side to stretch these muscles. Continue "picking grapes" for two minutes or for as long as you're comfortable. (Note: If you're restricted to sitting down—at a desk or in a plane or car for example—you can get some relief by "picking grapes" from your seated position. Forget what other people might think. Instead, know how much more relaxed your muscles will be for having stretched them!)

Limp Cat

Stand comfortably with your feet about six inches apart, your knees slightly flexed (not locked into position) and bend over, bringing your chin to your chest and letting your arms hang limp. Breathe in deeply, and as you exhale allow your body to bend even further, dropping your hands nearer the floor. Repeat for two more breaths, each time noticing how effortlessly your body bends as it relaxes and your fingers may even touch the floor. (If you're very limber, your palms may even touch the floor!) Imagine your body is as limp as a cat, simply hanging very loose, free of tension. Don't rush, allowing yourself plenty of time to engage in the deep breathing and exhalations which permit your body to loosen up through relaxation. You may find it easier and more relaxing if you close your eyes.

Elephant Walk

Position your feet so that they are shoulder-width apart. Bend over as in the Limp Cat exercise, relaxing your body as you exhale with four successive breaths, bending further each time you exhale. Raise up a little bit so that your hands are approximately 12 inches from the floor and loosely interlock your thumbs. With your upper arms alongside your head and your head hanging loose, begin to move your upper body from side to side. Imagine your arms as the trunk of an elephant, and slowly sway your "trunk" as you take very small steps, rotating the direction of your body. Take eight or ten steps, noticing how your body tends to roll effortlessly with each step and sway of your "trunk." You may feel a little light-headed, so proceed cautiously. Enjoy the feeling of stretching and litheness as you relax these normally unused muscles.

COMMUNICATION
DAY 12/
THE TRAPDOOR

Your cousin Phil had a party "just for the family," but he forgot to invite you.

You conducted a performance review with one of your subordinates and you neglected to praise her for her contributions to a team project.

Your neighbor borrowed your car in a pinch and returned it with an empty gas tank.

Your bowling buddy keeps forgetting to return that book he borrowed.

"So what?" you might say. These are all relatively minor incidents, certainly nothing to get excited about. These are what I call "unfinished business," and some of it goes back many years. Unfinished business can seriously affect, and sometimes even be deadly to, a relationship. It's worse, of course, if you have something negative or critical to say and choose to hold it in, thinking, perhaps, that you shouldn't be so sensitive or petty, but withholding something positive can also affect a relationship.

In either instance, negative or positive, whenever you're with that person, part of you is preoccupied with what you haven't said that, on some level, you wish you'd said. It's as if you're always aware of the trapdoor you must avoid whenever you two approach each other. It guarantees that you can't be fully present and in touch with that person at that particular time, which is what good communication is all about: being in touch with what's going on at the moment, being able to express it, and being able to respond to the other's feelings and the meaning of his words. It contributes to your blowing up later over some little thing because you haven't expressed previous resentments.

To assist you in this task, I suggest that you do the following:

271

1. Think of five people in your life, either at work, socially, or in your family, with whom you have some unfinished business.
2. Think of one incident with each person that has remained unfinished for you.
3. Now, with your knowledge of how to take responsibility by using "I messages" and expressing your feelings, rehearse the dialogue that you would like to have. Never mind that you don't think you *should* feel so upset; the fact is, you *do* feel upset. Say something like "I need to talk about something, and this is difficult for me to bring up."* Think of what you will say and how you will say it. A straightforward, nonpunitive style works best.
4. Anticipate what the other person's response will be. Think of three different responses to each of your statements so that you'll be less likely to be derailed. Be clear about the message you want to get across.
5. Be aware of your feelings as you think about this exchange. Do they change as you anticipate the three different responses? How can you remind yourself of the importance of completing this unfinished business when the other person may not be open to hearing it?
6. Think of any advantages for you in keeping the business unfinished. Do you enjoy playing the martyr?

---

* Refer to Day 9 of "Communication" regarding constructive criticism.

RELAXATION DAY 12/
*SOOTHE THE
SAVAGE BEAST*

While it's relatively well known that meditation can alter brain waves and produce altered states of consciousness, it's less well known that music can produce the same effects. But not just any music will do. Music by sixteenth- to eighteenth-century composers, called Baroque music, provides the required slow beat of sixty beats per minute in 4/4 time. As you listen to the slow rhythm, your body actually slows down. Your mind becomes more alert while your body relaxes, providing the same benefits of simple meditation—all without your consciously doing anything to make it happen.

In *Superlearning,* researchers Sheila Ostrander and Lynn Schroeder reported the result of their investigation into how to make learning possible in an accelerated, nonanxious, relaxed manner:

> Slow movements from Baroque instrumental music featuring string instruments gave the very best results. . . . Music with a slow, constant, monotonous rhythm, a nondistracting melodic structure (not the hum-along kind), and harmonic patterns based on specific ratios has so far given the best results.

Select music by J. S. Bach, Vivaldi, Telemann, Corelli, and Handel, as they have all written compositions that exactly fit the requirements of sixty beats per minute at 4/4 time.

Conversely, it's worth noting that music at higher tempos actually increases the body's state of alertness and induces agitation. Unfortunately, that's the kind that we usually hear.

LIFESTYLE DAY 12/
FIVE YEARS FROM NOW

"Would you tell me, please, which way I ought to go from here?"

"That depends a good deal on where you want to get to," said the Cat.

"I don't much care where—" said Alice.

"Then it doesn't matter which way you go," said the Cat.

From *Alice in Wonderland*
by Lewis Carroll

Get into a position in which you feel relaxed. Do some "belly breathing" to increase your relaxation. Feel yourself getting more and more relaxed.

With your eyes closed, go through your last working day in your mind's eye. See yourself awakening in the morning, getting dressed, having breakfast, going to work, going through your work day, taking coffee breaks and having lunch, ending your work day, anticipating the evening, having dinner, your evening activity, and, finally, climbing into bed at the end of your day.

As you visualize this day, think about how your body is reacting. When did you feel any tightness or anxiety? Who were you with during the day, and how did you feel about those people? Is your relationship with them one of mutual support, or do you feel that you give more? Are you willing to talk to them about a personal problem? How willing would they be to listen to your personal problems? How did you feel about the work you accomplished? Are you able to forgive yourself for whatever more you wanted to do but weren't able to? How did you respond to the interruptions or unexpected events that interfered with being able to do what you wanted to? How did you alleviate your stresses during the day? With whom are you able to share your feelings about this day? How does that feel?

274

Now imagine a typical day five years from now, and go through that day in your mind's eye. Where are you living? Where are you working? Are you with the same people you were five years earlier? Who are the people who like and trust you? How much time do you spend with them? What kind of work are you doing? What are the joys in your life? What level of tension or anxiety are you aware of as you go through this typical day? How do you feel as you think about your responses?

Now think about a typical day five years from now, but this time as a member of the opposite sex. How does it differ from your previous projection? In what ways is it the same? Do you find yourself limiting your thinking by concentrating only on the model of some one other person in your life, such as your spouse?

Contrast these two days in the future. How do you now feel toward the opposite sex after your brief experience of imagining that? Does this suggest any change in how you may act toward the opposite sex?

How do these five-year projections differ from your life at the present time? What are you doing now that will get you where you want to be in five years? What *can* you do?

Write down the goals you'd like to accomplish in the next six months. These could include what you want for yourself in several aspects of your life: personal, financial, family, career, social, community, and spiritual. Make vague goals concrete. From "look and feel better" to "weigh 160 and be able to run a mile three times a week." Divide big projects into smaller pieces. From "return to school" to "enroll in one course each semester." Once you've decided which goals you wish to pursue, slot the specific actions necessary to attain those goals in your date book. At the end of three months, pull out your original list of six-month goals to see how you're doing. You may wish to make some revisions. You are free to change or drop any of them at any time.

Only you can decide what you want to do with your time.

DAY 13

AWARENESS DAY 13/ YOUR PERSONAL ADVISOR*

Sit down, close your eyes, and use one of the relaxation techniques, such as "belly breathing," to become more free of tension. Picture yourself alone in some relaxing spot. It could be at the beach, in the woods, at the lake, or in your own garden—wherever you feel you can relax. Experience yourself feeling safe and comfortable in your special place. Look around and see if you notice something, a plant or an animal, for example. It could be a rabbit, a bird, or a pine tree. It will be your ally, your friend. It is your own personal advisor. Experience yourself talking to your friend.

You and your personal advisor are going to talk about what is bothering you. Ask him if it's all right for the two of you to meet from time to time, to talk things over. If he says "yes," ask your personal advisor if he has any advice he wants to give you. He may volunteer, "I want you to be kinder on yourself, not push yourself so hard."

You may have several questions to ask him, such as "How can I break the negative patterns I am in without jeopardizing my job?" or "What can I do to be more free of pain in my life?" or "How can I become less tense and more effectively cope with the stress I am experiencing?"

You and your personal advisor will continue to meet in this special place for a short time each day for one week. Each day the two of you can discuss the questions that matter to you. By the seventh day (or perhaps even sooner) your personal advisor will have presented some answers to these questions, and he may have suggested some answers immediately. Be returning to the same questions over a period of several days, he will present you with a broader array of answers.

---

* Adapted from the technique presented by Irving Oyle in *The Healing Mind* (Millbrae, Calif.: Celestial Arts, 1975).

NUTRITION DAY 13/ WATER, WATER, EVERYWHERE AND NOT A DROP TO DRINK

How much water do you drink in a day? Today, keep track of that bit of information. Every time you drink a glass of water, put a loose-fitting rubber band around your wrist. When you count them at the end of the day, you'll know just how many—or how few—glasses of water you've had.

If you're like most people, I'd guess you don't drink very much water in a day's time. The importance of drinking water is spelled out in the overview of "Nutrition." Your body needs at least eight glasses of water a day. See how you can increase your intake to that minimum.

EXERCISE DAY 13/
STRETCH AWAY YOUR TENSION (Part II)

Here are some more stretching exercises to get you going.

Back Arch

Stand comfortably, with your feet about six inches apart and your arms alongside your body. This is Beginning Position No. 4. Arch your back, rotate your head backward, and thrust your chin skyward, with your eyes on the ceiling. Hold for a count of ten, and then relax. *If you're recovering from a whiplash injury, avoid this exercise.*

I'm Flying

Standing in Beginning Position No. 4, raise your arms straight up and out from your sides, palms up, so that they're level with your shoulders. Keeping your elbows straight, make backward circular motions with both arms simultaneously, making the front of your circle in line with your body. Gradually increase the diameter of your circles, and feel your chest expand. Make seven circles. Then reverse direction, making forward circular motions with palms down. Make seven circles.

The Windmill

Standing in Beginning Position No. 4, make large circles by bringing one arm at a time back away from your body and then around, up, and across the front of your body; keep your elbows straight. When one arm is back, the other arm is forward, so that a windmill effect is created. As your body develops a rhythm, you may increase your speed. Repeat for ten rotations on each side. Then reverse direction, to achieve the same movement as a backstroke in swimming. Again, repeat for ten rotations on each side.

Diagonal Torso Stretch

Lying on your back on a flat surface without a pillow under your head, allow your arms to rest straight out from your body, in line with your shoulders. With your legs bent at a 55-degree angle, first cross your right leg over your left leg. Relax your legs so that they fall to the right side, and simultaneously direct your head toward your left arm, keeping your chin near your shoulder and your shoulders on the floor, creating a diagonal stretch on your torso. Hold for a count of ten. Then reverse direction, with your left leg over your right, and looking toward your right arm. Hold for a count of ten.

Individual Leg Stretch

Sit on the floor with your legs spread at a 90-degree angle to each other. Bring your left foot to your right knee to form a 'triangle. (This takes the strain off the lower back.) The toes of your right foot should point to the ceiling and your right leg should be straight. With your head down and your arms outstretched, reach toward your right foot. Hold for a count of ten. Then reverse, tucking your right foot into your left knee and reaching for your left foot. You may notice that as you exhale and relax, your reach is extended. As you become more limber, you'll be able to hold your foot in your hands.

Double Leg Stretch

Sitting on the floor with both legs together straight in front of you, toes pointed toward the ceiling and legs straight, bend at the waist toward your feet with outstretched arms. Keeping your head down, exhale, and relax, reaching for your feet. Hold for a count of ten.

Groin Stretch

Sitting on the floor, bring the soles of your feet together. Grasp your ankles (not your toes) with your hands to keep your feet together and lean slightly forward, keeping your back straight and applying a slight downward pressure on your thighs with your elbows. Hold for a count of ten.

COMMUNICATION
DAY 13/
IS ANGER ACCEPTABLE?

"Anger is the first emotion human beings experience and the last one we learn to manage effectively," wrote John E. Jones and Anthony G. Banet in their article, "Anger," in *The 1976 Annual Handbook for Group Facilitators*.

Think about how you feel when you get angry. See if you can recall a specific recent incident when you knew you were really angry. Picture the entire scene in your mind—where you were, whom you were with, what was going on, what the room or environment was like.

When you have a specific situation in mind, you may wish to consider these questions:

- How did you know you were angry?
- What did you feel on the inside when you were angry?
- What did you show on the outside?
- What did you say?
- How did you act?
- Did you want to change and become less or more vocal, physical, or talkative?
- How did people respond to you?
- How did you want them to respond to you?
- What joy do you get from your anger?
- With which person in your life are you the most angry? Why?

When you think of your intimate relationship, you may wish to consider these additional questions:

- What happens between the two of you that makes you the most angry?

- What part does anger play in your relationship? (Has it gone underground? Is it out in the open? Is there a lot of it or a little? Is it increasing or decreasing?)
- How do you want your partner to respond to your anger? (Leave the room? Watch silently? Hold you? Yell? Listen nondefensively? Ask questions?)
- How does your partner want you to respond when she gets angry?
- What does each partner feel when the other gets angry? (Numb? Frightened? Hurt? Angry?)

The next time you feel angry, I suggest you do the following:*

1. Admit that you are angry. Recognize the feelings and disclose them. For those of us who have been taught that it's "not nice" to be angry, this is especially difficult.
2. Pinpoint, if you can, what has made you angry. When you can locate the source of the anger, you've taken the most difficult step of all. You may have to spend some time on this, as the obvious answer may not be the true one.
3. Understand why you are angry. Which of your hidden expectations or feelings play a part in this? Is there a realistic reason for your anger? Finding the answer to this question can enable you to deal realistically with the anger.

---

* Adapted from the presentation by Nicholas Eltgroth in *"Growtogether" Education for Marriage Newsletter,* Vol. 3, No. 5, May 1981. Used with permission of the author.

RELAXATION DAY 13/
SATISFYING SENSORY PLEASURES

A "sensory pleasure" is any *sens*ation that stimulates the nerves in a positive manner. You've already read about two sensory pleasures: getting a massage and listening to soothing music.

Think now about other sensory pleasures you'd find relaxing. Some people like to take a long, hot bath—maybe even a bubble bath—or get into a sauna, steambath, or whirlpool tub. Lying in the sun with your skin protected from the sun's harmful rays is soothing to many people, supported by cushiony grass or cradling sand. Experiencing the new "isolation tanks," in which the body floats effortlessly in a solution of epsom salts, is another kind of sensory experience. Brushing your hair and getting a facial, manicure, or pedicure are sensory pleasures of grooming. Taking in a beautiful sunset, watching clouds floating by as you lie on your back, and caressing the smooth contours of fine sculpture are other sensory pleasures.

Think of something that would satisfy *your* senses. Write down a list of the things that you'd find soothing and restorative. Select one of these to do within the next three days. How do you feel as you anticipate giving yourself such a gift? What would it take for you to make this possible more often for yourself? How do you feel as you contemplate making such delights a regular part of your life?

LIFESTYLE DAY 13/
CHOICES

One of the hazards of living in a complex setting, as most of us do today, is that we are presented with an over-abundance of choices. Almost every aspect of our lives is characterized by being able to choose what we want or how we might go about getting what we want. We have much more information about what is possible in our lives than did our great-grandparents. Looking at the classified ads for a job, the travel section of the Sunday paper, or a university extension catalog brings home some of the many opportunities around us.

In my clinical practice I find that people often become paralyzed about making the decisions that affect their lives. It's as if they'd like some more powerful, wise, and concerned caretaker to take that load off their hands. The truth is that no one else can make an important decision for you any better than you can. Only you know all the variables, unspoken or perhaps even hidden from you at the time, that will affect your decision.

What are some of the current decisions you must make? Write down a key word or two on a separate colored 3-by-5-inch card for each decision.

Arrange them in order according to which are most urgent. (You may also have another pile of cards for decisions that are important but not urgent, such as redecorating your living room, visiting your relatives, returning to school.)

For each decision you must make, use one white 3-by-5-inch card to jot down a possible solution to the problem. Be as creative and expansive as you can be in writing down as many solutions as possible, each on a separate card.

Arrange the possible solutions in order of preference for now.

What's the worst thing that can happen if you make the "wrong decision"?

Go over your possible solutions again one day later. If the order no longer seems like the best possible solution, resort the cards until your decision feels right for you. Feel free to add new solutions.

What payoff is there for you if you make your decision rapidly? Remember, not making a decision is another way of making a decision.

DAY 14

AWARENESS DAY 14/ TAKE THE TIME TO NOTICE

Go to the food market, select five oranges, and buy them. When you get home, allot some time for yourself when you won't be interrupted. Place the oranges on the table. Pick one up, rotate it in your hands, and notice its texture. Study its pores, its coloration, its symmetry. How is one side different from the other? How does it smell? How heavy does it feel? How large is it in your hands? How firm is it?

Now pick up another orange and do the same thing, repeating the same process until, one by one, you have gone through all five oranges. Notice the differences among the oranges. Select one orange to be "your" orange.

Now close your eyes and relax, letting the tension disappear. Pretend you are very small, so small that you can crawl into your orange. You can become that orange. Envision yourself high up on your mother tree. Notice your surroundings as you are firmly supported high in the tree. The birds that nest in your tree appreciated your sweet fragrance even when you were still a blossom. A gentle rain is starting to fall, caressing your skin. How does that rain affect you? Does it change the ground in which your tree is rooted? Now imagine that the rain has stopped and the sun is peeking out from behind the clouds. Feel the warming rays of the sun remove the dampness of the rain, providing warmth to your core. You are becoming fuller and more delicious-tasting every day. You are good and desirable. You can recall everything you have experienced. Count from one to five, and on the count of five, open your eyes. You will feel alert and refreshed.

With your eyes open, once more look at the orange in front of you, "your" orange. Know that all the positive energy that went into creating this orange—the sun, the earth, the rain, the air, the contact with other beings—also contributed to *your* very being. You, like the orange, are unique. No duplicates! Every one of God's creations is a repository of life experiences and a genetic pool that make each living thing unique. Appreciate your specialness.

NUTRITION DAY 14/ YOU NEED YOUR VITAMINS!

How much and what kinds of vitamins are very controversial subjects for a lot of people. If you lived in a time when you breathed clean air and ate the proper balance of good wholesome food you grew yourself, you probably wouldn't need any supplemental vitamins. Since that's not the case for most of us, here is some information about the effect of stress on your body and about which vitamins and minerals may be especially beneficial.

Vitamin A. Larger doses of vitamin A, balanced with vitamin D, may be necessary during particularly stressful times. Vitamin A increases your resistance to infections, especially of the respiratory tract.

B-Complex Vitamin. Stress increases the need for a B-complex vitamin, especially pantothenic acid, which is often called the "antistress vitamin". It is needed by the adrenal glands and by the body's immune system. Pantothenic acid, folic acid, and pyridoxine are considered essential to the production of antibodies, which help fight off infection. All of these are in a B-complex vitamin in balanced proportions. Vitamin B-complex also helps form red blood cells, which supply oxygen to the tissues, and your body needs more oxygen when it's "under stress." Coffee, doughnuts, and cigarettes deplete the body of vitamin B and calcium.

Vitamin C. Stress causes the adrenal glands to produce more of the substance that uses up vitamin C. It is considered to be a natural medicine for the ailing heart, and—according to *The Complete Book of Vitamins* by the staff of *Prevention* magazine—vitamin C deficiencies have been linked to atherosclerosis. Vitamin C builds up the body's natural defenses and should be increased during times of stress.

Vitamin E. Evidence indicates that vitamin E is essential to good health, as it is important in preventing and curing various heart and blood-vessel ailments. It's an antioxidant for certain air pollutants.

Calcium. Calcium, the most abundant mineral in the body, is essential for the nerves, bone repair, regulating the cellular membranes, and an aid in clotting the blood. Stress overload depletes the reserve of calcium in the body, weakening the pelvis and spine.

Potassium. Stress causes a loss of potassium. A heavy intake of sugary junk food causes potassium loss. Potassium regulates the heart rhythms and water balance.

Magnesium. Magnesium is essential for proper nerve and muscle functioning. It improves the cardiovascular system and is necessary for metabolism of calcium and vitamin C, as well as that of phosphorus, sodium, and potassium. Magnesium is called the "antistress mineral."

Authorities offer these recommended daily allowances on these particular vitamins and minerals:

Vitamin A	5,000 units
B-Complex Vitamin	50 mg.
Calcium	800 mg.
Vitamin C	1000 to 4000 mg.
Vitamin D	400 units
Vitamin E	200 to 400 units
Pantothenic Acid	15–50 mg.
Potassium	20 to 40 mg.
Magnesium	150 to 250 mg.

Amino Acids, the building blocks of your body proteins upon which vitamins and minerals work, are also reduced by stress. The combination of L-tryptophan, niacin and vitamin B6 has been proven as effective as drugs in treating insomnia, pain, and depression.

Speak to an authority on vitamins, minerals, and amino acids or get one of the recommended books to find out which ones may be helpful for you. You will want to inquire about which vitamins are water soluble, which are retained in the body when an excessive amount is taken in, which should be taken only after eating, what effects they might have on your appetite, and so forth.

EXERCISE DAY 14/
ENERGIZE YOUR BODY AND CLEAR YOUR MIND (PART I)

Remember when you were a child the challenge to simultaneously rub your tummy and pat your head, and how it sometimes took a while to get your brain "hooked up right" to be able to do it? Cross crawls are a little like that, as they require your brain to move opposite extremities at the same time, thus, stimulating both hemispheres of the brain.

Cross crawls enable you to simultaneously energize your body, increase your flexibility, and think more clearly by using both sides of your brain. See if you find the following exercises somewhat like that childhood challenge. These are great exercises to do when you're feeling drained or tense, when you're unable to think clearly, or when your muscles are tight.*

You should wear clothing that doesn't interfere with free movement. Beginning in a comfortable standing position, with your arms by your side and nothing in your hands, do each one of the exercises for two or three minutes. After coordinating your leg and arm movements to get going, perform the exercises briskly to set up an energizing body rhythm.

---

* From *Touch for Health* by John Thie and Mary Marks (Los Angeles: DeVorss, 1980). Used with permission of the authors.

Cross Crawl No. 1

Cross Crawl No. 1

Keeping your legs parallel, bring your left leg forward and up while simultaneously raising your right arm. Then reverse, with right leg up and left arm up, like a high stepper in a parade.

Cross Crawl No. 2

Cross Crawl No. 2

Keeping your knees and elbows straight, raise your right leg to the side of your body while simultaneously raising your left arm from your side. Then reverse.

Cross Crawl No. 3

Cross Crawl No. 3

Keeping your knees and elbows straight, raise your left leg forward while simultaneously raising your right arm. Then reverse. If you wish, you can touch your foot with the opposite hand as you vigorously do this exercise.

COMMUNICATION
DAY 14/
YOU DON'T MEAN IT

Does this dialogue sound familiar?

Jan: Gee, I'm glad to see you. It's been such a long time! I think you look terrific!

Jon: Aw, you don't mean it.

How do you feel about accepting a compliment? For many of us, that's hard to do. We may have been taught that hearing and believing those things would give us "a swelled head" and make us self-centered. We're so busy not allowing ourselves to believe any kind words, and so ready to be self-critical, that it's no wonder most of us walk around with such low self-esteem!

On the other hand, how do you feel about giving a compliment? That, too, can be a tough thing for many of us to do. It's almost as if we feel that we're taking away something from ourselves if we acknowledge someone else's contribution to our lives. It really doesn't work that way. Giving sincere compliments about a specific quality or action you appreciate can make the other person feel better about himself. If he gets enough of these positive messages, he may risk stating his appreciation of others, and a bountiful, enriching ripple is started. This "ripple effect" is like a stone tossed into a pond, its ripple reaching outward in every direction, far from and sometimes unknown to the source.

People can adopt new behavior at any point in their lives. Margaret was beginning to feel old, having suffered a heart attack three years earlier, and now, as she approached her seventieth birthday, she wasn't feeling as well as she would have liked. She wasn't accustomed to talking about her feelings, as it wasn't something she had done during most of her life, and never with her own family. However, she had heard me tell her how much I appreciated her and as hard as it was to let those messages penetrate, she had somehow allowed them to.

She decided to call her older sister, who lived 2,000 miles away. They normally talked every two or three months on the phone, but this call was different. After they had talked for awhile, Margaret got to the reason for her call. That part of the dialogue went like this:

Margaret: I want you to know what a good sister you have been to me.

Sister: Now, Margaret, I'll be out there to see you in April. We can talk then. [Reassuring Margaret, denying the feelings of urgency Margaret felt, the sister's way of avoiding an emotional issue.]

Margaret: Now listen, this is hard for me to say, and I want to make sure you hear it. I love you, and you've been the best sister I ever could have hoped for.

Suddenly, unexpectedly, Margaret died two days later. Margaret was my mother. Later, her sister happened to tell me how strange Margaret had acted during that long-distance phone call. Margaret was clearly finishing her "unfinished business," saying the good things that she felt she must say before she left this world. Indeed, this was an example of the ripple effect.

What good things would you like to say to the people in your life? How do you feel as you contemplate putting those feelings into words? What is the worst thing that could happen if you stated how you felt? Are you willing to take the risk?

As you think about someone saying some kind words to you, can you be kind enough to yourself to say only "thank you," "I like hearing that," or "I appreciate that"? The next time that happens, I suggest you limit your reply to this type of simple acknowledgment. Let the feelings of being appreciated by another come in.

I suggest that you select three people in your life toward whom you have warm feelings. Think of one genuine, positive comment you'd like to make. Rehearse it in your mind, anticipating the other person's possible responses. Rehearse, too, your responses to his possible responses. Be aware of how you feel as you go through this process. Take time, if necessary, to become centered through "belly breathing" or another brief relaxation technique, and use the relaxation technique every time you find yourself becoming anxious as you anticipate the dialogue, until you're able to think through several alternatives to your satisfaction.

This may be awkward or difficult at first, especially if you fall into the category of those who proudly proclaim, "But I told you I loved you when we got married." Once is not enough. When you're able to express appreciation (and resentment!) as you feel it, you'll have the opportunity to develop fuller, richer relationships.

RELAXATION DAY 14/ MAKE YOUR WATCH YOUR ALLY

How many times a day do you look at your watch? How many times a day do you look at a clock? Stop for a moment and ponder those questions. If you're like most people, you probably do both a great deal. If you're constantly aware of the time, perhaps always feeling hurried and as if you "must dash," clocks and watches reinforce your feelings of anxiety about getting things done and being on time.

You can change all this if you wish. One way is to stop wearing a watch altogether. Impossible, you think! How could you ever get anything done if you went without a watch? I find that since I stopped regularly wearing a watch three years ago it's no problem at all. Everyone else has a watch, and it seems like clocks are everywhere. I have a clock in my office, and there's even a clock in my car. Instead of a watch, I have a pocket-size calculator with a clock/alarm function, which I carry in my briefcase or purse. I use the alarm function a great deal to inform me, for instance, when the parking meter is due to expire, when I must interrupt what I'm doing to move on to the next task, or when I plan to return a phone call. Curiously, I find that most of my colleagues who conduct stress-management training don't wear watches, either. This is one direct interference with the Type A personality's preoccupation with hurrying.

Another way to alter this process is to make your watch (or clock) your ally by affixing a small, brightly colored pressure-sensitive dot on the dial. Every time you look at your watch and see that dot, let it be your cue to engage in some "belly breathing." Taking three deep breaths every time you see that dot will retrain your responses so that clock-watching is a signal for you to relax your body.

LIFESTYLE DAY 14/
SAME AND DIFFERENT

Have you ever noticed that what you want most out of life sometimes isn't the same thing your spouse, mate, or lover wants? Maybe you're not aware of this until a conflict brings it out into the open. But, you don't have to wait until there's a conflict to find out.

Here's a self-evaluation to enable you to become aware of those areas in which you have agreement and those in which you have differences.

Below is a list of broad life goals. First, rank the items in their order of importance to you and then rank them in the order you think your spouse, mate, or lover would put them—and have your partner do the same. One of you can use a blank sheet of paper numbered for 1 to 16 for the ranking of self and partner.*

My Preference	Partner's Preference	
1 ——	——	Affection (to obtain and share companionship)
2 ——	——	Duty (to be dedicated to what I call my duty or life mission)
3 ——	——	Expertness (to become an authority in a field of endeavor)
4 ——	——	Independence (to have freedom of thought and action)

* Adapted from the self-evaluation developed by Nicholas Eltgroth in *"Growtogether" Education for Marriage Newsletter*, Vol. 3, No. 1, January 1981. Used with permission of the author.

	My Preference	Partner's Preference	
5	——	——	Leadership (to become influential)
6	——	——	Parenthood (to raise a family, to have heirs)
7	——	——	Health (to engage in wise self-care practices)
8	——	——	Pleasure (to enjoy life, to be happy and content)
9	——	——	Power (to have control of others)
10	——	——	Prestige (to become well known)
11	——	——	Job Security (to have a secure and stable position)
12	——	——	Self-Realization (to develop personal strengths and abilities)
13	——	——	Service (to contribute to the satisfactions of others)
14	——	——	Wealth (to earn a great deal of money)
15	——	——	Friendships (to have friendly and congenial associates)
16	——	——	Life Balance (to have balance between work, learning, and play)

After both of you have completed your rankings, compare your list with your partner's. You may wish to share your responses to the following questions:

1. How do you feel about the way your goals match or do not match?
2. How do you feel about the way your partner ranked his/her goals?
3. How do you feel about the way your partner ranked your goals?
4. How accurate were you in ranking your partner's goals?
5. What does this tell you about how well you understand each other?
6. What does the order tell about your relationship? Are there any goals you would like to change?
8. Are there any goals you would like your partner to change?
9. Which goals would you like to work on together?

DAY 15

AWARENESS DAY 15/ THAT'S NOT THE WAY I SEE IT

Man is not disturbed by events,
but by the view he takes of them.
—Epictetus

By now you may have noticed how unique you are. The things that make you tense or anxious may not affect someone else the same way. Since these events are so personalized, I suggest that you make a list of all the current situations in your life that trigger stress, including any stressful event you're likely to encounter in the relatively near future. Be specific as to the setting and people involved. Try to think of at least twenty situations, letting them range from mild discomforts and inconveniences to your most dreaded experiences. Rank the experiences according to how stress-producing they are for you, and then list them in a hierarchy. Each item on the list should represent an increase in stress over the last item, and the increases should be in approximately the same amount.

Joseph Wolpe calls this the Subjective Units of Distress Scale (SUDS). The most distressing event is rated at 100 SUDS and total relaxation is zero SUDS, with all the other items falling somewhere in between. You alone know how upsetting any particular event is, so you're the expert in deciding where each item will fit in the hierarchy. Your list might look something like this one, developed by a client of mine who is a woman elementary-school teacher.

Rank	Item	SUDS (Subjective Units of Distress Scale)
1	Waiting in line at the bank	5
2	Staying home from work, awaiting an appliance repairman	10

3 Rushing to take daughter to orthodontist — 15
4 Conducting Girl Scouts meeting Thursday afternoons — 20
5 Supervising recreation yard in cold weather — 25
6 Dentist appointment — 30
7 Catching up on weekend with shopping, errands, laundry, and correcting papers — 35
8 Tired at end of workday, but still needing to shop and cook — 40
9 Preparing house for Christmas dinner — 45
10 Deadline for performance appraisal of student teacher — 50
11 Disagreement with husband over sharing household tasks — 55
12 Taking a trip alone by plane to regional conference — 60
13 Extra work assignment: coordinating rehearsals for school play — 65
14 Preparation for Open House at school — 70
15 Feeling jealous about how much time husband spends with his hobby — 75
16 Meeting with parents to discuss their children's progress this semester — 80
17 Relatives visiting for a week during Christmas vacation — 85
18 Complaints from parents — 90
19 Principal critical of my work — 95
20 Daughter sick at home while I'm working — 100

A good list contains many different concerns because it's not limited to any one particular problem area in your life. The described situations are stated briefly but are clear enough so that you can reconstruct the scene in your imagination.

You may wish to use the technique of *desensitization* to make each event on your SUDS scale less threatening—that is, break the event down into smaller components, and allow yourself to become relaxed as you anticipate each small part.

For instance, on the SUDS list presented here, item number 12 ("Taking a trip alone by plane to regional conference") can be broken down into small segments. Make the scene vivid and real for yourself, imagining the various sounds, smells, sights, and textures you will experience as you pack for the trip, leave your house, go to the airport, check your luggage, check in at the gate, board the plane, find your seat, take off, be in flight, and land at your destination. Include what other people would be saying to you in each of these scenes. Know what your body movements would be. Retain each image for thirty to forty seconds. Notice the beginning of any anxiety or tension in your body, and use that sensation of tension as the signal to do some "belly breathing" and deep muscle relaxation. Relax away this tension, even as you imagine the stressful situations.

If you notice yourself becoming too uncomfortable at any step along the way, back up to the step where you were able to fully relax. Remember, this works when done gradually.

Recommended Reading

Wolpe, Joseph. *Psychotherapy by Reciprocal Inhibition.* Stanford, Calif.: Stanford University Press, 1958.

NUTRITION DAY 15/
NOT JUST
WHAT YOU EAT
BUT WHEN YOU EAT

Look over your Food Awareness Log to find out when you eat the most during the day. Most people follow the traditional American urban style that makes dinner the most important, in terms of quantity of food, regarding it as the main meal of the day.

However, eating a large quantity of food in the evening increases the likelihood that those calories will not be worked off as readily as those consumed earlier in the day. Also if your body is busy digesting food within three hours of bedtime, it's likely that your sleep won't be restful. Some experts say that the evening meal shouldn't be any bigger than breakfast, thus emphasizing the importance of both a hearty breakfast *and* a small supper.

All this is less feasible given our contemporary living patterns, whereby we tend to make "having dinner" a sociable, rewarding experience. Even so, it can still be accomplished. What counts is the environment and the people you're with. What and how much you actually eat isn't really that important in the larger scheme of things.

For an experiment, one day this weekend I suggest that you change your usual pattern of having a heavy evening meal. Instead, make lunchtime the occasion for your main meal and your dinner that night the equivalent of a light lunch. Notice if you feel any difference.

One professional husband-and-wife team I know make this habit part of their lifestyle. They each eat a full meal at lunch, and at night, when the two of them get together, they may have some fruit, a salad, or even just a bowl of cereal. They feel it has helped them keep their weight down and improve their health in general.

EXERCISE DAY 15/ ENERGIZE YOUR BODY AND CLEAR YOUR MIND (PART II)

Because cross crawls are fun to do, represent a different kind of challenge, and are helpful for so many common stress-related problems, here are some more you can do today.* Follow the same preliminary guidelines as in Day 14.

Cross Crawl No. 4

Cross Crawl No. 4

Raise your right leg to the side, bending your knee, while simultaneously raising your left arm, bending your elbow and raising your hand. Then reverse. Notice that your legs and feet will be at a 90-degree angle to each other.

---

* From *touch for Health* by John Thie and Mary Marks (Los Angeles: De Vorss, 1980). Used with permission of the authors.

Cross Crawl No. 5

Cross Crawl No. 5

Cross your body by raising your left leg up and to the right while simultaneously swinging your right arm across and up to the left. Then reverse.

Cross Crawl No. 6

Cross Crawl No. 6

Bend your left knee and raise your left leg behind your right leg simultaneously swinging your right arm to the left across the front of your body. Then reverse. This looks something like a sailor's dance.

COMMUNICATION
DAY 15/
GETTING INTO YOUR PARTNER'S SHOES

Being a good listener is more than simply allowing the other person to talk. That's a big part of it—not interrupting—but only one part. To be a really good listener means to know what it's like to be in that person's shoes.

What is she feeling at that time? What is she saying with her skin color, her facial expressions, her tone of voice, her gestures, her eye contact (or lack thereof), her body posture, her rate of breathing, *and* her words?

You may wish to follow these guidelines in order to become a better listener:

1. Notice as many clues as you can about what the other person is feeling. Don't allow yourself to be distracted by *your* response to what your partner is saying or feeling.
2. Listen without interrupting. Instead of being preoccupied with your thoughts or your next response, focus on how your partner feels.
3. Indicate that you are listening by nodding, making eye contact, and saying things like "um hmm" or "I'd like to hear more about that."
4. Repeat what you have heard in your own words so that your partner can let you know if you heard accurately, using such phrases as "It seems to me that you're saying . . ." and "I heard you saying . . ."
5. Comment upon what you notice, saying "I notice that . . ." (select one) "you're breathing faster" or "your gestures become more animated" or perhaps "your voice gets softer" and then finish with "as you talk about this." Comment on what you

313

can observe, and avoid making interpretations or assumptions about what your partner may be feeling because of those outward signs.

6. Reflect what your partner seems to be feeling, saying "you look as if you are feeling . . ." (select one) "anxious" or "excited" or perhaps "sad" and finish with "as you talk about this."

7. Check with your partner frequently for feedback to find out if you're on the right path, and help her explore the topic more fully by saying "Am I hearing you?" or "Is that what's going on?" or "Is that how it is?"

8. Don't assume your partner wants you to do anything about her problem unless she specifically asks for your help. Too often, instead of acknowledging that we genuinely hear our partners, we are eager to *do* something—offer advice, share our experiences ("the same thing happened to me, and *I* did . . ."), lecture, interpret, criticize, or analyze what they're saying. Being judgmental guarantees that your partner will not feel free to share what is important to her. Even positive judgments ("Gee, that's great!") shift the focus to *your* value system, removing her from her feelings.

9. Do not ask questions! That reflects your need to know more, not her need to talk about what is important to *her*. This is one of the hardest things to do, as people generally feel that asking questions is an indicator of their interest, concern, and desire to solve the problem. That may sometimes be the case, but asking questions will take your partner out of being in touch with her feelings.

10. Do not reassure or sympathize by saying "You'll feel better tomorrow" or "It won't be so bad after you've worked at it a while" or "I think your idea is terrific, and Jean is simply being envious."

These techniques of being a good listener create a climate of acceptance for the other person. A person who feels truly accepted is free to gain a fuller understanding of what is going on with herself, to explore new dimensions of the situation, to ponder possible alternatives that may not

314

have occurred to her before, and to feel in charge of her own growth. Each of us has that capacity, given the opportunity to be fully heard by another. A psychotherapist can provide this acceptance, which facilitates personal growth.

RELAXATION DAY 15/
LET IT HAPPEN

Can you *make* your body relax? I doubt it. Relaxation is something that comes more easily if you simply *allow* your body to unwind. In order to relax, your mind uses "passive volition" or "passive concentration," which is the opposite of the "active volition" or "active concentration" with which you are most familiar. Because you're so accustomed to living with excessive stress, relaxation is not a natural, passive skill. It must be practiced.

Your body needs four kinds of rest: physical, mental, sensory, and physiological. The techniques in this book enable you to practice skills that will fully rest your body. Here I'd like to offer some messages you can give yourself to allow your body to relax more often.

First, select a place where you can be undisturbed, someplace that is pleasantly warm, comforting to you, and without intrusions. Take the phone off the hook or unplug it. Position yourself comfortably, either sitting or lying down. Scan your body to detect if you're feeling any tension. If you're supporting your body in such a way as to sustain any tension, reposition yourself to let that go.

Begin by telling yourself these messages.

- "There's nothing to do, nothing to do."
- "I have all the time in the world."
- "I am able to simply let go and relax."
- "Letting go, letting go. There's nothing to do."
- "I feel my body slipping into deeper and deeper relaxation."
- "Nothing else matters, just simply letting go, letting go."

316

These phrases are useful in beginning any relaxation technique. I suggest you follow the preliminary steps of getting into a position in a place where you feel able to relax and practice saying a few of these phrases, feeling free to repeat them as indicated above. Add more of your own choosing.

LIFESTYLE DAY 15/ SO WHAT HAVE YOU DONE FOR ME LATELY?

If you are good, other people will notice and reward your efforts. Right? Wrong—or at least not necessarily. That's the Santa Claus theory presented in the Preface. If you know you are good, if you're making progress toward your goals, if you're redirecting your lifestyle away from negative health practices, you need to be able to reward yourself. What are some ways you can think of to do this?

If you're like most people, you may have a tough time with that question. We seem to be much better at thinking of ways to punish ourselves and be self-critical than to reward ourselves and be self-congratulatory. Self-rewards should be something readily available that you can provide for yourself (without depending upon someone else) and that provide immediate satisfaction or soothing.

Rewarding yourself can take four forms: (1) pleasurable activities, (2) positive self-messages, (3) symbolic rewards, and (4) material rewards.

Pleasurable activities include progressive relaxation, physical exercise, mental relaxation, and guided imagery.* Some of my clients have found these self-rewards enjoyable: listening to music; pleasure reading; going for a walk in a park, at the beach, or in the woods; giving oneself a massage; visiting an art gallery, a crafts shop, or the zoo; luxuriating in a bubble bath, with the bathroom lit by candlelight and the air fragrant with incense.

Positive self-messages are those that break the pattern of self-critical inner voices.** Material rewards are bonus

---

* Days 3, 5, 8, 9, and 10 of "Relaxation" discuss some pleasurable activities.
** Day 6 of "Communication" and Day 9 of "Lifestyle" present some positive self-messages.

gifts to yourself, something attractive enough for you to strive for but that you can do without. One client of mine loved to indulge herself with expensive blouses as a reward. She was concerned about losing weight, and every day she made the effort necessary to make that happen, she put one dollar into a velvet-lined box. Notice that she didn't depend upon the scale's verdict to dictate *whether* she deserved a reward. When she *knew* she had followed good dietary practices that would help her reduce, she deposited the dollar. When she had enough dollars for a coveted blouse, she rewarded herself by purchasing it, letting it serve as tangible evidence of her self-discipline.

Now is a good time for you to draw up a list of things you can do to reward yourself. Write down whatever comes into your mind—don't consider anything too outlandish. It's easy enough to limit yourself later, if you feel you must. For now, simply write everything down.

If you find yourself resisting this exercise, you may wish to engage in some of the relaxation techniques that will help you get in touch with your noncritical, peaceful center.

DEVELOPING YOUR PERSONAL ACTION PLAN

After you have finished reading this book, you may benefit from designing your own action plan. The first step is to note your accomplishments, which you may do by completing the checklists below. Here each of the six segments of the book are listed along with their daily programs.

Awareness

		Completed	Reread
Day 1.	How Do I Limit Myself	——	——
Day 2.	Know Yourself	——	——
Day 3.	Lemons or Lemonade?	——	——
Day 4.	What's Your Reaction?	——	——
Day 5.	I'm Gonna Change My Way of Livin'	——	——
Day 6.	My Many Faces	——	——
Day 7.	Every Body Is Different	——	——
Day 8.	The Bigger Picture	——	——
Day 9.	On the Home Front	——	——
Day 10.	What Would It Be Like?	——	——
Day 11.	Who's There?	——	——
Day 12.	The Blind Men and the Elephant	——	——
Day 13.	Your Personal Advisor	——	——
Day 14.	Take the Time to Notice	——	——
Day 15.	That's Not the Way I See It	——	——

Nutrition

Day 1.	But I Eat Like a Bird!	——	——
Day 2.	Calories *Do* Count	——	——

	Completed	Reread
Day 3. Somehow I Just Found Myself Eating	——	——
Day 4. A Rich Diet Can Kill You	——	——
Day 5. "White Death" Number One	——	——
Day 6. "White Death" Number Two	——	——
Day 7. Simpler Is Not Better	——	——
Day 8. Fins and Feathers Are Fine	——	——
Day 9. How Much Protein?	——	——
Day 10. Milk Is *Not* Good for Every Body	——	——
Day 11. How About a Cup of Coffee for a Pickup?	——	——
Day 12. What You Don't Know *Can* Hurt You	——	——
Day 13. Water, Water Everywhere, and Not a Drop to Drink	——	——
Day 14. You Need Your Vitamins!	——	——
Day 15. Not Just What You Eat, but *When* You Eat	——	——

Exercise

	Completed	Reread
Day 1. Ready or Not?	——	——
Day 2. "No Exercise" Exercise	——	——
Day 3. Window-Shopping	——	——
Day 4. Tell Me What It's Like	——	——
Day 5. What's New Under the Sun?	——	——
Day 6. The Best Exercise You Can Get	——	——
Day 7. How Hard Is Hard Enough?	——	——
Day 8. For That Pain in the Neck	——	——
Day 9. Relaxing Your Shoulders	——	——
Day 10. Strengthening Your Lower Back (Part I)	——	——
Day 11. Strengthening Your Lower Back (Part II)	——	——
Day 12. Stretch Away Your Tension (Part I)	——	——
Day 13. Stretch Away Your Tension (Part II)	——	——
Day 14. Energize Your Body and Clear Your Mind (Part I)	——	——
Day 15. Energize Your Body and Clear Your Mind (Part II)	——	——

	Completed.	Reread

Communication

	Completed	Reread
Day 1. Your True Friend	——	——
Day 2. Believing Will Make It So	——	——
Day 3. Whadjasay?	——	——
Day 4. I Am Worth It	——	——
Day 5. Free at Last	——	——
Day 6. A Bedtime Ritual	——	——
Day 7. You Are a Rainbow	——	——
Day 8. At the Next Gas Station	——	——
Day 9. You Did *What*?	——	——
Day 10. I Count	——	——
Day 11. I Am Responsible	——	——
Day 12. The Trapdoor	——	——
Day 13. Is Anger Acceptable?	——	——
Day 14. You Don't Mean It	——	——
Day 15. Getting into Your Partner's Shoes	——	——

Relaxation

	Completed	Reread
Day 1. You've Always Got It with You (Part I)	——	——
Day 2. You've Always Got It with You (Part II)	——	——
Day 3. Melt Away Your Tension	——	——
Day 4. Black Velvet	——	——
Day 5. My Own Special Place	——	——
Day 6. Rub the Tension Away	——	——
Day 7. Laugh and the World Laughs with You	——	——
Day 8. Find Your Center	——	——
Day 9. My Words Relax Me	——	——
Day 10. Healing Hands	——	——
Day 11. Pleasant Dreams	——	——
Day 12. Soothe the Savage Beast	——	——
Day 13. Satisfying Sensory Pleasures	——	——
Day 14. Make Your Watch Your Ally	——	——
Day 15. Let It Happen	——	——

Lifestyle Management	Completed	Reread
Day 1. You Do Have Enough Time		
Day 2. On Becoming Type B		
Day 3. People Need People		
Day 4. Forty Hours a Week		
Day 5. It's Always There		
Day 6. Seven Significant Habits		
Day 7. Where Is It?		
Day 8. Soar or Suffocate?		
Day 9. I Love Myself		
Day 10. Affirmation of Life		
Day 11. Who's Indispensable?		
Day 12. Five Years from Now		
Day 13. Choices		
Day 14. Same and Different		
Day 15. So What Have You Done for Me Lately?		

Your Action Plan

Reading this book is an important first step on your path to wellness. That alone, however, won't necessarily change your lifestyle. You may have found some sections of the book especially helpful—those you may have checked above that you wish to reread so that you can incorporate them into your everyday life.

The next step is to develop your own personal action plan. Here you set long-range goals, say of six months, and work toward those goals through a series of stages. I suggest you start with that. Below is an example.

To achieve your six-month goals, you need to break them down into "do-able" stages. Each of the stages is characterized by a plan or "self-contract" of two to four weeks' duration. That change is attempted, the results are reviewed, and a new plan is devised for the next two to four weeks.

If you should decide to coast for a while and not actively engage in improving your lifestyle, you may decide to write a self-contract saying that this is okay for two weeks. This way you still maintain control of your lifestyle and avoid falling into the trap of "letting things happen to you."

My Six-Month Goals

In the next six months, I wish to achieve these goals:

Run 30 minutes three times a week.

Weigh within ± 3 pounds of 165.

Keep a journal, making entries at least once a week.

Visit with a friend at least once a week.

Finish my work at the office — not bring it home.

Treat myself to a massage at least once a month.

Here is an example of a self-contract:

Two-Week Self-Contract
Plan to Increase Social Support

I will increase my contact with people who are significant and nourishing to me by reaching out to them, from my present once-a-week family gathering on Sundays to one more occasion during the week to be alone with another friend during the two weeks of this self-contract. I will enlist the help of_____.

My responsibilities:
1. To note in my date book the names of five people I haven't seen for more than a month whom I would truly enjoy being with.
2. To call three of those people within the first four days of these two weeks.
3. To set up a time once each week with one of them to get together for a social occasion. This should be

something where we could talk, such as breakfast, brunch, lunch, dinner, a walk through an art gallery or the park.
4. To keep those appointments.
5. To reward myself with listening to favorite music for fifteen minutes each night after dinner.
6. To record in my journal at 10:00 P.M. each night how I felt about increasing my social contacts.

My helper's responsibilities:
1. To reveal to me enjoyable activities in which he has engaged that would be suitable for me and a friend.
2. To listen to my feelings about reaching out, which is not easy for me to do, and to provide encouragement.
3. To review with me how I felt about these events after having met with a friend.

Date:_____ Signed:_____
Review Date:_____ Helper:_____

If you decide to write your own self-contracts, you may wish to note the various principles of self-directed change revealed in the contract above. No matter how minor the goal, it is important to seek small gains with good preparation, having clearly thought out what is required to make it happen. You want to avoid failing by sticking to manageable, short-term goals.

Selecting a helper increases the likelihood of your success in initiating and maintaining a change. You may wish to select someone who is a good role model for you in the area you wish to improve. For instance, in the above self-contract, you may choose a co-worker who has maintained a strong support group of friends over the years. That person can encourage and support your efforts. Select a helper whom you truly believe will be helpful. Feel free not to re-enlist that person's aid if his help is not to your liking.

The **self-reward** is an important element in achieving self-directed change. You can select whatever is meaningful to you, but it should be something that is pleasurable and that you can readily make happen. You should reward yourself every day for your efforts at self-directed change. These small rewards are more meaningful than, say, getting season tickets to the symphony for five performances a year.

Setting your goals at attainable levels should make it possible for you to reward your efforts. Allow yourself to progress gradually, not heroically. You can devise an action plan that will have high predictability of success. It has been consistently demonstrated that rewards are more effective in achieving behavioral changes than are punishments.

Evaluate your progress at the end of each period of self-contracting. You may wish to continue at the same pace and in the same direction or to add something new or change helpers. Return to the identification of the problem you wish to change, once again building commitment.

Refer to your list of the goals you wish to attain. Maintaining your progress is the key to achieving a more rewarding lifestyle. You may wish to review your goals on a monthly basis to see how well you're progressing toward achieving them.

Recommended Reading

Lazarus, Arnold, and Fay, Allen. *I Can If I Want To.* New York: Morrow, 1975.

Wheelis, Allen. *How People Change.* New York: Harper and Row, 1973.

FEEDBACK

> If I am not for myself, who will be for me?
> If I am not for others, who am I for?
> And if not now, when?
>
> —The Talmud

This book is more than a book to me. It is a process.
And you are a very important part of that process. You
have done so much already, and now I'm going to ask you
for a favor. When I close a workshop on stress reduction, I
ask for feedback. Similarly, I'd like to know your comments
and feelings about *Letting Go of Stress*. You may want to
wait two to six months before you complete this section, so
that you will have had a chance to evaluate what difference the book has made in your life. Address it to Dr. Jackie
Schwartz, c/o Pinnacle Books, 1430 Broadway, New York,
NY 10018.

Your answers to the following questions will provide me
with feedback about your personal experiences and help
me make this book continually more helpful to others.
Please complete the questionnaire and send it to me, signed
or unsigned. If you like, you may wish to write me a letter
relating how your life has been affected as you've engaged
in some of these new practices. This is your opportunity to
let me know what you'd like me to pass on to others.

1. *Letting Go of Stress* enabled me to achieve a more
   vital, satisfying, healthful lifestyle in my relationships
   with:
   (Check (√) as many as apply.)

——Myself
——Spouse, mate, or lover

327

——My children
——My parents
——Other family members
——Close friends
——Co-workers
——Employers, employees
——Students, teachers
——Other women
——Other men
——Others:_____

2. After reading *Letting Go of Stress* I find it easier to:
(Check as many as apply, and circle the checkmarks
of any behavior that is new for you.)

——Know more clearly who I am and what I want for
myself
——Reveal to others what I want for myself
——Reveal to others my true feelings
——Communicate more congruently
——Criticize another in a nonblaming way
——Detect my sources of stress at work
——Detect my sources of stress at home
——Detect my sources of environmental stress
——Detect my sources of stress due to rapid social change
——Anticipate the life changes that will cause my stress
——Detect self-induced stress
——Understand the interrelationship between mind and
body
——Know my body's early-warning signs of stress over-
load
——Know what I can do immediately to alleviate my dis-
tress
——Know what long-term changes I can make to alleviate
my distress
——Others:_____

3. I am able to recognize symptoms of stress in those
with whom I:
(Check as many as apply, and circle the checkmarks
of those observations that are new to you.)
——Live
——Work
——Regularly interact during the course of the day

328

—Infrequently interact
—Others: _____

4. Because of reading the "Nutrition" portion, I have been able to:
   (Check as many as apply, and circle the checkmarks of any behavior that is new to you.)
—Identify the harmful substances I take into my body
—Cut down on my smoking
—Stop smoking
—Cut down on my use of alcohol
—Eliminate hard liquor
—Limit my intake of liquor to a glass of white wine with dinner
—Cut down on my coffee intake
—Cut my coffee intake to two cups a day
—Eliminate coffee
—Increase my intake of water to four glasses a day
—Increase my intake of water to eight glasses a day
—Decrease my consumption of fats
—Decrease my consumption of fats to 30 percent of my diet
—Decrease my consumption of fats to 20 percent of my diet
—Decrease my consumption of fats to 10 percent of my diet
—Cut down on my intake of sugar
—Virtually eliminate sugar from my diet
—Totally eliminate sugar from my diet
—Cut down on my intake of salt
—Refrain from using the saltshaker at the table
—Virtually eliminate salt from my diet
—Increase my consumption of complex carbohydrates
—Decrease my consumption of red meats
—Decrease my consumption of red meats to three times a week
—Decrease my consumption of red meats to once a week
—Decrease my consumption of red meats to twice a month
—Eliminate red meats from my diet
—Decrease my intake of protein
—Decrease my intake of protein to 8 to 10 percent of total caloric intake

——Detect whether my body is sensitive to milk or milk products
——Cut down on my intake of milk products
——Identify which food additives are in the food I eat
——Eliminate food additives from my diet some of the time
——Eliminate food additives from my diet most of the time
——Modify my eating habits so that I eat more slowly
——Become more aware of how I feel when I am eating
——Become more aware of the food I eat while I am eating
——Reduce my weight to within twenty pounds of ideal weight
——Reduce my weight to within ten pounds of ideal weight
——Reduce my weight and maintain it within a few pounds of my ideal weight
——Cut down on my use of aspirin or other pain pills
——Eliminate regular use of aspirin or other pain pills
——Cut down on my use of sleeping pills
——Eliminate my use of sleeping pills
——Cut down on my intake of tranquilizers, marijuana, or other mind-altering drugs to once a week
——Eliminate regular use of tranquilizers, marijuana, or other mind-altering drugs
——Others: _____

5. Because of reading the "Exercise" portion, I have been able to:
   (Check as many as apply, and circle the checkmarks of any behavior that is new for you.)
——Understand the importance of a good exercise program
——Begin a program of regular exercise
——Engage in tension-relieving exercises when I want to
——Increase my "no exercise" exercise activities
——Others: _____

6. Because of reading the "Communication" portion, I have been able to:
   (Check as many as apply, and circle the checkmarks of any behavior that is new for you.)
——Keep a journal

330

——Examine my belief systems
——Recognize the negative inner voices I use to chastise myself
——Stop using those negative messages to put myself down
——Practice affirmations
——Ask for help more often, without any stigma attached
——Finish "unfinished business" more often
——Become more assertive in stating what I want from others
——Make "I statements" more often, being responsible for my own thoughts and feelings
——Become a better listener
——Others: _____

7. Because of reading the "Relaxation" portion, I have been able to:
   (Check as many as apply, and circle the checkmarks of any behavior that is new for you.)
——Understand the difference between relaxation and diversion
——Understand the importance of achieving deep relaxation
——Use breathing exercises to attain instant relaxation
——Sleep soundly without medication
——Relax my body with a progressive relaxation technique
——Relax by returning to my own imaginary "special place"
——Relax by listening to Baroque music
——Meditate
——Find new joy and laughter in my life
——Make massage a regular part of my life
——Become aware of my habitual tension responses, such as clenched teeth, tightened fists, frowning, or pursed lips
——Others: _____

8. Because of reading the "Lifestyle" portion, I have been able to:
   (Check as many as apply, and circle the checkmarks of any behavior that is new for you.)
——Be more comfortable with silence

——Enjoy my own company, not feeling that I "need" someone
——Schedule periodic appointments with my dentist
——Schedule periodic appointments with my doctor
——Increase my contact with friends to once every two weeks
——Increase my contact with friends to once a week
——Decrease the number of hours I watch television
——Decrease the number of hours I watch television to two hours a day
——Decrease the number of hours I watch television to one hour a day
——Decrease the number of hours I watch television to fewer than five hours per week
——Set long-term goals for myself
——Set short-term goals for myself
——Use a date book to organize my time effectively
——Organize my desk
——Organize my files
——Organize my closets and dresser
——Organize my cupboards
——Avoid "late charges" due to my carelessness
——Clean out my car
——Schedule routine maintenance on my car
——Decrease my incidence of Type A behavior by 25 percent
——Decrease my incidence of Type A behavior by 50 percent
——Change my behavior significantly to become more of a Type B
——Increase my contact with nature to once every two weeks
——Increase my contact with nature to once a week
——Increase my contact with nature to twice a week
——Increase my contact with nature to once a day
——Take one new risk a week
——Take one new risk twice a week
——Take one new risk every day
——Others: _____

9. Place an "X" next to the areas mentioned above that had the most meaning for you and an "0" next to those that had the least meaning for you. Mark items with a dash(——) if all areas were equally important.

332

10. What additional topics would you like to see included?

_____

_____

11. With whom have you shared this book? (Check as many as apply.)
____Spouse, mate or lover
____My children
____My parents
____Other family members
____Close friends
____Co-workers
____Employers, employees
____Students, teachers
____Other women
____Other men

12. What section of the book did you especially like?

_____

_____

What section of the book did you dislike?

_____

_____

13. Optional information about yourself: (Answer any and all.)
____Female
____Male
____Under 18   ____19–25   ____26–35   ____36–45
____46–55   ____56–64   ____over 65
____Never Married   ____Married   ____Separated
____Divorced
____Remarried, 1st time   ____Remarried, 2nd time
____Widowed
____Living Together
Occupation _____
Highest level of education completed _____
Name _____
Address _____
City _____ State_____ Zip_____
I completed reading this book ____ months ago.

On a scale of 1 to 10, with 1 being the lowest and 10 the highest, I would rate my stress level at:

——when I first obtained this book

——when I first completed this book

——now, months later, since I've put the suggestions in this book into practice.

I intend to use this book in my work in the following manner:

_____

_____

_____

Other books I have read concerning self-development:

_____

_____

Other books I have read concerning stress reduction:

_____

_____

_____

APPENDICES

APPENDIX A:
WHAT ARE YOUR
STRESS SYMPTOMS?

This scale measures the minor physical and emotional symptoms that indicate difficulty in dealing with everyday stress.* During the past month, how much of the time were the following statements true for you? Place a checkmark in the appropriate column.

	Most of the Time	Some of the Time	Almost Never
1. I felt tense, nervous, anxious, or upset.	——	——	——
2. I felt sad, depressed, down in the dumps, or hopeless.	——	——	——
3. I was low in energy, exhausted, tired, or unable to get things done.	——	——	——
4. I couldn't turn off my thoughts at night or on weekends long enough to feel relaxed and refreshed the next day.	——	——	——
5. I had difficulty falling asleep and/or staying asleep, and didn't feel rested when I awakened.	——	——	——
6. I found myself unable to sit still, and had to move around constantly.	——	——	——
7. I felt discouraged, pessimistic, sad, self-critical, inadequate, or guilty.	——	——	——
8. I was so upset that I felt I was losing control of my feelings.	——	——	——

*From *Healing from Within* by Dennis T. Jaffe (New York: Knopf, 1981). Used with permission of the author.

	Most of the Time	Some of the Time	Almost Never
9. I have been preoccupied with a serious personal problem.	—	—	—
10. I have been bothered by vague body aches and pains, nervous indigestion, or jitters.	—	—	—
11. I have been in unpleasant situations that I felt helpless to do anything about.	—	—	—
12. I felt tired in the morning, with no energy to get up or face daily activities.	—	—	—

To Score:

Total your checkmarks in each column. Enter here:

—	—	—

Allow 2 points for Most of the Time

1 point for Some of the Time

0 points for Almost Never

A score of 10 or more indicates a need to take active steps in order to improve coping.

APPENDIX B:
HOW CARDIAC PRONE
ARE YOU?

The scale below* is composed of a pair of adjectives or phrases separated by a series of horizontal lines. Each pair has been chosen to represent two kinds of contrasting behavior. Each of us belongs somewhere between the two extremes.

Putting a checkmark toward the left side of the horizontal line indicates the first set of adjectives or phrases that best describes you. Putting a checkmark toward the right side indicates the second set of adjectives or phrases that best describes you. Since most of us, for example, are neither the most competitive nor the least competitive person we know, put a checkmark where you think you belong between the two extremes.

1. Doesn't mind leaving things temporarily unfinished

— — — — — —

Must get things finished once started

2. Calm and unhurried about appointments

— — — — — —

Never late for appointments

3. Not competitive

— — — — — —

Highly competitive

4. Listens well, lets others finish speaking

— — — — — —

Anticipates others in conversation (nods, interrupts, finishes sentences for the other)

---

* This self-evaluation, entitled "The Glazer StressControl Life-Style Questionnaire," was devised by Dr. Howard I. Glazer, director of behavior-management systems at Executive Health Examiners StressControl Systems, New York, New York. Used with permission of the author.

5. Never in a hurry, even when pressured

    — — — — — — —

Always in a hurry
6. Able to wait calmly

    — — — — — — —

Uneasy when waiting
7. Easygoing

    — — — — — — —

Always going full-speed ahead
8. Takes one thing at a time

    — — — — — — —

Tries to do more than one thing at a time, thinks about what to do next
9. Slow and deliberate in speech

    — — — — — — —

Vigorous and forceful in speech (uses a lot of gestures)
10. Concerned with satisfying himself, not others

    — — — — — — —

Wants recognition by others for a job well done
11. Slow doing things

    — — — — — — —

Fast doing things (eating, walking, etc.)
12. Easygoing

    — — — — — — —

Hard-driving
13. Expresses feelings openly

    — — — — — — —

Holds feelings in
14. Has a large number of interests

    — — — — — — —

Has few interests outside of work
15. Satisfied with job

    — — — — — — —

Ambitious, wants quick advancement on job
16. Never sets own deadlines

    — — — — — — —

Often sets own deadlines
17. Feels limited responsibility

    — — — — — — —

Always feels responsible
18. Never judges things in terms of numbers

_ _ _ _ _ _ _

Often judges performances in terms of numbers (how many, how much)

19. Casual about work

_ _ _ _ _ _ _

Takes work very seriously (works weekends, brings work home)

20. Not very precise

_ _ _ _ _ _ _

Very precise (careful about detail)

To Score:

Total the number of checkmarks for each column below:

_ _ _ _ _ _ _

Notice that there are seven blanks. Assign a value of 1 to the blank at the far left, increasing the value to 7 for the blank at the far right. Each column would be scored as follows:

$$1 \quad 2 \quad 3 \quad 4 \quad 5 \quad 6 \quad 7$$

_ _ _ _ _ _ _

Multiply the number of checkmarks by the value assigned, and enter your total here:———

Scoring Key:

A score of 110–140 indicates you are Type A_1

If you are in this category, and especially if you are over forty and smoke, you are likely to have a high risk of developing cardiac illness.

A score of 80–109 indicates you are Type A_2

You are in the direction of being cardiac-prone, but your risk is not as high as Type A_1. You should, nevertheless, pay careful attention to the advice given to all Type A's.

A score of 60–79 indicates you are Type AB

You are a blend of A and B patterns. This is a healthier pattern than either Type A_1 or A_2, but you have the potential for slipping into A behavior and you should recognize this.

A score of 30–59 indicates you are Type B_2

Your behavior is on the less-cardiac-prone end of the

341

spectrum. You are generally relaxed and cope adequately with stress.

A score of 0–29 indicates you are Type B_1
You tend to the extreme of noncardiac traits. Your behavior expresses few of the reactions associated with cardiac disease.

This test will give you some idea of where you stand in relation to the discussion of Type A behavior that appears in the overview of "Lifestyle Management." The higher your score, the more cardiac-prone you tend to be. Remember, though, that even Type B persons occasionally slip into Type A behavior, and any of these patterns can change over time.

APPENDIX C:
NINE DOTS SOLUTION

Here is one solution to the problem of the nine dots.

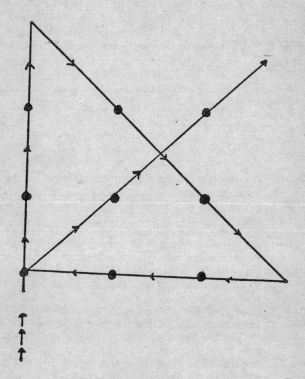

APPENDIX D:
HOW STRESSFUL
IS YOUR WORK?

Answer the following questions as they relate to experiences in your current job during the past twelve months.* Place the appropriate number on the line preceding each question. The numbers correspond to the following descriptive terms:

6=Always
5=Frequently
4=Often
3=Occasionally
2=Seldom
1=Never

—— 1. Do you feel overqualified/underqualified for the work you actually do?
—— 2. Do you feel lack of identification with your profession?
—— 3. When you compare yourself with your co-workers and personal friends with respect to their accomplishments, are you unhappy with your career?
—— 4. Do you think you won't be able to satisfy the conflicting demands of the various people around you?
—— 5. Does your job interfere with your personal life?
—— 6. Does your personal life interfere with your job?
—— 7. Do you feel you have to do things that are against your better judgment?
—— 8. Are decisions or changes that affect you made without your knowledge or involvement?

* Self-evaluation developed by Tom Isgar, © copyright 1979. Used with permission of the author.

—— 9. Are you expected to accept others' ideas without being told the rationale?

——10. Do you feel you have too little authority to carry out your responsibilities?

——11. Are you unclear about what is expected of you?

——12. Do others you work with seem unclear about what you do?

——13. Do you feel unclear about the scope and responsibilities of your job?

——14. Does management expect you to interrupt your work for new priorities?

——15. Must you attend meetings to get your job done?

——16. Does your job require travel?

——17. Do you have too much to do and too little time in which to do it?

——18. Do you have too little to do?

——19. Do you think the amount of work you have to do may interfere with how well it gets done?

——20. Do you have differences of opinion with your supervisors?

——21. Do you lack confidence in management?

——22. Do you feel unable to influence those decisions and actions of your immediate supervisors that directly affect you?

——23. Do you have unsettled conflicts with people you work with?

——24. Do you have an inappropriate amount of interaction with the people you work with?

——25. Do you feel you may not be liked and accepted by the people at work?

——26. Is there conflict between your unit and others it must work with?

——27. Must you go to other departments to get your job done?

——28. Are the people you work with trained in a different area than yours?

——29. Do you worry about decisions that affect the lives of other people?

——30. Do you feel you have too much responsibility for the work of others?

——31. Are you unaware of the manner in which your performance is evaluated?

——32. Are you in the dark about what your supervisor

thinks of you—that is, how she or he evaluates
your performance?

———33. Are you unaware of the degree to which your performance is evaluated as acceptable?

To Score:
Total all your answers and divide by 33. The higher your
score, the more stress you are experiencing. If your score is
between 1.8 and 4.4, you fall within the normal population.

Remembering the bell-shaped curve described in the Introduction, you know that too little stress can be as detrimental to your health as too much. If your score is greater than
4.4 or less than 1.8, you might begin to look at the stressors
or lack of stressors on your job.

The questions measure different aspects of job stress as
follows:

Questions		
1 – 3	measure your fit with the job	
4 – 6	role conflict	
7 –10	lack of authority	
11–13	role ambiguity	
14–16	interruptions	
17–19	work load	
20–22	supervision	
23–25	peer relationships	
26–28	relationships with other units	
29–30	responsibility for others	
31–33	evaluation	

You might want to see if your high/low scores correspond
to any set of questions. This will help determine specific
sources of job stress for you. You may wish to discuss these
scores with your supervisor or co-workers, in relation to the
particular stress-producing areas of your work.

APPENDIX E:
HOW PEOPLE REACT
TO STRESS OVERLOAD

Here I have reprinted selected responses to the sentence-completion exercise that appears in Day 7 of "Awareness." This is an instrument I have used in my workshops on Understanding and Managing Stress for the past five years. Participants in these workshops included members of professional organizations, students in graduate schools of business, people in the helping professions and women's social organizations, and executives in different fields from all over the United States. Regardless of the nature of the group, the responses bear marked similarity. I have repeated verbatim some of the responses here, including a representative range of replies. The asterisks indicate those replies that predominate.

1. *My biggest concern about stress is*
    * the manner and extent to which it will adversely affect me both physically and mentally
    that I feel like I'm going stir crazy and I take it out on the children
    not to let it overcome me—to gain control
    * how to recognize it and do something to minimize it
    not handling it and having a nervous breakdown
    * its relationship to hypertension
    * that it does not affect my health and impair my effectiveness with my subordinates and my family
    * its effect on performance, ability to relax, and happiness—how to hang in there
    * that it reduces the quality and length of my life
    it slows down my personal growth as a manager
    * that other people will notice it
    feeling so trapped and not being able to talk to anyone about it

347

that I do not know I am under stress until I am approaching the breaking point
to learn how to deal with it now so it doesn't crop up later

2. *When I'm experiencing excessive stress:*
   My physiological clues are
   heat wave over my body, sweating, tightness in my stomach, hemorrhoids, teeth clenching, disturbance of speech pattern
   * tightening of stomach muscles, tight gut, tight feeling in my head, headache, hives, excessive stomach problems
   * lack of appetite, sleeplessness
   rapid heartbeat, clammy palms
   lack of proper sleep, stiff neck, tight shoulders
   * hyperactiveness, can't sit still; shaky hands;
   jaws become tight; tense; becoming pale; dry skin
   * my chest feels tight and I perspire a lot
   eye twitching, muscle aches, shortness of breath
   flushed face, hands and voice shake, heart beats very fast
   * feel shaky all over
   * high blood pressure, feel nervous, stomach upset, indigestion
   * knots in my stomach
   * waking up in the middle of the night, having a lot of energy
   * headaches, tension in my lower back and in the back of my head at the base of my neck

   What I show on the outside is
   hurriedness, frustration
   * being "short" or snapping at others, dictatorial
   * very little, reasonable and calm, "Mr. Cool"
   * stern look, being overly abrupt with people
   reserved or subdued behavior
   * I am not sure
   bad temper, short on patience, soft voice, loud arguments
   tight face, cold stare
   calmness, become very quiet
   strong organization, large amount of activity
   * anger, hostility, being defensive

348

generally calm demeanor though disturbed speech pattern is occasionally evident
* worried, stressful expression, irritable
hesitant, confused
* preoccupied
* not what is happening on the inside

People usually respond to me by
not commenting
giving extra effort to solving our problem
walking away
telling me not to let certain individuals get to me
* leaving me alone
trying to get inside my preoccupied "wall"
avoiding me
* indifference
anger
staying out of the way
avoiding interaction
ignoring me
being intimidated
getting upset but not pushing me
getting defensive
backing off
working around me

3. *When I'm under a great deal of stress, I'd be embarrassed if people knew that*
   * I am
   * I can't control it and feel incompetent
   I really feel like getting aggressive
   * I was often not as sure of myself as I attempt to reflect in my outward behavior
   * I had a fear of failure
   I wanted to go for a very long walk
   I had feelings of inability, shortcomings
   I eat and eat and eat
   I was not handling the problem effectively
   I was afraid of something
   * I felt so insecure
   I am nervous
   * I was letting the job get to me and that I was suffering
   I feel like passing out

I cannot make decisions as quickly as I would like or as
surely
* inside I felt out of control
I drink secretly

4. *My organization suffers from stress overload through*
   * ineffective dealings with employees/poor communications between upper-middle and lower management personnel
   the kids get into trouble at school
   * too many false alarms
   * crisis management—priorities change daily
   management behavior that squelches interest and creativity
   * lack of productivity and harmony within the organization
   tight deadlines, not knowing how to solve a problem, lack of experience, people shortage, high turnover, shortage of competent resources
   * personnel problems, health problems, heart attacks
   overaggressiveness
   ineffective planning
   fragmented efforts, zilch morale
   * poor performance, exasperatingly bad communication
   too much work, union-management conflicts, lack of direction

5. *The people I work with show their stress overload by*
   * I haven't noticed
   * not doing a good job and/or not completing assigned tasks
   reacting strongly or withdrawing
   decreased productivity
   shouting arguments with others in public work areas
   bitching about top management, being grumpy about not enough personal time
   * attacking, placing blame
   * either complete withdrawal or shouting matches
   * taking days off on sick leave and not responding in an aggressive manner
   bringing problems to me that they should solve themselves
   becoming either very excited and irritable or very quiet and noncommittal

fatigue, poor planning, procrastination
running away from their responsibilities
becoming tense, red-faced
not accomplishing their business efforts
getting obnoxious, throwing things, shouting
* turning white, holding back, covert hostility
making excessive demands on other people
* complaining to me, insubordination, and/or quitting
griping, drinking, emotional outbreaks
becoming moody, quiet, testy
* goofing off
* poor workmanship

How do you feel inside as you read about people just like yourself? Are you aware of any increased tension in your body as you have been privileged to "get inside another's skin" for a brief time?

In my seminars, I ask people to complete these sentences anonymously at the beginning of the workshop, and then I read them their responses, grouped together under each sentence stem as above. Generally, the participants are both relieved and saddened to know that they are not alone.

What stands out repeatedly is that people generally feel that it is inappropriate for them to express their true feelings, thereby increasing their stress levels. Therefore, the very people who could be supportive move away from them, sensing their incongruity and not knowing what to make of it.

APPENDIX F:
HINTS FOR AVOIDING
BACK STRAIN

John Thie suggests these guidelines to avoid back strain.

When Standing

Don't stand with your knees "locked" into position. Keep your knees relaxed and your lower back flat.

To relieve swayback when you are standing or working, place one foot on a low stool.

Don't stoop forward from the waist unless you also bend your knees.

Avoid high heels. They tilt the pelvis forward, putting a strain on the back.

When Sitting

Don't sit in very low or soft overstuffed furniture. A firm straight-backed kitchen type of chair is best.

Sit back with your spine supported by the chair and your knees slightly higher than your hips. A footstool or ottoman may help.

Sit with your feet flat on the floor. Crossing your legs at the knees puts a strain on the lower back. Don't sit on your legs or in a twisted position.

When Sleeping

Use a firm mattress to *avoid having your buttocks sag. A well-designed chiropractic mattress is now available in all parts of the country. A three-quarter-inch plywood board under the mattress will make a soft mattress firmer.*

Sleeping on your back is the preferred position. A conventional pillow or two under your knees will flatten the lower back, relieving the strain. Use a cervical roll pillow under your neck to keep your neck flexed and your spine in a straight line. Some five inches in diameter, these pillows are available from chiropractors and in the notions or bedding departments of some department stores. You may make a substitute by folding a bath towel in half vertically, rolling it up, and securing it with safety pins.

When sleeping on your side, you may be comfortable with one or both knees bent and your hips flexed. The pillow under your head should be the same height as the space between your head and your shoulder so that your spine will be in a straight line. If the weight of your top leg pulls down on your lower back, you may wish to use a small pillow (two or three inches thick) as a spacer between your knees.

It is extremely bad for your back to lie on your stomach.

In getting up from a lying position, roll over on one side and use your hands to push up to a sitting position, keeping your back straight. Let your feet swing to the floor. This can be done in  *one smooth, rhythmical motion (see illustration).*

When Driving

Your car seat should be firm and positioned so that you can operate the pedals with your knees slightly bent. With the natural backward slant of most car seats, you may wish to use a foam wedge or an orthopedically designed car seat to provide a more upright and firmer back than is available with seats that are standard equipment. "Sacroease," an orthopedically designed car seat, is available at orthopedic supply houses. It is custom-shaped to your body.

On long drives, stop every two hours, get out of the car, stretch, and move around. (You should also get up periodically to stretch and move around during plane flights.)

Get in and out of the car with your back straight. Swivel in the seat with your back straight. Do not stoop.

How to Lift

Lifting should be avoided as much as possible. When it is unavoidable, your legs should do most of the work. Bend your knees and lift with the strong leg muscles, not with your back. You can support your elbows on your thighs. Keep the load close to your body. Don't stoop and lift unless your knees are bent, and always move carefully.

Soreness or Pain in Your Back

Moist heat is often effective in relieving pain. It can be provided with a hydrocolater or a "wet heating pad," both of which are available at a pharmacy. Don't use a dry heating pad. If you have strained your back (or any other muscle) you may relieve the swelling and increase your circulation (to help the body heal itself) by alternating moist heat and ice for twenty minutes every hour until the pain and swelling are alleviated. Flexible ice packs filled with "blue ice," which conform to the body's contours, are available at large pharmacies and hospital pharmacies. Use a Handi-Wipe or some other thin fabric between the ice and your skin. The unpleasant intensity of the cold sensations lasts for only three or four minutes, until the affected area is numbed.

Exercises to Strengthen Your Back

1. Lie on your back, place your hands behind your knees, and hug your knees to your chest. Repeat ten times.

2. Hug one knee to your chest by placing your hands behind your knee. Keep your other leg straight and raise and slowly lower it, keeping your abdomen tucked

354

in. Repeat five times with each leg.

3. *Lie on your stomach with your legs fully extended and your hands clasped behind you at the small of your back. Raise and lower each leg alternately. Repeat five times.*

4. *Using the same position as in number 3, raise your head and chest from the floor, and return. Repeat five times.*

5. Regular exercise within your ability and tolerance is vital to keeping your back limber and strong. Start exercising slowly, giving your muscles time to warm up. Don't push yourself into exercising more than you can tolerate comfortably. Walking should be increased to a minimum of two and a half miles per day, perhaps in two mile-and-a-quarter walks. Remember the importance of walking with nothing in your hands or arms!

6. An overall exercise program, such as brisk walking, swimming, and bicycle riding, may be your best insurance for increased mobility and strengthened muscles, as these three activities increase the natural motion of the spine while using all the body's muscles. Jogging may be too severe, as it can jar the spine or other parts of the musculoskeletal system.

   I was told that I should never jog, due to repeated back injuries from automobile accidents. I joined the YMCA planning only to walk briskly and do warm-up and cooling-down exercises. But, with everyone around me running, I calculated that the worst that could happen was that I'd experience a few days of pain, so I decided to risk it. I soon discovered that running was the ideal exercise for me, and my back is stronger than it has ever been. All this points to the necessity of discovering for yourself what works best for you. No expert or book is certain to be true. Your body knows.

BIBLIOGRAPHY

Adams, John. *Understanding and Managing Stress: A Workbook in Changing Life Styles.* San Diego: University Associates, 1980.

Airola, Paavo. *How to Get Well.* Phoenix: Health Plus, 1974.

———. *How to Keep Slim, Healthy, and Young with Juice Fasting.* Phoenix: Health Plus, 1971.

Albrecht, Karl. *Stress and the Manager: Making It Work for You.* Englewood Cliffs, N.J.: Prentice-Hall, 1979.

Arensen, Gloria. *How to Stop Playing the Weighting Game.* Los Angeles: Transformation Publications, 1978.

Assagioli, Roberto. *The Act of Will.* New York: Viking, 1973.

Beiler, Henry G. *Food Is Your Best Medicine.* New York: Random House, 1965.

Bellet, S., et al. "Effect of Caffeine on Ventricular Fibrillation Threshold." *American Heart Journal* 84:215–227, 1972.

———. "Response of Free Fatty Acid to Coffee and Caffeine." *Metabolism* 17:702–708, 1968.

Belloc, Nedra B, and Breslow, Lester. "Relationship of Physical Health Status and Health Practices." *Preventive Medicine* 1:409–421, 1972.

Benson, Herbert. *The Relaxation Response.* New York: Morrow, 1975.

Berkman, Lisa F., and Syme, L. Leonard. "Social Networks, Host Resistance, and Mortality: A Nine-Year Follow-up of Alameda County Residents." *American Journal of Epidemiology* 109:2, 1979.

Bernhard, Yetta. *Self Care.* Millbrae, Calif.: Celestial Arts, 1975.

Bliss, Edwin. *Getting Things Done.* New York: Bantam, 1976.

Bolles, Richard N. *What Color Is Your Parachute? A practical Manual for Job-Hunters and Career-Changers.* Berkeley, Calif.: Ten Speed Press, 1972.

Bresler, David E., with Richard Trubo. *Free Yourself from Pain.* New York: Simon and Schuster, 1979.

Bricklin, Mark. *Natural Healing*. Emmaus, Pa.: Rodale Press, 1978.

Brown, Barbara. *New Mind, New Body: Biofeedback—New Directions for the Mind*. New York: Harper & Row. 1974.

Brown, W. J.; Leibowitz, David; and Olness, Marlene. *Cook to Your Heart's Content: On a Low-Fat, Low-Salt Diet*. New York: Van Nostrand Reinhold, 1976.

Capacchione, Lucia. *The Creative Journal*. Athens, Ohio: Swallow Press, 1979.

Cheraskin, E.; Ringsdorf, W. M. Jr.; and Brecher, Arline. *Psychodietetics*. New York: Bantam, 1976.

Cleave, T. L.; Campbell, G. D.; and Painter, N.S. *Diabetes, Coronary Thrombosis, and the Saccharin Disease*. Bristol, England: John Wright and Sons, 1969.

Coates, Thomas, and Thoresen, Carl E. *How to Sleep Better: A Drug-Free Program for Overcoming Insomnia*. Englewood Cliffs, N.J.: Prentice-Hall/Spectrum, 1977.

Cooper, Kenneth. *The New Aerobics*. New York: Bantam, 1970.

Cousins, Norman. *Anatomy of an Illness*. New York: Norton, 1979.

Crosby, W. H., and Segal, Julius. "Biofeedback as a Medical Treatment." *Journal of the American Medical Association* 232:178–180, 1975.

Davis, Adelle. *Let's Get Well*. New York: Harcourt Brace, 1965.

Davis, Martha; Eshelman, E.; and McKay, M. *The Relaxation and Stress-Reduction Workbook*. Richmond, Calif.: New Harbinger Publications, 1981.

Dychtwald, Ken. *Body-Mind*. New York: Jove, 1977.

Editors of *Consumer Guide, The Vitamin Book*. New York: Fireside/Simon and Schuster, 1979.

Farquhar, John. *The American Way of Life Need Not Be Hazardous to Your Health*. New York: Norton, 1978.

Feltman, J. "Tryptophan—A New Natural Weapon Against Depression and Sleeplessness." *Prevention* 28:55–60, 1976.

Ferguson, Marilyn. *The Aquarian Conspiracy: Personal and Social Transformation in the 1980s*. Los Angeles: Tarcher, 1980.

Fixx, James. *The Complete Book of Running*. New York: Random House, 1977.

Freudenberger, Herbert J. and Richardson, Geraldine. *Burn-Out: How to Beat the High Cost of Success*. New York: Bantam, 1980.

Friedman, Meyer, and Rosenman, Ray. *Type A Behavior and Your Health*. New York: Knopf, 1974.

Friedmann, Lawrence W., and Galton, Lawrence. *Freedom from Backaches*. New York: Pocket Books, 1976.

Garn, Stanley. *The Earlier Gain and Later Loss of Cortical Bone in Nutritional Perspective.* Springfield, Ill.: Thomas, 1970.

Geisinger, M. *Kicking It: How to Stop Smoking Permanently.* New York: Grove Press, 1978.

Glasser, William. *Positive Addiction.* New York: Harper & Row, 1976.

Goldberg, Philip. *Executive Health.* New York: McGraw-Hill, 1978.

———and Kaufman, Daniel. *Natural Sleep: How to Get Your Share.* Emmaus, Pa.: Rodale Press, 1978.

Gordon, Thomas. *Parent Effectiveness Training.* New York: McKay, 1970.

Gottman, John; Notarius, Cliff; Gonso, Jonni; and Markhaus, Howard. *A Couple's Guide to Communication.* Champaign, Ill.: Research Press, 1976.

Graedon, Joe. *The People's Pharmacy: A Guide to Prescription Drugs, Home Remedies, and Over-the-Counter Medications.* New York: St. Martin's. 1976.

Greenwald, Harold. *Direct Decision Therapy.* San Diego: EDITS, 1973.

Hittleman, Richard. *Introduction to Yoga.* New York: Bantam, 1969.

Holmes, T. H., and Rahe, R. H. "The Social Readjustment Scale." *Journal of Psychosomatic Research* 11:213–218, 1967.

Hunter, Beatrice Trum. *Fact/Book on Food Additives and Your Health.* New Canaan, Conn.: Keats, 1972.

Jaffe, Dennis T. *Healing from Within.* New York: Knopf, 1981.

James, Muriel. *Breaking Free: Self-Reparenting for a New Life.* Reading, Mass.: Addison-Wesley, 1981.

Jones, John E., and Banet, Anthony G. Jr. "Anger." *The 1974 Annual Handbook for Group Facilitators.* La Jolla, Calif.: University Associates, 1974.

Joy, W. Brugh. *Joy's Way: A Map for the Transformational Journey.* Los Angeles: Tarcher, 1979.

Kaye, Beverly. *Up Is Not the Only Way.* Englewood Cliffs, N.J.: Prentice-Hall, 1981.

Keller, Jeanne. *Healing with Water.* West Nyack, N.Y.: Parker, 1968.

Kraus, Barbara. *The Dictionary of Sodium, Fats, and Cholesterol.* New York: Grosset and Dunlap, 1974.

Lakein, Alan. *How to Get Control of Your Time and Your Life.* New York: Signet, 1973.

Lance, Kathryn. *Running for Health and Beauty: A Complete Guide for Women.* New York: Bobbs-Merrill, 1977.

Lappe, Frances. *Diet for a Small Planet.* New York: Ballantine, 1971.

Lazarus, Arnold, and Fay, Allen. *I Can If I Want To*. New York: Morrow, 1975.

Lettvin, Maggie. *Maggie's Back Book*. New York: Houghton Mifflin. 1977.

Lowen, Alexander. *Bioenergetics*. New York: Penguin, 1975.

Mace, David and Vera. *How to Have a Happy Marriage*. New York: Ace, 1977.

MacKenzie, Alec. *The Time Trap*. New York: McGraw-Hill, 1975.

Mahoney, Michael and Kathryn. *Permanent Weight Control: A Total Solution to the Dieter's Dilemma*. New York: Norton, 1978.

Miller, Emmett E. *Feeling Good: How to Stay Healthy*. New York: Spectrum, 1978.

Mirkin, Gabe. *The Sportsmedicine Book*. New York: Little, Brown, 1978.

Mitchell, Curtis. *The Perfect Exercise*. New York: Simon and Schuster, 1976.

Moskowitz, Robert A. *How to Organize Your Work and Your Life*. New York: Doubleday, 1981.

Oyle, Irving. *The Healing Mind*. Millbrae, Calif.: Celestial Arts, 1975.

Ostrander, Sheila, and Schroeder, Lynn. *Superlearning*. New York: Delacorte, 1979.

Pelletier, Kenneth. *Mind as Healer, Mind as Slayer: A Holistic Approach to Preventing Stress Disorders*. New York: Delta, 1977.

Phelps, Stanlee, and Austin, Nancy. *The Assertive Woman*. San Luis Obispo, Calif.: Impact Publishers, 1975.

Price, Weston A. *Nutrition and Physical Degeneration: A Comparison of Primitive and Modern Diets and Their Effects*. Santa Monica, Calif.: Price-Pottenger Foundation, 1945.

Pritikin, Nathan; Leonard, Jon N.; and Hofer, J. L. *Live Longer Now: The First One Hundred Years of Your Life*. New York: Grosset and Dunlap, 1974.

————with Patrick M. McGrady, Jr. *The Pritikin Program for Diet and Exercise*. New York: Bantam, 1980.

Progoff, Ira. *At a Journal Workshop*. New York: Dialogue House, 1975.

Rainwater, Janette. *You're in Charge: A Guide to Becoming Your Own Therapist*. Los Angeles: Guild of Tutors Press, 1979.

Ray, Sondra. *I Deserve Love*. Millbrae, Calif.: Celestial Arts, 1976.

Rodale, J. I., and staff. *The Complete Book of Minerals for Health*. Emmaus, Pa.: Rodale Press, 1977.

Royal Canadian Air Force Exercise Plans for Physical Fitness. New York: Pocket Books, 1972.

Rush, Anne Kent. *The Basic Back Book.* New York: Summit, 1979.

Satir, Virginia. *Making Contact.* Millbrae, Calif.: Celestial Arts, 1976.

————. *Peoplemaking.* Palo Alto, Calif.: Science and Behavior Books, 1971.

Schafer, Walt. *Stress, Distress, and Growth.* Davis, Calif.: Responsible Action, 1978.

Scheele, Adele. *Skills for Success.* New York: Ballantine, 1980.

Schultz, J. H., and Luthe, Wolfgang, eds. *Autogenic Training in Psychotherapy.* New York: Grune & Stratton, 1959.

Schwartz, Jackie. *The Relaxation Log.* Los Angeles: Kasriel Productions, 1978.

Selye, Hans. *Stress Without Distress.* New York: Signet, 1974.

Shealy, C. Norman. *Ninety Days to Self-Health.* New York: Bantam, 1978.

Simons, George F. *Keeping Your Personal Journal.* New York: Paulist Press, 1978.

Simonton, Carl and Stephanie. *Getting Well Again.* Los Angeles: Tarcher, 1978.

Spackman, Robert R. *Exercise in the Office.* Carbondale, Ill.: Southern Illinois University Press, 1968.

Spino, Michael. *Beyond Jogging: The Innerspaces of Running.* Millbrae, Calif.: Celestial Arts, 1976.

Staff of *Prevention* magazine. *The Complete Book of Vitamins.* Emmaus, Pa.: Rodale Press, 1977.

Steinmetz, Lawrence L. *The Art and Skill of Delegation.* Reading, Mass.: Addison-Wesley, 1976.

Stevens, John O. *Awareness.* New York: Bantam, 1973.

Stuart, Richard B., and Davis, Barbara. *Slim Chance in a Fat World: Behavioral Control of Obesity.* Champaign, Ill.: Research Press, 1972.

Terkel, Studs. *Working: People Talk About What They Do All Day and How They Feel About It.* New York: Avon, 1972.

Thie, John F., and Marks, Mary. *Touch for Health.* Los Angeles. DeVorss, 1973, expanded and revised edition, 1980.

Toffler, Alvin, *The Third Wave.* New York: Bantam, 1981.

Travis, John W., and Ryan, Sara. *The Wellness Workbook.* Berkeley, Calif.: Ten Speed Press, 1981.

Tubesing, Donald. *Kicking Your Stress Habits.* Duluth, Minn.: Whole Person Associates, 1981.

Verrett, Jacqueline, and Carper, Jean. *Eating May Be Hazardous to Your Health.* New York: Doubleday/Anchor, 1975.

Wegscheider, Sharon. *Another Chance: Hope and Health for the Alcoholic Family.* Palo Alto, Calif.: Science and Behavior Books, 1981.

Wessel, Janet. *Movement Fundamentals* New York: Prentice-Hall, 1957.

Wheelis, Allen. *How People Change.* New York: Harper & Row, 1973.

Wilson, Stephanie. *Getting Organized.* New York: Warner Books, 1979.

Wolpe, Joseph. *Psychotherapy by Reciprocal Inhibition.* Stanford, Calif.: Stanford University Press, 1958.

Yankelovich, Daniel. *New Rules: Searching for Self-Fulfillment in a World Turned Upside Down.* New York: Random House, 1981.

Yudkin, John. *Sweet and Dangerous.* New York: Bantam, 1973.

Index

Asthma, 16
Atherosclerosis (see Cardio-
    vascular Disease)
    caution re—, before begin-
        ning exercise program,
        57–58
    chest pains as a symptom
        of, 87
    increased by cigarette
        smoking, 33
    related to diet, 36
    reversal of —, through
        diet, 36–37
Autosuggestion, 50, 186–87,
    229–31
Austin, Nancy, 162
Awareness, 22–27

Baby foods, 38
Bach, J. S., 273
Back pain, 32, 46, 75, 240,
    242
    (see "Hints for Avoiding
        Back Strain,"
        Appendix F)
Banet, Anthony G., Jr.,
    Communication Day 13,
    284–85
Barbiturates (sleeping pills),
    51–52, 258
Baroque music, 273
Behavior modification—see
    Environmental cues for
    eating, Belief systems,
    73–74, 111–12, 115–16,
    246–48
Belloc, Nedra B., 176
"Belly breathing", 118–19,
    126, 150–51, 176, 216,
    229, 259, 274, Aware-
    ness Days 13, 15, 279,
    307; Communication
    Day 14, 298–300; Relax-

ation Day 14, 301
Belly laugh, 201–202
Berkman, Lisa, 98
Berne, Eric, 70
Biofeedback
    as a tool to lower stress
        level, 90, 91
    interrelationship of mind
        and body, 24
Birth defects, 46
Bisch, Jeff, 12
Blood sugar level—see
    Glucose
Breathing exercises
    Alternate Nostril Breath-
        ing, 119
    Basic Relaxing Breath Ex-
        ercise ("Belly Breath-
        ing"), 118–19
    Breath Mindfulness, 217
    Controlled Sigh, 136
    Efficiency Walk, 136–37
    Progressively Deeper
        Breathing, 136
    What's Going On At My
        Nostrils, 218
Breslow, Lester, 190
Broad Life Goals, Lifestyle
    Day 14, 302

Calcium, 294
    correlation to bone thick-
        ness, 44
    deficiency caused by excess
        protein intake, 44
    requirements, 44–45
Calories, 38, 42–43, 129–30
Cancer
    as stress-related illness, 16
    Cancer Counseling and
        Research Center, 16
    "Cancer Personality", 16

363

364

367

368

370

371

THE NEW SEXUAL LEPROSY

HERPES:
CAUSE & CONTROL

WILLIAM H. WICKETT, JR., M.D.

"HERPES: CAUSE & CONTROL is the best explanation of herpes and what to do about it that I have ever read. It's written in language that everyone can understand and should be required reading for every high school and college student." —Abigail Van Buren, "Dear Abby"

The insidious herpes virus has spread in recent years to epidemic proportions, afflicting more than 20 million Americans, with another 500,000 new cases diagnosed every year. Now, in the most comprehensive and up-to-date discussion of herpes ever written, a medical doctor offers new hope for the millions — from preventive measures to recommended treatments.